LEADERSHIP THROUGH THE AGES

LEADERSHIP THROUGH THE AGES

SIR GEORGE MACMUNN

GYAN

Published by

GYAN

Gyan Publishing House
5, Ansari Road
Daryaganj, New Delhi-110002
Phone: 011-47034999, 9811692060
E-mail: books@gyanbooks.com

Distribution Network
gyanbooks.com
India, USA, Canada, UK, Australia

ISBN: 978-93-7014-649-5 (HB)

First Published, 1935

2nd Impression 2025

Printed at: Gyan Press, Delhi.

LEADERSHIP THROUGH THE AGES
Author: SIR GEORGE MACMUNN

LEADERSHIP THROUGH THE AGES

LEADERSHIP THROUGH THE AGES

BY

LIEUT.-GENERAL

SIR GEORGE MACMUNN

K.C.B., K.C.S.I., D.S.O.

COLONEL COMMANDANT, ROYAL ARTILLERY

CONTENTS

CHAPTER I

CONCERNING LEADERS

Famous Men
Occasions
The Make-up
Some Components
Women as Leaders

CONCERNING LEADERS

Famous Men

'Let us now praise famous men . . . such as did bear rule in their Kingdoms . . . honoured in their generations . . . the glory of their times.'

The subject of the World's leaders is always a thrilling one, and one on which the moderns have an insatiable curiosity. How and why do they come, and what do they do? Far deeper even than the story of their lives, their successes, their failures and their ends, is the 'how' and the 'why.' What were the conditions that called them into being, and what was the psychological cause of their leadership? What was the magic and the charm in their personality? Where lay 'it'?

Without crises of some kind, or some unusual occasions, leaders do not arise. Here in England we have no leaders in the magnetic sense at the moment, because we do not want one. We have several *khojas*, several worthy men, of character and sense, who hold the wheel and help to keep the car of State in the middle of the fairway. The engine does the rest of the work—the great, sane British people. Given other circumstances, Sir Oswald Mosley would not perhaps be crying in the wilderness. Did we want the leading, no doubt the genius of the nation would find its fugleman, or even its *Führer*.

In endeavouring to study the secret of the World's great leaders through the ages, rather than their biography, there will be two matters to present: first the circumstances; second the secret. The greatest leader of all, whose secret of secrets is beyond our ken, Jesus Christ the Righteous, must be ruled out of court, since before Him all human leaders can but shine dim, and since no human hand can hope to present that secret. But to Holy Writ we may fairly go for a highly documented example, that of Moses—the *Musa* of the Semite world—and begin our study with the man who could tarry in the desert till he had grown a generation free of the slave taint of Egypt, to do his business. After that, as the years unfold, the leaders whose charm and power and secret can be assessed can be put on the screen, to make a modern holiday.

The inclination, as we ponder of leaders and leadership, is to think of the famous men of action, and of great statesmen and commanders, great victors and empire-builders. They bulk larger in charm and circumstance, but the same principles and gifts sublimated to other purposes, must equally drive those who lead in the walks of peace, and religion, and who turn men's minds to the channels that await them.

Occasions

The occasions which bring forth leaders must of necessity be very varied, but it is safe to say that there must nearly always be some crisis in national life. Great conquerors there have been, of course, to whom ambition and self-interest have been the moving spirit, and here Alexander of Macedon leaps to mind—the man who overran the Near and Middle East—yet perhaps in his bonnet there stirred a bee akin to Nazi-ism or Pan-Germanism. The idea that Hellenism must be forced on the world for its salvation may have been the inward spur working consciously or otherwise on the gift of war and the glory of youth in the purple. The circumstance of the Greeks in Asia, even if they did not want to be saved from Persia, was there all the same.

The occasions of the uprising of Moses were far more obvious. The chosen people, fostered from the descendants of twelve philoprogenitive brothers into a numerous colony under the great ægis of Egypt, with a change of dynasty became helots, groaning under a perpetual *corvée*. It had obviously the right dynamic complex to be handled by a leader, when the God of Abraham, Who had chosen them for His experiment, gave the word and sent him.

In more modern times 'Old Oliver' was the most unlikely person to be drawn from his farms and his occasional Calvinistic introspection and his study of the 'Authorised Version' to become a leader of Horse, let alone a Lord General and Protector, had not the incompetence of the Parliamentary leaders stirred the gift that was in him. We have seen the same story in our own lives, and how David Lloyd George of the dynamic spirit was called to lead a nation—nay, an Empire—which mistrusted him, because no one else would or could. And, incidentally, if you study the genius of the British race you will find it wants to be led, and if someone competent does not grip it and save it from being bothered, it will, before long, demand the reason why. Between knowing that something is wrong, and the determination to put it right, a considerable period will elapse while the British grumble and their spleen augments and dissatisfaction gathers *momentum*.

We have seen some such feeling prompt the old Tory party to let Benjamin Disraeli seize the helm of their ship—and a man of Israel lead Britain lest worse befall—and in so doing build better or greater than they knew, adding line upon line and precept upon precept.

The occasions that make a Joan of Arc bearable, and her 'voices' from pagan Lorraine effective, are intelligible enough—a nationalism that was dead, and none to rekindle it! Thus too to-day we see Germany, conscious of her humiliation, sure that neither Socialism nor Jewry could show her the road, experimenting with Herr Hitler, as one who, right or wrong, speaks with no uncertain voice. There we see one of the great factors of leadership of a kind, the sure and certain voice that calls to those lost in a wood.

We see an Italy drunk not with real freedom but with the licence that comes of the loosening of the silver cord, turning eagerly to the rod in pickle of a Mussolini, giving up freedom so that Sardinia shall educate her lesser breeds in that national discipline which must come before freedom. A leader! A leader! My kingdom for a leader! A great occasion and the long-dormant spirit of Ancient Rome springs up. *Aut Teucro duce aut nihil.*

But a leader must not only lead, he must be able to build. It is one thing to summon spirits from the deep, and quite another to send them back again, or to cabin and confine them, as even grim Oliver found. So, Holy Russia gone to dust, and

China in a thousand pieces; for those who have led a people to break cannot lead them to rebuild.

It is doubtful if Lenin or Trotsky or Stalin can come within the circle of leaders whom history will accept, however dynamic or subtle their personalities, and we have yet to wait and see what will come of it.

Then, if we would change our train of thought: where shall we place little Tseu-Hi, Dowager Empress of China, the little maiden torn by ambition from her Manchu boy, a *kouci-jen*, or concubine of the lower class, whose chance of chambering with the Emperor seemed *nil*? How shall we estimate the occasion that developed this little piece of Tartar complaisance and may-blossom sweetness into a shrewd, dominant and often ruthless power and spectre behind the screen of the Imperial Palace? How far was she woman and how far devil? Did she save China? Did she sustain or lose the Tartar power, or did she break China into those hundred thousand crinkum-crankums, which are so hard to piece together? Whatever she did do, little may- or peach-blossom, good or evil, how came she to do it? What indeed was the occasion, and her secret of power?

The Make-up

We find as we look in the Tussauds of history that heroes and leaders have a very definite tessellated make-up, sometimes apparent, often to be found only as the real story of life and achievement is unfolded. Perhaps we may divide them into two broad classes: the first those who, great and inimitable though they be, consciously and definitely do add trick-work to their conduct, and limelight for their accompaniment. The latter is sometimes due to their entourage, who try to arrange for them as a manager arranges for a star. In the second are the still greater—those free of all guile and consciousness of effect, and super-genuine in all their doings; and then we can see too, even in the first category, the froth passing, as the man finds himself and perhaps realises that he is born to a mission. That must have been so with Benjamin Disraeli.

The author of *Ecce Homo* has shown to us how the human portion of Our Lord's nature was not, seemingly, aware of His two personalities for some time, but only as human mind and stature came to fullness, did full realisation of His own identity come to Him. All that we are vouchsafed of the story shows that this may be so, and to our human understanding this seems natural enough.

With human leaders and heroes it must be thus, and one day the call comes to leave the plough or the desk, and follow insistent fate, and the weal, or maybe the woe, of the world. Joan in her village and her father's woods, Oliver on his acres and by his village pump, Elizabeth from the prison of the Traitors' Gate, Moses from his Chaldæan deserts and his Chaldæan wife, *quo fata vocant.* Often the 'call' describes it best of all, the mysterious 'call,' not merely to Orders, but to serve. To look a leader, either in war, in politics, in religion, is obviously an asset on the side of influence, yet how many has the world revered whose value lies all in the fire and wisdom within?

The call and the occasion are not the same. Without the occasion it is true there is no call—

but there are many occasions and none to call or be called. The Great War was an 'occasion,' the 'call' to David Lloyd George came almost by chance. England wanted a leader in her confusion, someone who could see straight and march straighter, however pernicketty.

But if an ardent young man were to say to a wise man among those in the past-masters' chairs 'How can I become a leader?' the answer would be 'You cannot.' You can train yourself in many things, awaiting the occasion, and the call—and praying that you have 'guts' to answer. Prepare and wait, and in ninety-nine cases you will be disappointed; mend your nets and count your catch, and all of a sudden comes the call to 'Follow me.' And as the call came to the fishers to be fishers of men, so comes the call to lead; yet for thousands that have the gift, but one perhaps gets the call, or even knows he has the gift.

Round us are those of great capacity whom call and occasion will yet never require, and who will go to their grave with their gift and none the wiser, though probably the happier.

Some Components

There must be several obvious qualities that make for fugleman, and such would be courage, both physical and of the mind, earnestness and genuineness. There are many occasions in which knowledge of the world and how men must be handled are essential, and yet enthusiasm and earnestness can take its place, while the world laughs and follows. Thus, in part, Abe Lincoln.

The leader who has to be in close touch with his

followers needs the gift of camaraderie, on occasion, even, of what in our army used to be called '*Flat-catching*,' which is but a whimsical term for imposing on your public at typical occasions. A standard example of this would be Napoleon's holding the musket of an outpost sentry at the edge of a wood who was sleeping wearily on the snow, and jeopardising the safety of the army—such must receive the death-penalty for very safety's sake. Yet Napoleon, visiting his outposts alone, is in truth *bon camarade*, takes the musket, and does the soldier's duty till the N.C.O. of the guard brings up the relief. Sympathy? Yes; for none knew better than he the weariness that can overcome the soldier who has marched all day. Yet also none knew better how the story of the 'Little Corporal' taking the musket rather than calling for a firing-party, must have flashed round the bivouacs and the marching columns next day. To genuine sympathy the Emperor must have added the flair of propaganda. How great the mastery of the soldier's psychology was that plucking the cross from his own breast to pin on that of a hero. His staff must have had a dozen spare tucked away for him in their sabretaches.

Such things are 'Flat-catching' *in excelsis*—the catching of the flat by clever gesture.

We may imagine that Abraham Lincoln, with his tongue of humour in his cheek, had it in somewhat different guise in that inimitable gift of his, of telling some simple farmyard story, often with Rabelaisian flavour, that showed how impossible a course of action urged on him might be.

The shy Briton rather shrinks from such gestures. Not for him to kiss the soldier on both cheeks as he gives a reward. The tribe of Flynns, it is said, know their own whisky-skins; the French general knew his own men, and what stirs the Gallic hearts; we in Merrie England miss much that is human in our over-developed sense of the ludicrous. There are stories, also, born of the heart alone which can touch strong men's hearts with glory till they weep. What do you make of our Prince visiting a Disabled Soldiers' home, and hearing one inmate had not been shown because—without eyes or mouth or hearing—how could he be presented?—a lump of flesh with naught but a precious spark of God-life attached—and the Prince insisting and—kissing what was left of a hero. Sublime sympathy here, with no sense of the effect that stirred a nation—and with such do we class dying Sir Philip Sidney giving his water to the wounded soldier.

It would seem that Oliver Cromwell had moments when the Old Testament fervour of some of his men was more than irksome, yet he adopted the snuffle, and also the vigorous similes of the major prophets, for the sake of the influence it gave him. Such is but another aspect of the principle that makes the candidate kiss the voter's baby.

But when all is said and done, however wise, however clever, however courageous, yet to every leader that has taken the world or a people to great things there must be some intangible quality that is psychological, and that we in modern slang so often refer to as 'it.' 'It' without judgment is no use. King Charles I. had a glamour that is *dieu-donné*, and yet could not lead to success because he could not compromise, or see the wood for the trees. And 'it' has various forms, from that calm soothing influence that Field-Marshal Lord Raglan exercised on all around him in hours of trouble and excitement, to that fire that Lord Nelson poured on all his subordinates.

But among the many forms of the psychological 'it' there is perhaps none so important as oratory —to explain what you want and put your own verve and enthusiasm over your hearers. Would Adolf Hitler be the leader he is if he could not say it before all the world, with the very magic of fairy-land behind his voice, his gesture and his sublimation of self? Could Spurgeon in his pulpit have torn the jewellery from off the women in his audience without the magic gift, or William Ewart Gladstone have led his millions with what was often little more than verbosity, had he not possessed all the gifts of oratory? There are not many among the Saxons with the gift. It may be a lure due to Hebrew blood in the make-up, it may be Celtic, perhaps even Hitler's blood may belong to a Semite group! Since Gladstone we have none; save only our incomprehensible Celt with the magic tongue that at times dominates him, and blots out all his prudent resolutions—David Lloyd George, whom all England distrusted and followed to a man. Nor in this case was it oratory that let him pilot the whole Empire to a victory greater than ever dreamed of, but sheer power of concentrated drive. Yet since Gladstone, only Lloyd George can hypnotise his audience and make them believe that black is white. The astounding gift of tongues, so far different from that of good speaking; what power can it give to the qualities of heart and head!

In Britain we are particular, and no one could

aspire to lead who does not bring sincerity and uprightness to the other qualities of greatness.

Women as Leaders

The examples in history of women as great leaders are by the nature of things comparatively few, for, as has been set forth, it is occasion and opportunity that bring out the dormant quality. There have been royal women born to greatness whose common sense has enabled them to let their ministers carry on, but these are outside the question of leadership inherent. For the purposes of this book, two only will be presented, those whom fate had called and whose inherent flair had the requisite modicum of psychological uncanniness to satisfy the conditions. These are Queen Elizabeth and, the most wonderful creature of all, the Dowager Empress of China. Joan of Arc and Queen Victoria would come within the circle, but their lives have been so thoroughly portrayed that except as brief, thumb-nail examples, they will not be explored, yet both had uncanniness, something superhuman in their make-up. We talk of Victorianism and our Victorian age to-day glibly, and those who think modern England grew of herself, disparagingly, but a reign of over sixty years covers several different ages. The magic comes in, not with the lonely and in truth pathetic figure of the Widow at Windsor, but the glory of the busy lass, a-horse and a-bed, that so led England's trend towards dignity and righteousness, in the days when all was young. The magnetism involved will be worthy a brief glance.

But when all is said and done, the humblest of

women has a magnetism inherent, an uncanniness, which at all times may be evoked, and bring her to special influence directly or indirectly. The temple wherein lies the spark of life, and the power of charm that nature has intertwined therewith, have compelling possibilities. In Queen Elizabeth it was the *joie de vivre* of youth, and woman's mystery, that enabled her to lead the spirit of that England emerging from the dark days of the Roses, and palpitating with the escape from a dominating religious system.

CHAPTER II

MOSES

The Bible Story
The Call
The Making of a Ruler
The Leading in the Wilderness
The Ringing to Evensong

MOSES

The Bible Story

The story of Moses is a household word and a children's happy lesson among us, and even because it is so, does it call for some examination at our hands, since household words, though pithy, must often be but outline. It has been said that a great leader cannot and does not appear unless there be an occasion, and often a dire occasion, a need and a call for deliverance and direction. How real was the need of his countrymen under a dynasty that knew not Joseph, history has told us.

Let us look for a moment at this occasion known as it is to us and our fathers of old since childhood. For several generations the families of the sons of Israel had colonised Goschen, that tract close to the line of the Suez Canal from which we, to this day, view those astounding mirage cities, those 'wonders in the land of Ham' which the children of Israel saw of old. Their colonies had been formed under the protection of desert kings of their own *bedawin* race, the Shepherd Kings of Egypt. But the Shepherds had been driven out, and the old Pharaohs re-established, those who knew not Joseph. Partly, no doubt, for dislike of foreigners, and not improbably because these men of Shem had been admitted to too large a share in officialdom, hostility towards them was pronounced, even as in Hitler's Germany. Because it was so, the settlers were, under duress, working away at frontier-fortified cities and posts that would in future keep out the Shepherds and perhaps, even then, the races of Babylonia and Syria. The system of labour was apparently a rigorous *corvée*. Never again would Egypt be overrun. What is more suitable than that Israel should make the works to keep out their *Bedu* kin? The store cities, where the grain of this fertile province should be held against the lean years, would also serve as a second line and a support to the frontier posts.

Now under the system of *corvée*, controlled by supervisors of the public works department—the taskmasters of Holy Writ—the Israelites had become slaves, and a generation had grown up with a slave mentality. Mass slave-labour in some form or other was the tradition of the country, and the great granite blocks for the Pyramids, and the great pylons of the Temple, could have been drawn only by thousands of slaves working under the lash. To this day does the tradition remain. An Egyptian labourer carrying a sack on board or out of ship must needs have a lash every time he passes the tallyman by the gangway, usually it is true on the sack, unless he be idling, but the gesture is traditional and self-explanatory.

It is not to be wondered at that the free colonists 'murmured' at the conditions imposed on them, murmured and caballed, but fell back before the hopelessness of revolution in face of the hosts of Pharaoh.

So much for the conditions; now for the equipment of the deliverer. The story of the finding of Moses in the bullrushes, no doubt a true folk-legend, has delighted Jewish and Christian children for many hundreds of years. Here is a fragment as it used to be sung by an old ballad-singer of Dublin years ago which produced the atmosphere with some more wealth of detail than the Book of Exodus, yet with the true colour:

> In Aygypt's land on bank of Noile
> King Pharaoh's Royal daughter went to bathe in sthoyle,
> She had her dip, and hied into the land,
> And to dry her royal pelt she ran along the sand,
> A bullrush thripped her, and at her feet she saw
> The little Mōses in a wad of sthraw.
>
> 'Thunder and Turf, girls! Which of ye owns the child?'
> The criturs blushed, but ne'er a word they said.
> The Princess surveyed the child from foot to head.
> 'Holy St Bridget! 'Tis a Hebrew Jew!
> Tear and ages! Fwhat am oi to do?'

—and so forth. There is the story in its colour. We have the beginning of the equipment. The Hebrew waif, cherished by the kind-hearted princess—we may scorn the suggestion that Moses was her own child, and accept the Bible story of the real mother, entertained seemingly as foster-mother—educated and trained at Court, with all the learning of Egyptian science teachers to hand, equipped, as he grew, with ideas of empire, religion and affairs. No better *milieu* for the mental development and equipment of a race leader can be imagined than that of the young Hebrew.

That he was of understanding nature and quick sympathy we know by his recorded indignation at the cruelties inflicted on his fellow-Hebrews—but we also learn that his palace upbringing had separated him from his fellows. His story was obviously known and he was looked on askance, and when he interfered it was, 'Who made thee a prince and a judge over us?' and also, 'Thinkest thou to kill us, as thou killed the Egyptian?'

He must have been brought up by his mother in the Israelite belief, such as it was, for the Hebrew religion as we know it later had not yet developed. But the teaching was of God Almighty, of El, the God of the Deserts, and of his promise to the seed of Abraham. The God of the Patriarchs as taught to the Jews was *El Shadai*—'The Almighty'—not yet known as 'I Am That I Am,' the Great *Jehovah*. God was *El*, to Israel as to Muhammad, and *Beth El*, the House of God, was His dwelling-place. But the young Moses would have taken part also in some of the Egyptian religious ceremonies. Priests of Osiris and Apis must have been his teachers. Moses himself, though probably not brought up by his benefactress as an Egyptian in religion, must have been familiar with the Egyptian mythology—had possibly imbibed an extreme distaste for it. However that may be, Moses was not as other Israelites, which is the explanation of the obscure passage in Exodus: 'Now thou art truly a bloody husband to me.'[1]

We know from Holy Writ how, as the years went on, Moses' sympathy with the oppressed fellows of his race increases, and indignation at the treatment accorded them culminates in his killing the tyrant; a killing apparently observed, despite Moses' precautions, that gave point to the gibe already quoted. Then it was that Moses fled to the desert, whence came his obvious and invaluable experience of desert and camp life and ways of living, that was to stand him and his people in such stead, when he came to lead them to Sinai

[1] Exodus iv, 25. This obscure verse is quite clear if we realise that 'fork' has for decency been rendered 'feet,' and are familiar with the early desert custom of the mutual blood rite at marriage.

and keep them there for forty years. Several years in the tents of Jethro, with a desert wife to teach him, left him little to learn.

The Call

For years of semi-modern research it has been the fashion to say that the tradition that Moses wrote, which meant dictated and edited, the Pentateuch was a myth, and that it was a much more recent post-Exilic writing-up of old stories. The clever German students and those who so eagerly followed up their line, with its 'P,' its 'E' and its 'J' narratives and the like, had not enough linguistic and archæological lore to let them prosecute their studies with the best evidence. So much water has since run under the bridges of archæology and linguistic research that the old story has come by its own as first-class history, both in the Pentateuch and of course in Exodus, and also in the Bible as a whole. Many of the most puzzling statements have been proved meticulously accurate, and so much is this the case that others not yet so cross-checked may be accepted also.

In the stories of the Pentateuch it is the 'Egypticity' that proclaims the period, and is equally evident in 'E,' 'J' and 'P,' and one or two of these may be quoted to illustrate the confidence in the detail on which we base a study of the Patriarch's character. One instance is the long and uninteresting desert itineraries given in Numbers (xxiii), which could only have been written at the time, probably in a diary, and are not likely to have been compiled hundreds of years later, or even inserted from some ancient document.

Indeed all through the Pentateuch the assertion that Moses wrote the story appears so repeatedly, that all the later writers who refer to it as gospel must have lied together. Sixteen of the laws in Exodus have the phrase 'when ye come to the Land of Canaan,' obviously therefore written before the arrival, unless the author was an expert faker in realism. The laws are not arranged in any regular order, but rather as the events which called for them dictated, and are often definitely dated (Numbers ix, 1, etc.). Several of the laws are laws for the marching period and quite unsuited for a settled country, and could hardly have been recorded hundreds of years later; and so on, in countless indications. The reference to 'the evil diseases of Egypt which thou knowest' must be genuine or by a very skilled intentional faker.

In this attempt to study the development of the character and leadership of Moses, the divine inspiration direct and repeated is accepted as historic, and not merely emanating from the trend of a devout man, who attributes all his successes to divine support, of that nature for which good men pray.

Now, as we know, Moses sojourned in the desert, with what really were the Beduin, and the Beduin moved long distances in the year. Jethro was a priest of Midian, but the priests of Chaldæa, of any status or sanctity, were trained at the priestly college at Ur of the Chaldees, which we now know to have been a great centre of civilisation, and of power, might and dominion, many many centuries before Abraham lived and left the neighbourhood. It is extremely probable that young Abraham was sent by his father, Terah, to the college school, or to the priestly college itself, or both. We may even surmise, without any sort of stretching the evidence, that young Abraham may have at any rate undergone some priestly training, or even been ordained as a priest after the order of Melchisidek. That takes us a step further. The higher and inner priesthood, while supporting the uneducated in their worship and fear of the forces of nature, and in the giving to portions of the divine power separate names and obediences, as rulers of nature—as the Hindus do to this day—also knew and worshipped the Great God of all, the 'El' from whom all powers proceed. Their knowledge may easily have descended from the Patriarchal conditions told of in Genesis.

But that is not all. It is more than probable that Moses with the culture and knowledge of Egypt, also visited and studied at Ur, where he may have reinforced the ancient knowledge of 'El' that the Hebrews had. He may easily there have learnt of the Tetragrammaton, and the 'Name of Power' so familiar in other forms to anyone conversant with Egyptian theology, whether by mere converse with the priesthood, or by the direct gift of God. Sir William Wilcocks, who alone has studied Chaldæa with a theodolite, hazards the suggestion that *Jahweh*, *Je-ho-vah*, or however we may guess at that still concealed spelling of the Tetragrammaton, was the Eah-Hueh, the God Almighty of the Chaldæans, to whom the name had come from the Patriarchs, and that the proceedings in the desert by the burning bush were born of lore learnt at Ur.

Jewish tradition said that this 'Name of Power

was born on Aaron's rod, and that when the rod was lifted up, then the Ineffable Name, the *Shem Hamephorash*, worked its might. This is the explanation of the obscure line in one of the Psalms, 'When the sea saw that it fled'—viz. stood up to give dry passage, only to fall down as the rod was lowered.

Fascinating as this line of thought is, we must leave it and follow the story of Moses as revealed, leaving the mysteries of the 'Word of Power,' whose correct pronunciation the camel knows, to those whom such lore calls.

Apart from such happenings as these, we know that Moses sojourned a long while in the desert, that the priest's daughter, Zipporah, bore him two sons and that Jethro, or Raguel, his father-in-law was a well-educated man of the world, as his advice to Moses to be quoted later clearly shows. The traditional hospitality of the desert is charmingly and naturally shown when the priest chides his daughter, for not bringing in for a bite and a sup the stranger who had helped at the well.

And now we come to the 'call,' when old Pharaoh had died, and the young Pharaoh made the yoke still more burdensome for the Hebrews, so that they cried aloud grievously. Then we come to the the day when Moses, in desert simplicity, far away from the fleshpots of his palace life in the days of his youth, is feeding his flocks on Horeb. To him comes the divine summons and intimate conversation. It shows how vague was the Hebrew conception of the God of Abraham, that when he is told who it is that addresses him, He who says 'I am the God of Abraham, of Isaac and of Jacob,' Moses should ask, 'When they shall say unto me, "what is his name?" what shall I say unto that?' And then comes the Name of Power, the Word of four letters with the lost vowel points, 'I Am That I Am.'

But as yet Moses is a diffident young man, and also suffers from an inferiority complex, for he is not as other Hebrews nor as the Arabs of the desert. Several times does he remind God that because of the neglected rite he can dictate neither to Pharaoh nor to his brethren, and he is evidently very conscious of this inferiority, while his wife also taunts him at coming to her, a desert maiden, thus, or at best chaffs him about it, in the passage already referred to. Moses is equally diffident as to his powers of speech and effectiveness, till the Almighty is angered with him. 'Is not Aaron the Levite thy brother, and I know that he can speak well.' And so at last, the hesitating and diffident Moses takes leave of his father-in-law, and returns to Egypt. Then taking his brother he goes through the long wrangle with Pharaoh that we know of, working on him, with the help of Aaron and his rod, the long series of plagues and pressure, protesting constantly to God that he is not fit for the job, and reaffirming his disability. Nor is he at all well received of his own people, who do not appreciate his good offices and attribute to him the new duress put on them by Pharaoh. Pharaoh's heart was 'hardened' by God possibly with the object of developing resolution in Moses, till we work through all the plagues and the further hardening of Pharaoh's false heart to the death of the first-born and the final spoiling of the Egyptians. The Hebrews accept the developing leader, who however apparently is now over eighty years of age, though that may well be one of the errors in handing down the story.[1]

The Making of a Ruler

The period of proof is over, 'And Israel feared the Lord and believed the Lord and his servant Moses,' as well they might. But they were kittle cattle this slave race, more than easily upset and of mordant tongue, they who cried when Pharaoh and his chariots came after them, 'Were there no graves in Egypt that thou hast taken us away to die in the wilderness?' If Moses knew what was before him it is not to be wondered at that he pleaded to be excused the leadership. Yet withal a mighty patience was growing up within him, and his confidence was now established. And the murmuring of the hungry people brought the flight of tired quail,[2] too weary after their flight from Macedon even to run away when huddled under the scrub, and the Manna, '*Man-Na?*'—'What is it?' And the taste was like wafers and honey as it is in Chaldæa to this day.

The desert is always a place where water and rainfall is short, and the murmuring of Israel was not unnatural, but power is given to Moses at Marah to sweeten it and at Meriba to find it. And all the while the Amalek are raiding and fighting the Children of Israel, not unnaturally, since a new claimant to share their water in the oases

[1] The difficulties over numbers and dates in the Old Testament indubitably point to some error in the transpiration or interpretation of figure signs. It is not practical to think that the situation took sixty years to develop, before Moses led the people.

[2] Which incontrovertibly shows that the route taken was by the Mediterranean at any rate for a while.

was a fair grievance. Yet is it one more milestone in the building up of the character of this uncircumcised man.

Once more is Moses to have a lesson taught him, and this the most important of all for those who lead a nation, and one that every man who aspires should read and re-read—the secret of decentralisation. And this is how the story goes. Jethro learning that Moses has succeeded in his mission and is now in the desert, brings to him Zipporah and his two sons, and Moses went to meet him and kissed him, and they asked each other of their welfare. One can hear it: 'Are you well?' 'Are you happy?' 'Are you sure you're well?' 'Don't be tired.' 'May you never be cast down,' and so forth, after the manner of the tribes. Next morning comes the lesson, when Moses sat all day surrounded by the crowds of Israel each with their plaints and their desires.

Jethro sees the absurdity. 'What is this thing? Why sittest thou by thyself alone, and all the people stand by thee from morning unto even?' And Moses explains how busy he is, 'When they have a matter they come unto me, and I do judge between them.'

But Jethro is a man of the world, and sees that it cannot go on. 'The thing that thou doest is not good, thou wilt surely wear away, both thou, and this people that is with thee. . . . Hearken now unto my voice, I will give thee counsel. . . . Be thou for the people to Godward . . . teach them ordinances and laws . . . provide out of all the people able men . . . place them to be rulers of thousands . . . of hundreds, of fifties and of tens and let them judge the people . . . every great matter they shall bring to thee . . . every small matter they shall judge: so shall it be easier for thyself, and they shall bear the burden with thee.'

And Moses was wise enough to listen to the experienced administrator who spoke, and learnt the first rule for all who would lead armies or peoples. Which brings us to the marvel of the law-giving on Sinai, and the twentieth chapter of Exodus, and those remarkable laws which rule the world to this day, and without which no civilisation can exist. And then too came this marvellous Covenant, of which the Hebrew even to-day is the outward and visible remembrance.

The Leading in the Wilderness

The teaching of Jethro, the giving of the Law, the constant communication with the living God, which is such a feature of the story, have now made the diffident palace-born scribe, added to his subsequent sojourn in the desert, the competent, confident leader. Unhesitatingly, fully primed, does he lay down the rules and the laws that are to bind the people of the Covenant, murmur as they may. Fighting men are trained, the ark and tabernacle of a marching host are made,[1] and then does the *Führer* send out spies who report to him of the promised land. It seems that he shall now lead them to that victory which has been promised them. The spies return with glowing reports and fruits of the land, yet some one among them makes mischief, and speaks of the struggle

[1] The ark with the rings for the poles found in Tutank-amen's tomb is not unlike that described in the Book of Exodus—*and it is of considerably older date*; so that the story that the 'Secret' of Abyssinia is the existence of the Ark of the Covenant may easily be true.

before them and the fierce fighting men. The people—in our modern language of contempt, this 'herring-gutted' people—murmur against Moses for having brought them away from the protection of the fenced cities of Egypt. Caleb the leader strives to reassure them, but of no avail. How incensed must Moses have been at this 'give-away.' And then we are told that the Lord lost His patience too, and decreed that none of this faint-hearted generation save Caleb and Joshua should ever see that promised land, and that for forty years should the race sojourn in the deserts and oases, till all were dead and men of grit were born and come to their prime. For Moses it must have been a bitter disappointment, for he had no doubt looked to seeing his people well settled and himself their judge before the Lord. And if you take the view that this story is but allegory, and that the direct intervention and communings with God did not actually take place, why all the more must you marvel at the resolution and wisdom which, 'off his own bat,' the leader had developed, and at his decision to wait for a better race of men to be bred before he could go up against the Canaanites and the Amorites and all the rest of them.

An interesting story is that of Moses trying to avert God's anger lest the people of Egypt jeer at the God of Israel for promising more than He could perform, for all His pillars of fire and of cloud, of which the tale was well known. And so God relented and did not destroy them, but ordered them back to the Red Sea. Then too the men of Israel were ashamed and did actually try to prove their courage and their war-worthiness to take that which was promised them, but having no blessing were heavily defeated and fain to accept their fate with the best grace they could, which was not much.

Moses, in addition to his own overwhelming disappointment, was to have for forty years the sort of time that Cromwell as Lord Protector could scarce endure for five, rebellions and murmurings and cabals and pestilence and punishments. If as has been said he was mere man and not God-directed, how great must have been the character and influence that he had developed in the stress that he had experienced. We may leave it at that.

The Ringing to Evensong

They were to go through much, this chosen people, before at long last came the order, when all save Moses and Joshua and Caleb that came out of Egypt had passed away, to move on. First do we see Moses establishing Reuben and Gad and the half of Manasseh in Trans-Jordania, in the territories of the King of Sidon and of Og, King of Bashan, that country of lush grazing and fat cattle, where both bulls and cows, in this twentieth century, chew the cud and gape at the passers-by, in a way that sounds not so terrible as when 'fat bulls of Bashan gaped.' In fact Reuben and the half of Manasseh well knew what they were about, when they asked for the lands east of Jordan.

But the great leader who was now the snow-bearded Patriarch was not to see the land of promise or the fenced cities carried, or the walls of Jericho [1]

[1] From which perhaps the very slang of 'jerry-building' is derived, since the pushed-out walls lie flat under the drifted sand to this day, even as written in the Book of Joshua.

fall flat from the thrust of overbuilding within and a jerry-builder's foundation.

He had sinned against the living God by that terrible sin of presumption, and on Mount Nebo was he to view from afar the land to which he might not lead his people. He yielded up his soul unknown to his following somewhere 'over against Beth Peor,' although at the end 'his eye was not dim, nor his natural force abated,' this man 'whom the Lord knew face to face.'

It is the story of a leader of leaders, developed by mighty forces beyond the ordinary ken, 'and there arose not since a prophet in Israel like unto him.'

CHAPTER III

ALEXANDER OF MACEDON

The Chronology
The Epic of Alexander
The Macedonian Setting
The Equation of Olympias
Alexander starts his Career
To Arbela and all Persia
Alexander's Marriages
The Road to India
Back in Persia
The Collapse

ALEXANDER OF MACEDON

The Chronology

The following are the principal dates connected with the life of Alexander:

356 B.C. Alexander born.
336 B.C. Succeeds to the throne of Macedonia.
334 B.C. Starts his invasion of Asia. Battle of the Granicus.
334–332 B.C. Overrunning of Asia Minor, Sicilia, Tyre and Sidon. Battle of the Issus.
332 B.C. Captures Gaza. Surrender of Egypt. Visit to the oasis of Siwa.
331 B.C. Invades Babylonia and Susiana. Battle of Arbela.
330 B.C. Starts for Ariana and Bactria.
327 B.C. Starts for India.
323 B.C. Dies at Babylon.

The Epic of Alexander

After Moses, Alexander of Macedon's character and story is the best documented of all the heroes and leaders of ancient times. History, by those who wrote before Christ, took its details from the material written by those who had accompanied the conqueror. Not only do we know well the condition of the Greek world and the city-states, and the people who did and still do pronounce their 'th' as the Anglo-Saxons, but we also know the long story of the Persian empires. Just as in the case of Old Testament history, the spade and the more modern form of the Higher Criticism justify rather than disparage those testimonies, so from Herodotus to Aurel Stein almost every gap in our knowledge is being filled in by archæologist and numismatist. The stones have spoken to us as eloquently as the desks of the dead. We are thus able to master the details of the occasions, to see something of the mental equipment, and to follow the mind and the genius of the individual.

What is it that Alexander did? He succeeded to his father at the age of twenty, and to the leadership of the Hellenic peoples, so far as he might be able to keep it. He succeeded also to his father's plans and preparations to invade Asia Minor and rescue the Greek settlements in Asia from Persian dominion. He eagerly followed out the programme. He beats the Persian troops on every occasion, and he then moves into Syria. He is not upset by the fact that the Greeks in Asia Minor are not in the least desirous of being emancipated from the easy control of Persia, or that thousands of Greek mercenaries are still with the Persian armies and like to remain so. He bustles the Phœnicians out of Tyre, thereby fulfilling the prophecy in Ezekiel[1] in a remarkable way, a prophecy which had remained half-fulfilled for several hundred years. He proceeds to drive the Persians from Egypt not, as some would have it, as a digression from his purpose, but in a long-formed determination to visit the shrine of Jupiter at Ammon, in the half-belief that his mother's story of his birth might be true. Treated at first by Darius and many others as a naughty wayward boy, his career of triumph soon astounds the world. He marches towards Persia, overwhelms the Persian

[1] Chap. xxvi. The Tyre on land was destroyed by Nebuchadnezzar (v. 4), but v. 12 is not fulfilled till Alexander takes the stones of Old Tyre and uses them for a causeway to reach the new island-Tyre—and brings the soil too to fill up the interstices.

hosts at Arbela on the Greater Zab, destroys the puissant Darius, declares himself Great King and pushes on to what is now Afghanistan, founding some of his many cities of Alexandria. He marches over the Hindu Kush, or as it was then called the Parapomisus, and then crosses the Oxus to Samarkand. He sets up his governors, he raises local troops, he marches down to India, crosses the Indus and, either defeating or appeasing those who would resist, actually reaches the Ravi in the neighbourhood of Lahore before a great *caffard* seizes his Macedonian troops and compels him to turn back. Down the Jhelum he marches to the Indus, fiercely entreating *en route* all who oppose him, and then returns to Persia by the terrible desert way of the coast, and finally, after vicissitudes with his homesick and unutterably weary Europeans, died at Babylon. He died of what was probably malaria in a frame racked with excesses and weakened by the effects of many wounds, in the thirty-third year of his age and the eleventh since he crossed the Hellespont, an undoubted leader of men and child of fortune. What he would have done with his conquest if he had lived is beyond computation. It was altogether a 'one-man show,' as we should say in the slang of to-day, for without his power of leading the vast accretion could not hold together. The fissiparous tendencies were too strong for anything but a superman, and perhaps even for a superman. For those who like to ponder on the 'ifs' of history, that of the Near and Middle East had Alexander lived is a pleasing excursion.

But even with Alexander gone, and his empire breaking up in the hands of his generals, there remains the record of these amazing eleven years. What the secret and what the occasion? It will profit us to study them.

The Macedonian Setting

What in the case of this astounding Alexander was the occasion that started him on this meteor-like path that was something far more than the mere conquest of such as Attila and the Huns? To Alexander we see that Hellenisation and development went hand-in-hand with his lust for fighting and love of battle. The period was a very great one in history. It was not long since, for the first time, Aryan empires had arisen and challenged the great Semite empires that had held so much of the Near East. Babylonia and Nineveh and even Egypt had fallen to the Eastern Aryan of Persia, and now the Western Aryan was to appear on the scene.

The occasion that called for an Alexander must be first viewed in its Macedonian setting. Philip the Second of Macedon, the ruler of a sturdy if barbarous people whose leaders had assimilated Hellenism, had to a great extent dominated the old city-states, and Philip dreamed of a Pan-Hellenic union under his leadership. The tamed Macedonians of the Court were more Hellenised than the Hellen. Philip and Alexander wanted Pan-Hellenism because they believed it good for the world, as well as profitable for their people. Persia, the territory of the 'Great King,' had conquered the whole of Asia Minor and had even brought hitherto mighty Egypt under her dominion. But the Asiatic shores of the Eastern Mediterranean and of the Euxine were studded with Greek colonies and cities under Persian dominion. Persia itself was already honeycombed with Greeks. Large numbers of them served in the Persian military forces and in the Persian navy that swept the Levant. Greek merchants traded everywhere in the Persian Empire, and Greek officials were numerous.

To Philip it seemed that all these Greeks should be under the dominion of their own people, and be subjects of an Hellenic Empire. His Macedonians and Greeks were organised into a very highly trained efficient force, a force that had made him acceptable to his otherwise arrogant neighbours, the city-states.

We know the story of the young Alexander, son of Olympias, and putative son of Philip—putative because Olympias declared that he was the son of Jupiter Ammon, the form of Zeus whose sanctuary was in the Siwa oasis of Eastern Egypt. We can easily imagine the genuine, if not necessarily deep, affection which this handsome, growing lad, agog to excel in athletic manly sports, must have inspired in the experienced soldiers and statesmen of his father's hardy Court. A young prince, however feeble his parts, must always get an undue meed of adulation, but much more so when the lad is more than worthy, and more than attractive, does he get it to the full. The young Alexander thus started with everything on his side to help him to lead, had he but even a moderate share of the necessary brain and character.

The Equation of Olympias

Let us now look at the mother's equation and her claim, and indeed assertion, that he was the son, not of a god—but of the great Deity of the Greek World, no less than Jove or Jupiter, in that lateral habitation of his in the oasis of Ammon in the Egyptian desert. Alexander, declared Olympias, was the son of Jupiter of Ammon—of the Deus-piter himself.

We of the Christian world, who readily accept the claim of Another to be the son of the Living God, need not laugh at the presumption of Olympias. The Greek world certainly did not, at any rate when the offspring in question began to display an outstanding personality, though naturally there were scoffers in the market-places. Greek sentiment was used to the anthropomorphic form of gods, and even of the great god, and many of their religious allegories and traditions were based on such happenings. The world of Alexander was not astonished, such things were known to be. Those that did not take the matter seriously knew that temple priests [1] were but enjoined to help bless childless women, as they are in some of the Hindu temples to this day. If the prayers of an anxious woman are blessed vicariously through a priestly office, it is no great extension of thought to assume that the resultant childbirth is due to the deity to whose worship the temple is dedicated. Incidentally it is not too much to say that the Christian Verity was the more readily acceptable, at any rate to Greek minds and

[1] These are the Sodomites of the Old Testament, the kept fathers of the temple service.

Greek train of thought, by reason of this very belief in the possibility of godly anthropomorphic paternity, just as the idea can be developed that all mankind are the children of God and all life His gift.

We can therefore see that the golden-haired athletic youth and would-be soldier would easily have his prestige enhanced by his mother's claim, and few to jeer thereat. When fortune smiled on his career, and his victories over great odds astounded the world, the story at once became doubly honoured and probable. We shall see that at times Alexander himself was profoundly stirred with the idea and convinced thereof, and this must be taken as a reason for that boundless confidence in himself and his destiny that sustained him at all times.

We may consider too the question of heredity in her son's composition. Olympias was the daughter of a king of Epirus. Epirus would correspond to Southern Albania, and in Epirus was the famous oracle of Dodona widely consulted by Greeks. The women of this land, according to Plutarch, were much addicted to the orgiastic rites of Orpheus and Dionysius, and their Latin name would be Bacchantes. Plutarch described Olympias as a 'zealous devotee of these wild and orgiastic excitements,' which were usually connected with sex ideas. It is not therefore stretching the point too far if we imagine her as a young woman of some fervency in this direction. In the shadow of the oracle her mind may well have been touched with that mysticism which can be so intimately connected with sex elation. In modern parlance, she was probably an over-sexed young woman with a taste for cocktails. Of the sublimation of carnal to spiritual exaltation a good deal has been written, and Arthur Weigall has perhaps aptly described her as 'a woman who was deeply religious and profoundly mystical, yet whose pious ardour was indistinguishable from self-indulgence.' We may leave it at that, and we can see that her son, whether born of Zeus or not, would be likely to inherit some strange proclivities.

She is said to have met Philip in Samothrace and was in his company in 'the dark sanctuary of the Cabiri in Samothrace.'

On her marriage night it is stated that she dreamed the old dream of the thunderbolt, and may have told the same to Alexander.

At twenty years of age we have an Alexander that differs considerably from his fellows. He has refused to grow a beard, the normal adornment of all Greek soldiers and the ambition of all Greek lads, having his chin and lip shaved or plucked. His intercourse with and his interest in women was far below that of the youth of the times, but all agree that he was singularly free from that homosexuality which was the fashion and custom of the age—a custom that has so detracted from the object lessons of Greek civilisations. Even his unusual and unalienable and almost freakish friendship for Hephæstion, that endured all his life, was never regarded as in any way perverted. He neither then nor in his later years showed evidence of inheriting the ardent trait of sex that all attribute to his mother. On the other hand, there is ample evidence that he had a full share of her mysticism, as well as a tendency to orgies of drink, and excitement, which in other forms were features of Olympias' character, and in fact all her more excitable tendencies were sublimated into this form of mental instability. It is on record that when Philip and Olympias had their final quarrel, Alexander spent some of his more impressionable years in retirement with her, before returning to his father and commencing his martial training. So bitter was the estrangement between his parents that Alexander and his mother were both credited, probably unjustly, with the murder of Philip.

The foregoing gives us some inkling of the temperamental forces that were comprised in the young hero's make-up.

Alexander starts his Career

When the handsome boy succeeded to his father at the age of twenty he was something more than an eager young athlete, for he had been trained in the quiet Mieza by Aristotle himself. He had served in Philip's campaign in Bœotia and Phocis, and in the battle of Chæronea he had led the charge of heavy cavalry which won the day, and then he had realised that, for his purposes, the heavy cavalry charge was more effective than the great wedge of his father's unbeaten phalanx. He had trouble on the Danube that postponed any Asiatic plans, and while he was leading his force into Illyria, on the far side of the Danube, Thebes revolted. Alexander marched back through the mountains, crushed Thebes and destroyed the city. To Athens, which had been toying with similar intent, he granted easy terms, and the rest of Greece, save only Sparta about which he did not bother, sent abject embassies.

In a year he had shown his generals, who were quite ready to support him but who had greatly wondered what sort of a man he might be, that he was something more than an eager boy. They had wondered and now they knew.

At the same time there is not to be noticed anything more than might be expected from staunch generals and stout troops pushing a figurehead before them, with an intriguing and adoring mother behind. Demosthenes is openly scoffing at any pretensions.

But now we are to see something of an occasion as well as a spur. With his enemies in Europe crushed, and the Greek states frightened into acquiescence, his father's design now stands out before him. The plans are laid; omens, to which as the son of Olympias he must needs attend, are favourable. The Pan-Hellenism of his entourage, and his own feelings, stimulated by the teachings of Aristotle, are stirring excitedly. The world to be saved by Greek civilisation and ways of thought! The Hellenes in Asia rescued from a foreign yoke! It is a mighty urge. Alexander crosses the Hellespont never to return, and yet to leave the one story in the world that is remembered of all creeds and races.

In April in 334 B.C. he bids farewell to Olympias with the trifling march of 350 miles before him ere he reaches the shores of Europe that he is to leave, hard by Cape Hellas. With 40,000 men he crosses the narrow straits, and on the Asiatic shore stimulates himself and his troops by pouring libations to the gods of Hellas. Then, camping his troops on the plain of Troy, he endeavours to fire their enthusiasm by the story of the deeds of their fathers. Was it enthusiasm or trick-work? Did he believe that all who had gone before would help him now; in the shade of his ancestor Achilles behind? We, who are wrapped in the deeds of the old time before, can accept it. Was there trick-work and 'flat-catching' in it? Maybe too, for we have considered how necessary to most leaders is 'flat-catching' at the right moment, especially when troops are weary and disheartened. The secret is to use the right appeal. His youth, his beauty, his appeal to the past and to great traditions, all went to build up that enthusiasm that was to win him, without style or finish, the forthcoming battle on the Granicus.

Turning eastwards from Troy town he is to find, after marching a short distance, the local commanders and satraps drawn up in force on that river. He is all agog, and will wait for no scientific handling of his phalanx and his squadrons, no stratagem and no tactics, other than the good old method of riding at the vital point and damn the consequences, the spirit of which our fixed bayonets and drawn sabres are the outward and visible sign. He leads his heavy cavalry straight over the river and into the ranks of the Persians, making for the commander-in-chief and his staff. They have formed their line, have they! Then, with Napoleon, *Enfin je les tiens!* They wait for me?—*bon!* And so, Boy Alexander at their head, go the heavies, as at Balaclava, right into the mass of Persians, into the heat of their line. It is routed and is driven from the field, with heavy slaughter, for it was hard to escape in days gone by, with no rearguard firing steady volleys to cover you. It was the first of the battles of Western discipline and efficiency against the ineffective courage of the masses of the East. It was the story of Plassey and Assaye and many another victory of the Western few against the Eastern many.

Only one body still kept the field. Some 'axed' officer, trained under Philip, had a large body of Greek mercenaries in the Persian service—the very men who were to be saved by Alexander from Asia and join the great Hellene cause of civilisation! But they would have none of it. Their ranks were trained as the Macedonians and they were keeping their agreement for which they were paid like all true mercenaries—*Pas d'argent pas de Suisses*, as they said on the Continent in the Middle Ages. But there was plenty of money in the Persian service, and they were true to their salt. In vain the Macedonians swarmed round them. *They* did not make much of Pan-Hellenism as a cult, perhaps they knew too much about it, any way it was like the cheek of the Macedonian barbarians to pretend to be honest-to-goodness Hellenes. The Greek contingent fought on, and it was not till but 2000 remained that they surrendered, many sore wounded.

Alas! Alexander was mad with fury and chagrin and the lust of blood. The fools are flouting him and the great god of Hellas; they seemed to say that the Asiatic Greeks did not want him, the apostates! And to the sword they were put. Hell hath no fury like a Hellene scorned, and scorned by his own co-opted people!

Incidentally it may be remarked that it was not a good way to encourage other Greeks, of whom there were many thousands in the Persian service, to come over, as the late Mr Æsop should have taught him, by the episode of the East Wind.

Apart from this tragedy, all was magnificent. By his success, however much the older and experienced leaders might shake their heads at his rashness, and vow that battles should not thus be won, their respect was immensely increased. The lad really is a soldier, a fighter, and if he can be made to listen at times, this enterprise, which Philip could have undertaken, can be made to win through in these young hands!

In the camp, where the rank and file were gossiping and talking, this leadership on the top of the Troy flummery was having effect. Alexander worshipped the heroes of legend, and wanted them to do the same! Well, he was not backward in emulating them. Does fortune follow the brave? Was there anything in that old tale of the Queen's? And some old soldier grey in the wars of Philip would expectorate and say, as soldiers have said through the ages, 'Twas like his father that . . . anyway he's good enough for me.'

It has been well said that those who drive fat horses should themselves be fat, and that those who preach of glory, and of treading the paths of the heroes of old, must be up to the part, and Alexander had now given proof thereof. He was on the road to be an inspirer of men. We need not mind what the older soldiers thought; rules are made for the average men. The Wellingtons and Napoleons are rules unto themselves, for that is the prerogative of genius.

And so the evening and the morning of the

Granicus were the first day. The young man had justified himself, that choice young man and goodly, like Saul of Israel, and was accepted of the rank and file and thus on the way to leadership with a big 'L.'

The ruthlessness that massacred his Greek prisoners must be deplored and we shall see ruthlessness growing on him on occasion. Leaders must be ruthless when needs be, but it must be the ruthlessness of reason and not that of wrath, and history attributes this massacre to the latter.

We are but following this story of Alexander to bring into the high lights the points that help us to understand the phenomenon of the epic, and we can begin to recognise the components of his make-up—his father a successful leader and organiser, his mother a highly strung imaginative woman—the belief in himself and in his destiny, his imagination making the lives of old a living presentment, his commanding physical beauty—and then behind it the legendary story of his divine birth, which developed in his mind into fact as he proceeds. There is also the tactical flair that makes him realise how Asiatic troops can best be tackled, and how little numbers count. Fortune had kissed him on one cheek at least, and kisses are intoxicating.

From the Granicus our hero marches his small, elate, but disciplined army along the coast of Asia Minor, the coast that is studded with Greek cities modelled like those of European Greece, which withstand him in their Athenian and Spartan insolence! He storms them, and, when they submit, enlists under his own banner any of their troops that will follow him. The massacre of the Granicus is seldom repeated.

Sardis and Halicarnassus too are besieged and stormed, and the next year as he marches along the coast he is to meet the Great King himself on the Issus. We need not trace the circumstances. The Persian force has manœuvred itself across the route to Macedon in his rear. Once again Alexander leads a charge of heavy cavalry that penetrates almost within sword-thrust of the chariot of Darius. The Great King is extricated by the self-sacrifice of Persian chivalry, and escapes up the Persian turnpike, abandoning his camp to the Macedonian.

In the Persian camp were the family of the Great King, mother, wives, daughters, to whom Alexander showed courtesy and protection, refraining from the rape and transfer that the world, and perhaps the women, expected of him, and an affection between him and the mother of Darius arose, which says much for the human side of the Macedonian.

It was a first-class victory and indeed had Fortune now kissed the other cheek. Darius had ordered his generals to capture the presumptuous boy and whip him soundly, and now Alexander makes retort in no uncertain terms. He writes that he will proclaim himself Great King by right of victory. There is a good deal to be done, however, if the ground made is to be consolidated. The following of Darius and preventing his military recovery is not practicable.

The Persian Empire may be considered as consisting of three distinct parts, the whole of Asia Minor, the country of the basins of the Tigris and

Euphrates, that the Greeks knew as Mesopotamia and the Arabs as the Country of the Cliff (Mr James Breasted has invented for it the name of the 'Fertile Crescent'), to which may be added Syria, Judæa and Egypt, and thirdly the great upland of Persia Ariana and Bactria, with such trifles as Media and Susiana added. The first was now in Alexander's hands, but since a Persian fleet was in being under the Greek admiral, Memnon, his supplies must come by land, be obtained locally, or else run the gauntlet of the Persian cruisers. The fact of this fleet and its admiral was a disturbing factor *vis-à-vis* the Greek states on the Asian shore, who, as has been explained, had not yet absorbed the Pan-Hellenic germ. Therefore Alexander dallied awhile in Syria, making good his communications, learning much of what so many soldiers forget, the machinery of supply, and then suddenly marched south along the coast for Egypt. There was no need for this if he was intent on an early march to the Persian table-land, for there were not enough Persian troops in Egypt to threaten his rear seriously. But it seems extremely probable, knowing as we do his worship of the past, that the legend of Jupiter Ammon attracted him, and his mother may easily have pressed the course on him. The story of his quip with Parmenion has a strain of humour that lasts and is modern enough. Asked for his views Parmenion says, 'If I were Alexander I should do so-and-so,' and Alexander replies, 'If I were Parmenion so should I.'

The mystical side of Alexander's nature seems to have been developing, and the secret seems to have dawned on him, that the God of Abraham was also the God of all the world however dimly revealed. He sacrificed to the god of each town that he took, whether of the Hellenic pantheon or not, and also pressing on his mind must have been the idea that he, already the spoilt child of fortune, might also be the darling of the gods, nay, be god-descended, as his mother so often insisted to him. Was what he had at first taken as a pleasant legend, with which to emphasise in half-jesting guise his wishes and ambitions, really literally true? He began to think so, and to the oasis of Siwa he would go and sacrifice in all humility in the temple of Jupiter Ammon. And so he did, storming *en route* the great frontier city of Gaza, now holding a Persian garrison. In Egypt he was readily received as a deliverer from an unwelcome yoke. And thus began that long Greek tradition in Egypt which to this day Egypt knows might be revived if the kindly Briton withdrew, babble the effendi never so loudly.

The visit to Siwa, his sacrifices there, the flattery of the priests, so strengthened his belief in the truth of his mother's story that it was, as we shall see later, to develop, under Brahminical influence, into the belief that he was an actual incarnation. Those who study Alexander's career from this point of view of his growing belief in his semi-divine—and even divine—origin may see in spurious earthly guise the same process at work as the writer of *Ecce Homo* traces in the Carpenter's Son. So in some unreal and presumptuous way, born of Greek ideas and his mother's enthusiasms, worked the mind of this poor amazing Alexander of the Two Horns.

To Arbela and all Persia

By 331 B.C. Memnon was dead and the Persian fleet sufficiently disposed of for Alexander, now bounding with super-self-confidence, to start to make good his letter to Darius, and show himself to be the real and only Great King. His army was in fine order, many drafts had marched in and come by sea, and the rumour of the good fortune that attended him was kindling every lad of spirit. Alexander had achieved the first stage of the successful leader to whose standards men flock. His generals were agog for more enterprise, and his troops had had enough of the women and wealth of Syria and Egypt. Training and discipline was as good as ever. In attention to detail Alexander had proved himself right. He was not one of those miserables of whom it is written by the egregious, 'No detail was too small for him to attend to.' He knew what should be, and left it to others to see to it, only assuring himself that those others did it. The lesson that Jethro gave Moses, already referred to, was more to his liking, that lesson which stands to this day to those who lead in war or administration: 'Appoint the captains of thousands to judge the people—you cannot do it all yourself.'

So once more a conquering army marched out of Egypt, by the way of the Philistines, on Babylon the Whore, as Rameses and Tothmes and Necho had done before—but the hosts of Greece and Macedon marched by the ladder of Tyre. They crossed the Fertile Crescent, and over the Euphrates to the Tigris and those forgotten mounds of Nineveh, so forgotten that even Xenophon who had passed by never mentioned them, until they came to the banks of the Greater Zab, that flows to the Tigris from the mountains of Persia. There on the far side were the hosts of Darius collected from the far quarters of his empire.

Here again the tactics of Alexander were crude and direct enough. Once more as the lines engaged he led his horse straight for the Great King, the lust for personal engagement stirring him mightily. Long was the day of contest, long was the tally of the slaughtered, but the charge of the heavy cavalry as usual decided the day. The Great King fled, and Alexander sped after him. Far up the great Imperial Road Darius fell to the sword of a traitor just as Alexander, who had ridden hard on his heels for days, was coming up. It only remained to bring his body, generously enough, to his family for honourable obsequies.

The great capital of the Fertile Crescent, Babylon itself, that had fallen once before, fell into his hands, and then Susa and Persepolis, the latter burned in a drunken frolic, Alexander acquiescing—and then on, on across the deserts and plateaux of high Persia and after a while to Herat and the Oxus. The Macedonians held by their leader more than ever: wealth had come to all the leaders save himself, who cared naught for it. The rank and file had as much as they could carry.

Alexander was lofty enough. Not for him the usual gratifications, not for his bed the wives of kings, whether to crown his victory or for their own beautiful sakes, as they themselves expected. Like so many young men of the Nordic races, women interested him still but little—not that he eschewed them, but he had other fish to fry. He had refused to marry and have a replica before he left, and when, as we shall see, he did marry his wives cut no ice in his daily round. These good Nordic fish-men can be dull husbands, which explains many things in the world of Europe. In the East it was not understood.

But the gracious dignity accorded to the family of Darius was to come back as coals of fire on his head, in the more than acquiescence with which his rule over Persia was regarded, and the god-theory was now falling in more understanding soil. Alexander's freedom from the habits of his officers served in some sense to hedge him with more than ordinary royal divinity. His occasional roistering among his troops endeared him to the sturdy Macedonians, but the drunkenness which he used to develop did undoubtedly detract from his dignity. As long as victory was with him, that did not much matter, though the end was to be death at thirty-three.

With Persia settled and acquiescent, the Great Road along which Greek traders had for ages marched and which Greek transport agents managed, and the Silk Road to China, now lay before them. By Meshed to the valley of the Heri Rud, to Herat, to found Qandahar, which men say was an Alexandria, to march to what is now Kabul and thence over the Parapomisus to Balk, and later over the Oxus to Samarkand and deep into what are now the Soviet Republics of Turkistan is too far a cry to be told of here. The abounding restless energy of the leader held good, and it was greatly needed. Though many princes quailed before his name there were plenty to rise behind and fall on his garrisons, which often set him fiercely counter-marching. His confidence in himself and his paternity held good, his forces still looked to him as the god-sent guiding star. Leadership was still leadership on the well-recognised lines.

His vast accretion of territory called for large bodies of local troops, some, as with our own Asiatic forces, officered by young Macedonians; vicissitudes not unlike our own experiences in Afghanistan overtook him, only to be mastered furiously. His powers of fast marching were heavily tasked, but the upland climate allowed his Europeans, with their great leader at their head, to outmarch even the tribesmen.

Thus the years passed. Many Alexandrias were founded, and if we marvel thereat, we must remember that the Greek model was the city-state, like a market town round which the countryside rallied. Elderly or tired Macedonians, amply married, formed the colonists, and each Alexandria exuded a Greek culture. We see that the conquered countries eagerly adopted Greek ways and culture, as the Indian intelligentzia have spread themselves in English learning, in their search for the 'Secret.' So much did this obtain that we see Parthian and Sassanian kings finding Greek on their coinage as essential as we find Latin, and we may almost reckon Alexander's flair for world-wide Hellenic culture as the wise recognition of a general need. Thus in the pacification and Hellenisation of the Oxus valleys and the Bactrian table-lands we see the years pass by. Hypnotised by his glory, Macedonia and the Greek States stood reasonably by Olympias and the home government, although they were never to see their young King again.

To flair for rule and organisation, and to still supreme self-confidence, Alexander was adding some considerable political sense. Persian nobles were encouraged; he had long adopted, save when on some lightning march, Persian luxury, and very suitably—sniff his Macedonians never so jealously—on occasions wore Persian dress. Matrimony of the Nordic kind referred to had overtaken him, in which politics as much as love were the mainspring.

In these Persian years the belief in his divine descent, that had so sustained him under Persian and still more later under Indian hyperbole and suggestive flattery, becomes more pronounced. This megalomania developed to the extent that he claimed for himself not only divine descent but divinity itself. His Macedonians listened grimly enough, his Asiatics applauded, and since greatness and success is God-given, and Eastern deities took anthropomorphic form even more easily than those of Greece, why not? And Alexander evidently gained in some of his moods more assurance therefrom. In others he may have but thought it a useful aid to his supremacy. But with it all came more moodiness, more fierce rage, more repressions and executions. Contradictions of a god were obviously worthy of death. And the historian's tale of this changing mentality is a sad one. Nevertheless the charm lasted, the leader's influence, added to the stories of wealth, was to bring the Macedonian hosts in triumph to the Ravi, and behind it all must have been the young man's intense belief in himself, that still enabled him to hold and to bind.

Alexander's Marriages

Marriage and love, those great mainsprings of the world of high and low, are still the 'best news' from a human and journalistic point of view, and the conduct of heroes in their relationships is always a popular study.

Alexander's small interest in women has been referred to, which does not mean that he avoided them altogether, but among men of action his moderation is unusual. Great men of action have usually been great lovers in their moments of relaxation. We may well remember wise Francis Bacon's remarks hereon as regards soldiers: 'I know not how it is, but men of war seem to be given to wine as they are to women. I suppose it is that perils demand to be paid with pleasures.'

If we look to some of the great soldiers we shall readily see how essential to them was woman's companionship. Napoleon I. was a more than ready lover, and to him the company of women in his few leisure moments was indispensable. The Duke of Wellington in his younger days was affectionate to promiscuity. More than one of the great men of our own days have been similarly accredited. In fact the world admits to men of action a standard of their own, for 'perils demand to be paid with pleasures,' and those who can deliver great goods must order themselves their own way, even to their own undoing.

Alexander's first wife was Roxana, a lady of great beauty, daughter of a Sogdian prince, into whose territories came Alexander after he had marched through Persia. To her all accounts admit he gave his affection, and it was by her that he had a posthumous son, who under a more settled administration should have succeeded. Then he married, at the time of the 'mass marriage,' to be described later, Statyra, daughter of Darius, and by Barsine, the widow of Darius' great Greek general, Memnos, he had a son born out of wedlock. But since his early death prevented his having an adult heir, there was none to preserve the edifice. As has been said, there were no stories of amorous traditions and connections. The marriage with Statyra was political entered on to lead off in the 'mass marriage' aforesaid.

In India many princesses were available and many lesser delights, rarely partaken, though there is a strange story of a Brahmin family in Northern India that claims descent, preserving in its young men the likeness, carrying also that epileptic taint with which Alexander is said by some to have been afflicted, and which accounted for his greater vagaries.

This we do know, that by common consent his women—even Roxana his love—had no great interest for him in the constant rush of affairs and doings that surrounded him. If you marry the world's Alexanders you must be prepared for that.

The Road to India

It was India that was to make the 'wonder of the world' and finally to break it; not by her strength, for India accepts all conquerors and men of the sword, but by that terrible *caffard* that in all ages comes to overstrained soldiers.

By now the Macedonians were a small part of

the Alexandrine entourage. People of innumerable races were in his train. Many thousands of the Bactrian and Scythian folk, as aforesaid, followed Macedonian officers, and the King marched as an Eastern despot, a ruthless despot too he was becoming, violent and high-handed, believing himself a death-dealing deity—and now India was drawing him whether his troops liked it or not.

It was midsummer of 327 when he left his cool Afghan uplands for the hot banks of the Indus. It is indeed one of his executive failings that weather and climate were not his servants. If the spirit moved him he marched, regardless of the season, the which was probably his undoing at the last. For soldiers are but human, even if the leaders be supermen. Many of the princes of Northern India had visited him in Afghanistan and many had sworn to be his men, as they had been to an earlier Darius. But it was the King of Taxiles, hard by our Rawalpindi, who alone had kept his word, perhaps because he too was a Jăt and a foreigner. There was plenty of fighting with the hill tribes—with the Aproetæ, whom we call Afridi, and the Pactydæ, whom we call Paktans or Pathans—on what we now call the North-West Frontier, or rather the northerly extremity thereof, and there was the storming of that mysterious and only recently identified stronghold Aornos. Here was Alexander back in the heart of his troops, his Persian extravagance left behind, his golden helmet and his white plume always in evidence, especially at the storming of the isthmus at Aornos.

The Macedonians, who had constantly received drafts by the long march from Europe, were with him heart and soul, and his power and fame were carried to fabulous heights, in fact and in the world's opinion. When was it all to end?

It was his strategical sense that prevented his leaving the tribal refuge of Aornos undealt with on his flank, and now the Indus was left behind. With his friend Taxiles the Macedonian was making for the Hydaspes (the Jhelum), behind which what we should now call the Rajput forces were assembled under King Poros.

Before this, however, in the winter of 327–26 he had penetrated to Chitral, and on his way to the Jhelum had turned aside to Nyssa, on an ivy-clad mountain where rites like to the Bacchanalian were, he heard, in use.

The Jhelum crossed by stratagem, came the victory over Poros, and the defeat of the first tanks—the great armed Indian elephants. Where this was fought, fought also the British in 1849, singing round their camp-fires:

> Bayonets fixed and sabres drawn,
> Fight, where fought Alexander,
> Oh! Paddy Gough's a cross betwixt
> Hero and salamander.

No longer Alexander the god-like, the moody, the luxurious, but the simple soldier whom the men loved, all India seemed at his feet. Over the Acesines, which is now called the Chenab, the 'water of China,' down to the Hydraotis, which we still call the Raovi, on which now stands Lahore, the men marched willingly enough.

Alexander now heard of a Great King farther south in Sir-Hind, the Head of Hindustan, and to meet him he would go. But he had come to the place called stop! The Macedonians, his fighting spearhead, had had enough. *Caffard* had seized them of a sudden, as it usually does, and home they would go; and the generals broke it to the leader.

The god-man, infuriated, resisted, wept, stormed, sulked, and sat alone in his tent swallowing the bitter pill. The spell was broken, broken on the rock of tired feet—*pas manda*, as the Persian has it. He, Alexander!—Dionysius reincarnate—had to give way and march if not homewards, at least Persia-wards, even as Napoleon had to march back from Russia. Alexander's march down the Punjab and through Sind was, however, not at first on a par with the retreat from Moscow. He, with prescience that would alone stamp him as a great commander, had built and impressed boats on the Jhelum and Chenab, boats of stout deodar timber that would take the sea, and down to the sea with the armies they went. What to-day we should call the 'C3' men stayed as garrison of the subdued provinces, bidden to make colonies as lustily as possible.

On the way down, the Malloi, presumably the folk of Multan, offered resistance. Alexander turned aside his unwilling soldiery to storm their stronghold,[1] being severely wounded himself for his pains. We need not dwell on the great journey, of Nearchus setting forth in his deodar ships for the unknown Persian Gulf, of the heavy train being sent *via* Quetta and Qandahar,[2] of the lighter troops, and curiously enough the hosts of women, marching along the terrible desert coast of Mekran and of S.E. Persia. Perhaps Alexander dreamed of establishing cities on the coast, perhaps he knew that

[1] To this day at Paniala in the Derajat men say that the dates sprang from the date stones of his camp.

[2] A few years ago a heavy bronze Hermes was found on the Khojak.

Mekran would finish off the concubines and their brats. In any case it was a march of pitiful death starvation and thirst, as disastrous as the drag from Moscow to the Beresina.

Grim and determined, Alexander marched at their head, and devil take the hindmost. The Eastern women dropped by the way, as the French light-o'-loves died in the Russian snows in 1812. The personality of the leader brought the strong men and women through, to indulge in terrible saturnalia at Pella, to drown their memories. Also once more had the Alexandrine star shone bright, for news came that Nearchus had won through also, and was waiting on the coast. But once more too as their strength recovered did the Macedonians demand to be led back to Greece.

Back in Persia

Alexander, however, was now back on sure ground. He was the Great King, the semi-Persian, the divine.

Recognised as the successor of Darius he could and would be Persian, and his Macedonians liked it not. He had by his side his Persian 'Companions,' now trained, organised and selected like those who had accompanied him from Europe, and his Macedonians might go hang. He was the Great King, and there was no other way. If he was to be the Star of Persia he could not be wholly or very greatly Macedonian, and if he was to spread Hellenic culture he must meet that of Persia half-way, and the 'political' flair, that has already been referred to, was now strong within him. It is also to be remembered that both Greek and Persian, other than the Persian-Turk, were Caucasian or Aryan, and it was not so very long since they had left the same matrix. Fusion by physical union was in his mind, and to this end he now organised what is known in history as the 'Mass Marriage of Pella,' the marriage of East and West, even as John Company thought to do in early Georgian times.

Two princesses, one Statyra, daughter of Darius, the other Parysadas, daughter of Artaxerxes III., climbed to his marriage bed of *convenance* rather than love, for Roxana alone held what passed for affection with him. Their marriages brought together the two rival houses of the old Persian dynasties. The marriages of his high officers, with suitable Persian ladies and princesses, were celebrated by himself as officiant. To the thousands of his soldiery came thousands of Persian girls, willing or otherwise. The Greeks marrying οἱ βάρβαροι! —yet Alexander insisted that it was not so much *barbaroi* as all that. The half-bred colonies would but cement his power, or so he thought, and yet most of his Macedonians eventually left him for their homes, leaving their wives behind them.

The Collapse

The administration of Persia kept him more than engaged, when he endured the bitter shock of the death of Hephæstion, and this added to his failing, for with all his acquired wisdom and power of rule, he had lost his rule of himself. Drinking bout on drinking bout, the joy of boon companions, which was at the bottom of it, added to the shocks of many severe wounds, were too much for even his magnificent frame and constitution. Following on two nights of carouse, a bout of what was probably malaria was more than his system could overcome. He died as his army filed past him.

With him went his empire, and most of his family in an orgy of heathen cruelty, but he had built better than he knew. He had Hellenised much of Asia for a while, and his heritage in culture still, in some sense, remains, while the provinces into which his Empire broke up remained, some for centuries, under the dynasties of his generals. Seleucia, the province seized by Seleucus, remained a great empire for generations, and Egypt to the day of Julius Cæsar. Even distant Bactria, from the Oxus to the Indus, remained for years in semi-Hellenic guise, and over two hundred mints therein long struck Greek coins, which you may find to this day along the British frontier.

So at Babylon was the end of it. Often has it been asked, What has the world gained or lost by the death of this astounding *enfant gâté*, this mixture of all the great gifts with some of the worst traits? No man can say.

In any case we have something very definite to take to ourselves in the study of leadership, some grip of the elusive fairy gifts that compel fate and fortune and lead or drive mankind.

Reviewing the occasion, it may be said that there was no demand for a great leader in Western Asia. The Asiatic Greek demanded no Pan-Hellenism and no release from foreign control, the world was not cognisant of its need for Hellenic culture.

The policy of the former was but the reflection of Philip's ambition, the latter of his son's imagination. War, the desire of a young soldier to experience more of it, must also have been a stimulant to start the great adventure. Trained of Aristotle, the young King no doubt thought that Hellenism was something worth while. It is then possible that Alexander had a genuine crusading spirit that sanctified the desire of military glory for glory's sake. The sword and the spear, the phalanx, the thousand that march as one, the squadron that rode knee to knee—they had their urgent call for him.

But nothing of this would have availed had he not the two essentials, the gift of command and of courage, and above all good fortune in his saddle-bow.

'Don't tell me he is a good general,' said Napoleon, 'tell me if he is lucky.'

To all his brilliant qualities Fortune put the coping-stone of her favour. Whence derived his compelling self-confidence?—and the answer is laboured herein—the intoxication of the Jupiter Ammon legend, steadily becoming more and more an article of faith in his highly strung mind, driving him ever on as the belief in his blessedness becomes confirmed by success.

Since we are primarily studying leadership, let us try to sum up the qualities and concomitants that in some sort encompassed and contributed to the result. We may perhaps enumerate some factors in the ungaugeable, something as follows:—

(i) His youthful charm, his father's prestige, and the prepared weapon that his father left to his hand.

(ii) The call of Hellenism, the call to spread the Hellenic outlook and culture, which the cultivated Macedonian had acquired—more Greek than the Greeks.

(iii) The fortune that shone on his efforts, especially his early efforts, that hypnotised his followers.

(iv) The overwhelming courage and *élan* that he always displayed, that captivated his soldiery.

(v) The development and strengthening of his self-confidence, due to his early successes and to his growing belief in the truth of the Ammon legend.

(vi) The feebleness of Eastern armies before Western organisation.

(vii) His obvious flair for government, which enabled his Eastern provinces to remain Macedonian after his death.

(viii) The fact that he not only made war support war, but he made it very profitable to his followers of all grades, in the items of the Persian alliterative saying, *Zăr, Zăn, Zămin* 'Gold, Women, Land', all that men of those days, or indeed any other, really cared about.

But of all these many characteristics and concomitants the underlying gift of a compelling personality, round which the said concomitants can accumulate, was there, born within him, in that strange gift of life that we, even now, understand not at all.

That in brief is the story, so far as we can understand it, of Alexander of Macedon, dead in Babylon the Mighty of a fever, in the thirty-third year of his age.

The evil traits in his character, developed under the stress of his career, are patent, and perhaps kindly death saved him from the pit they were digging for him. The speculations as to the world's 'if' had he lived, and been able to break away from his views, can be without end. But, when all is said and done, there is no other example in the world of the fortune and subsidiary occasions of any man being able so to dominate and enthuse the world's races.

CHAPTER IV

QUEEN ELIZABETH

Chronology and Data
Harry's Daughter
The Occasions of Elizabeth
Elizabeth's Early Days
Elizabeth in the Saddle
Elizabeth as a Woman
Elizabeth the Stateswoman
The Last Days

QUEEN ELIZABETH

Chronology and Data

The times and dates of Elizabeth and her compeers and her predecessors are most confusing to the reader, and a few notes thereon will not be out of place.

(1) The principal dates of births and successions are as follows:—

Henry VIII., born 1491, acceded 1509 aged 18, died 1547 aged 56; reigned 38 years.

Edward VI., born 1537, acceded 1547 aged 10, died 1553 aged 16; reigned 6 years.

Mary, born 1515, acceded 1553 aged 38, died 1558 aged 43; reigned 5 years.

Elizabeth, born 1533, acceded 1558 aged 25, died 1603 aged 69; reigned 44 years.

(2) Henry VIII.'s sisters were married as follows:—

Margaret to James IV. of Scotland (grandmother of Mary Queen of Scots).

Mary to Louis XII. of France, and secondly to the Duke of Suffolk (grandmother of Lady Jane Grey).

(3) The Duke of Suffolk (Charles Brandon) was beheaded by Henry VIII.

(4) The Duke of Somerset (Seymour) was Lord Protector to Edward VI. till 1549, when the Duke of Northumberland (Earl of Warwick) succeeded him as Minister but not as Protector. He had Somerset beheaded in 1552.

(5) Henry VIII. had declared both Mary and Elizabeth illegitimate and unable to succeed, but in 1544 an Act of Parliament reaffirmed their

right of succession, and made Lady Jane Grey their successor in case of their not being available.

(6) Edward VI. at Northumberland's instigation had nominated Lady Jane Grey as his successor. Northumberland had been indiscreet enough to marry her to his son the Earl of Dudley, who was executed after Lady Jane.

(7) The Duke of Norfolk was beheaded by Elizabeth for a plot to marry Mary Queen of Scots and take the throne.

(8) Anne Boleyn, Elizabeth's mother, was niece of an earlier Duke of Norfolk.

(9) The young Earl of Essex, the favourite of Elizabeth's old age, was Robert Devereux, second Earl, and was beheaded for a foolish rising in 1601. His mother after the death of the first Earl had married the Earl of Leicester, the Queen's early favourite, so involved were the personalities of those days.

Harry's Daughter

It is not possible to survey the rise of Britain and the British Empire without feeling how seldom this essentially self-governing self-sufficient people required a magnetic leader in a crisis. Groups of men of good sense, and filled with the sense of the commonwealth, have almost always taken the place of such. Few then as are the Britons to be classed as great leaders, because the need of them so seldom arose, it is still more rare to find occasion for women. England has never had her Semiramis, her Isabella, her Catherine the Great, but she has had Harry's Daughter, not only to pull her out of a crisis, but to set her with enthusiasm on a new course and start her in a new race. Victoria the

Good ruled commercial England, set a tone of good morals and high endeavour, reigned but rarely ruled, because there was no occasion. Her reign it is true was the reign in which Elizabeth's sowing blossomed a hundredfold, but it happened largely of its own accord, *Consule* Victoria, and not *propter* Victoriam.

When, however, we turn to Elizabeth, we have an occasion and a leader who rose to it, some peculiar circumstances, and perhaps some subtle power, which it is worth our while to explore. In what lay the genius and this power of Good Queen Bess, whom our people idolised during the first two-thirds of her reign?

She was Harry's Daughter, that was it is true a great start in the race, for England had revered their great tempestuous King, who never quite grew up, but who defied Rome and all its temporal pretensions, and cleared out the abbeylubbers—that Harry to whom Laughton with all his acting has not done full justice. Harry, even when chambering with Anne of Cleves 'for England's sake,' was a great king, and a man after the heart of the Anglo-Saxon of the period; and here was his daughter, who came after, Mary Mary, quite Contrary. How the nursery rhyme records England's tolerance of Mary with her nuns and her shrines!

> Mary, Mary, quite contrary!
> How does your garden grow?
> With fairy belles and cockleshells [pilgrims' shells]
> And pretty maids [nuns] all in a row.

Elizabeth ruled and led England. What was the occasion and what was her secret? Merely to be a woman, is always to hold a secret, the great secret of life and its call, and in her case the frustrated call, to a maiden, but the secret must have been more than that. Charm and beauty and the real meaning of 'The Jewel within the Lotus' are great things, great spurs, but there was more than that to this young queen.

The Occasions of Elizabeth

Now Harry of England had reigned for thirty-eight years, and in that period great things had happened. It is true enough that Henry's quarrel with Rome over his need for a new wife and a son did start the Reformation in England, but it only let loose a great pent-up stream of reaction against the ways of Rome. It probably saved England from the discords and inconsistency of the Continental reformations, it kept Calvinism from us till it had been humanised for three-quarters of a century, and it permitted the ancient Church to emerge purified and more dignified in its own right, despite the inheritance of strife in later days. He had also made a new nobility and gentry to take the place of those that the Wars of the Roses had destroyed.

He had disinherited the Church lands, which these sad wars had swelled unduly, but even the unreformed Church knew it had too much. He had turned Thomas Cromwell loose among the abbey lands and dissolved abbey and nunnery, those nunneries concerning which inspectors from Rome itself had written such terrible things. England loveth him therefor; it hated all the abbeylubbers. He was a sportsman, a roisterer on occasion, so were they. He loved women, so did they. On the Continent he and Wolsey had maintained prestige and he had founded the British Navy. His long reign was prosperous, popular, amusing, for all its mistakes. The heads that came off were Court and noble heads, and that did not affect the people, who were still happy in the peace and quiet of the Mortimer Rose. And on Henry's death, all was well. One of his wills disinherited, so far as such disinheritance was valid, Mary and Elizabeth, his daughters, declaring them illegitimate—Mary because he had divorced Katherine, Elizabeth because he should not have; a subsequent Act had made them heirs. But there was a male heir, delicate, but competent under a protector. Edward VI. reigned at the age of ten, and while he reigned, Mary and Elizabeth were his properly cared-for sisters. But there was trouble to come, and the delicate boy reigned but six years. The country, for all its acquiescence in the Reformation, was Catholic in its religion, and had loved the old Church. Mary was chosen as Queen, the old Catholic families looked to a restoration of the old *régime,* and restored it was with a vengeance, to the kindling of the martyrs' fires.

Now Elizabeth, as all the world knows, had been brought up in the Reformed Church, Protestant in that it protested against the powers and errors of Rome, Catholic in that it accepted the universal doctrine, the Apostolic Succession, and the mystery of the Holy Communion. Archbishop Cranmer was her godfather. Suspect she was, and not unnaturally the subject for anti-Roman plots. In those days of torture, of denials and assertion and confessions under the question, it was easy for Elizabeth, now grown up, to be implicated;

and not only to the Tower did she go, but to the Tower by way of the Traitors' Gate, she indignantly protesting. Many, including especially the Spaniards, clamoured for her death. In fact, but for Mary's stout refusal to sign her sister's death warrant, the support of the Howards, and the Governor's refusal to obey a warrant unsigned by the Queen, there would have been no Good Queen Bess for the future to dissect and start theories on. However, after two months she was put in the care of Sir Henry Bedingfield at Woodstock, and when Mary was reported *enceinte*, she was brought to Court as no longer harmful.

Poor feeble little Mary with her Spanish husband, who would have made England an appanage of Spain, and under the Roman Obedience, was happily not to reign for long. In four and a half years she had passed to her sour rest.

Parliament now declared Elizabeth, erstwhile prisoner in the Tower, Queen of England, and all the common people, and all Henry's new-made squires, battening on the Church lands, shouted for joy. It was true that Thomas Cromwell had distributed lands venially, by sheer friendship and favour of the King and himself, but you can turn any respectable Briton, however humble his family, into a country gentleman, or even a great nobleman, in three generations, and the new and the old squires were a stout and sturdy lot. Among them, rich on Church loot indeed, was the grandfather of Oliver Cromwell. Here clearly is the occasion calling for leadership evident—an England, shaken by Mary's fierce ways of returning to the Roman Allegiance, anxious for peace and prosperity to come again, and threatened by the enmity of the then mighty Spain.

Elizabeth's Early Days

So at twenty-five years of age, Elizabeth, Harry's Daughter, succeeds to Harry's throne. What like was this maiden just coming into her prime of womanhood, destined to lead and guide good ministers, and to demand the great allegiance of all the young men of England? Was she gay and beautiful, was her temperament that of a sheltered girl? She had been into the Tower by the Traitors' Gate, with the valley of the shadow closer perhaps than she knew. It may have sat lightly on her, it must have affected her nature, may have been responsible for the harshness that at times shadowed her normal good sense.

It was 1558 when she came to the throne. Had her childhood and girlhood been otherwise normal? It had not. She was two and a half when her mother was beheaded, and though she had probably no actual remembrance thereof, yet there may well have been in her subconscious mind the effect of what those around her must have said in her hearing, and in her earlier years she must have often heard the story. When she was twenty came the tragedy of Lady Jane Grey. There were two granddaughters of Henry VII., and two great-granddaughters, all eligible heirs if the mother's marriage of the first two were to be considered legitimate. These were Henry VIII.'s daughters, Mary and Elizabeth; Lady Jane Grey, whose grandmother, sister of Henry VIII. and widow of Louis XII. of France, had married the Earl of Suffolk, *en secondes noces*, and Mary Stuart, whose grandmother was also sister to Henry VIII., and married to James IV. of Scotland.

As has been said, the first two by certain declarations had been declared illegimate by their father. To avoid the succession of Catholic Mary, Northumberland tried to make Lady Jane Grey Queen, and Queen she was in some sort for twenty days. Then came the counter-revolution of the Catholic Cause, and poor innocent Lady Jane Grey goes to the scaffold, followed by her spouse, and later by her sponsor.

In Elizabeth's mind and soul these tragedies must have left some mark, as also some episodes when she was with Katherine Parr, who had married the roistering Lord High Admiral, brother of the Protector, and who brought up her royal step-children.

Elizabeth in the Saddle

To have led the chequered life just outlined from childhood, to have spent some months of young maidenhood in the Tower, with a very real danger of death ever present, and then to emerge to the joyous acclamations of a people, was strong, nay, glorious diet. All England was to welcome her, and round her Court the young folk of the noble houses new and old, and a brilliant *corps diplomatique*, were ready to sport themselves in all the silks and satins of the markets. And sport they did. To be twenty-five, to be her father's daughter, as well as born of beautiful, vivacious Anne Boleyn, to be just released from bondage, auburn of hair and pink of complexion, all glorious without and within, in an England that intended to be Merrie and forget; what more wonderful!

Moreover to this now peaceful country was to come at last, with both hands full, the spirit of the Renaissance, and as the years grew and the chimneys in Zion were hot, there were Marlowe and Spenser, Shakespeare and Francis Bacon—*Tamburlaine*, *Venus and Adonis*, *Faerie Queen*, and what not, for posterity to wonder at, though curiously enough we are often baffled as to personalities. The gift of portraying the stars on the film is rather lacking. The choice young men and goodly who thronged the Court and the country gatherings were after the girl's heart, and it was a very large and generous one for choice young men.

But when we come to Elizabeth's grip on the saddle, matters are somewhat different. For some not very intelligent reason, historians seem to group round her personality all the doings of the leading spirits of the age. We have seen Jethro explaining to Moses that a man must delegate. Even the greatest of autocratic sovereigns does not really 'run the show' himself; how can he? He or his chief minister, the latter usually, having sucked all the good from the ideas of his assistants, proposes policies. The monarch hears proposals, accepts, and then, if a wise one, directs his own and his Court's influence in support thereof. If the monarch is a lesser, but a wise spirit, the more active lead must come from the minister. The Wellingtons gather much from their staff, even the flair of Napoleon was not all his own. The Haigs and the Pétains, surrounded by machines of intense complexity, must do so still more.

The twenty-five-year-old Elizabeth could have known little of statecraft. All she could have known was that England wanted an agreed-on religious system with an anti-Roman incline; that the country had no desire to be an appanage of Spain, and that, above all, peace and trade and agricultural development were what was demanded of England's Queen and England's ministers. These main points being agreed on, then the Ministry could get to work, and we shall see that the Elizabeth of the iron heart and hand was largely fiction, certainly for many years.

In all our studies of history, the tendency, hard to avoid, is to telescope time. The Romans ruled and developed England for twice as long as the British have developed India. To us, Roman and Norman are none too far apart, away back in the mists of time. Yet it is still *further* from the coming of Aulus Plautus, let alone Julius Cæsar, to the Norman Conquest than it is from the latter event to our own times. There was no Victorian Age; there were at least three ages, as there were three generations covered by that long reign. Similarly the term Elizabethan Age is equally loose. Elizabeth reigned for forty-five years, and the Armada came when she had been on the throne for thirty years. The story of the lion-hearted young Queen stimulating troops at Tilbury and sailors of the British Navy is but imagination. Elizabeth was then fifty-five years of age, a fine woman still, but already on the way to be that terrible 'raddled' old woman of fifteen years later. As Kipling, the understanding, sings:

> The Queen was in her chamber and she was middling old.
> Her petticoat was satin, and her stomacher was gold.
> Backward and forward and sideways did she pass,
> Making up her mind to face the cruel looking-glass:
> The cruel looking-glass which will never show a lass
> As comely or as kindly or as young as what she was!
>
> *The Looking-Glass* (R. K.).

Further, an equally unrealised period of time occurred, which we often also forget, between the coming of Mary Stuart, her first-cousin-once-removed, to Elizabeth, and the latter's regretful assent to removing the cause of much plotting. Close on nineteen years elapsed before the cruel though almost unavoidable decision. Elizabeth was fifty-four then, and the old suggestion of jealousy of a beautiful rival had no basis.

When Elizabeth was young, what was the situation? There were two different sets of millstones grinding—the upper and the nether millstones of Rome and Calvin in things spiritual; in things temporal, France and Spain. To Elizabeth's great minister, Burghley, and of course to her own common sense, the one thing to do was to save England from being ground to powder between either set. To it was added her personal antipathy to her brother-in-law, Philip, and her vigorous personal determination on no account to succeed to the bed of her sister Mary.

Perhaps ninety per cent. of all Elizabeth's wisdom and cunning was due to that remarkable stay behind the throne, William Cecil, Lord Burghley (1521–1598), who trained at Cambridge (where he did not take a degree) and Gray's Inn, had become a legal light, and a man of shrewd affairs, and eventually Lord of the Exchequer, to whom Elizabeth herself said, 'The judgment I have of you is that you will not be corrupted by any manner of gifts, and will always be faithful to the State.' In the rough times of his earlier life he was, as the Marquess of Winchelsea once said of himself, 'More of the willow than the oak,' tough, but bending somewhat to the storm and the stress.

Burghley's great dominating feature was caution, the caution that England so needed, and the extremely capricious moods of the Queen, often exaggerated for political reasons, enabled him to back and trim before the blasts of his mighty neighbours, and mightier faiths, by using her caprice as a cloak to his own craft—'I should like to do it, but my wife . . . Well, you know what women are,' and we may be sure that Burghley made the most of so heaven-sent a device. Elizabeth could rarely make up her mind, thought the outside world, and a decision usually meant a war, which was what England did not want. We may imagine that Queen Victoria's Foreign Ministers at times used her womanhood also as a useful cloak. Nothing is sacred to a Sapper—or a Foreign Minister.

Elizabeth as a Woman

Since undoubtedly one of Elizabeth's chief assets as a leader was her femininity, the glamour of the temple of life, and her indecision one of her useful assets to her ministers, it is necessary to consider that aspect of her life and character—to estimate, if it be possible, the effect of the great 'daie spring' of sex. That side of her has been explored in popular writings of late years, with a lamentable neglect of that delicacy with which this facet of a woman's life and nature should at all times be regarded. But at the same time it cannot be overlooked.

To begin with, as in Victoria's youth, the question of her marriage stirred considerably the chancelleries of Europe. Marriage that would secure the friendship of these pugnacious and wealthy islands was a very right matter for competition. Indeed did Burghley find it so. To starve Spain the assistance of France was needed. For twelve years did Elizabeth, perceiving the strategical point, and enjoying the joke, succeed in engendering the belief that she was in love with the Duke of Anjou. Even Philip for a while was fed on such honey-dew.

But apart from this, queens have not quite the privileges of their female subjects in modern days. They cannot, unless singularly strong of purpose, please themselves. The Crown demands a son, and a son they must do their best to provide. Her ministers were anxious enough that the Queen should so exert herself, could a suitable consort be found.

And now we come to the great sad secret of the Virgin Queen. It is generally accepted that she was not quite as other women are, for surgical reasons which modern science could have removed. Ben Jonson the gossip is probably right when he records that she had a 'membrana,' and the Spanish Ambassador, Feria, wrote to his master, as the years of maidenhood rolled on, '*Intendo qu'elle no terna hijas*,' and so whispered the wind, and murmured the waters.

Elizabeth herself told Sussex, 'I hate the idea of marriage for reasons that I would not divulge to a twin soul,' and so the poor lady spent her life on the all-alone stone, feeling, it was said, that, to her at any rate, a husband would be but a drag that there was nothing to be gained by, if there could not be the crown of children—and all the world may well bow the head in decorous sympathy.

On the other hand, it was not to be expected

but that the daughter of Harry and Anne would take an interest in the other sex, and she evinced an amorous nature that on occasion was distinctly scandalous. Indeed it has been said, probably with truth, that her admirers at times were allowed some intimacy after amorous dalliance. They might carry 'The outworks and bastions yes! The citadel no!'

The exact truth will never be known, nor does it concern us, save that at first the possibility of her marriage, then the excitement of possible courtship and favour, were, to her ministers, useful assets in diplomacy and to herself. For her country, they exacted services of adventure and daring that money could not buy. So here we have in her own sex-self, and even her abnormality, a spur and a stimulant that was one of the factors of her almost uncanny power.

At the same time it is generally recorded that, after the charm of her first youth and *joie de vivre* had passed, there was not the charm, say, of Mary Queen of Scots. For her men went mad, but not for Elizabeth. The Gloriana and Bel Phœbe business, at first genuine in the intoxicating excitement of her youth and royal glamour, had to be kept up long after any spontaneity was dead. There were many men for whom she felt attraction. For Robert Dudley, Earl of Leicester, she had a real passion; there was the stately Hallon, Heneage of the good looks, De Vere, young Blount with the nut-brown hair; a goodly procession such as any comely woman, let alone a queen, has a right to. The story of Elizabeth at fifty-three and the ambitious young Essex aged twenty is in another category. Before the years had been eaten by locusts there was ample enough of the woman to yield that mysterious influence of sex that in a queen gives leadership. In humbler life, deprived of the added glamour of place, it would have lost much of its power.

Elizabeth the Stateswoman

Queen Elizabeth lived till she was sixty-nine, a considerable age for the period, so that all the stories of her ill-health and maladies are controverted thereby. At the most she probably suffered from 'nerves,' which the tragedies of her earlier life and the non-fulfilment of her natural life may easily have engendered.

The impression that the Queen was a lion-hearted woman of splendid gestures is not borne out by facts. The Spanish Ambassador described her as pusillanimous, given to dissimulation, and flexible. She has, however, been called a sane woman in a world of maniacs. But she, in fact, could rarely make up her mind, and it has been said how Burghley sometimes profited in his dealings with the outer world, on his own account, by this defect—and also how decision at this period might easily have meant war. But Elizabeth was Harry's Daughter, some said also his grand-daughter, and there was a dash of his vigour and pertinacity as well as the sinuosity and vacillation more readily apparent. She floated in a sea of indecision, occasionally reaching hectically for some object, and she could tack, deny and shuffle with any politician. Nevertheless she could show courage when necessary, but too often had to turn her back on the ways of strength. In fact it would often be hard to say when her vagaries were her own, or called forth by the politics of the hour. Even Burghley at times found her variability and caution more than he could adapt, and he served her for thirty years.

The breaking of the Armada was the apotheosis of Queen Elizabeth's fame and influence. For thirty years had she and Burghley watched and feared. The adventurous, seafaring folk of England had made up their minds, however much the statesman might deprecate, that the Don's monopoly in South America was not to be borne. So, during many of these years of hesitancy, it was fear of what the persistent British piracy might provoke that complicated matters. Drake, Frobisher, Hawkins, and the rest, were but heroic pirates most of the years, and it was not much use she and Burghley humouring the Don, while her subjects were making a profitable living by singeing his beard. No doubt Francis Drake's periods in the black books were due to his escapades under what was very like the 'Jolly Roger.'

The threat of invasion brought out all the best in the Tudor Queen. Her personal courage and energy brought her to horse with her troops, though fifty-three. The years had worked their will on the laughing Queen of twenty-five, and now, though able to languish among her young men, she was a rough, hectoring Tudor dame, a stern-faced woman of business. As such she appealed to many as what England, seafaring England, wanted, and yet withal in these thirty years she had other amazing characteristics and sides to her character. She was the cultivated lady of the Renaissance. She could speak six languages, several fluently;

she was a real connoisseur of music; her beautiful calligraphy is still a model; she had unerring social sense, and the gift of speech, especially of official speech, as the years rolled on and experience gave more and more confidence.

At home, her agreement with Burghley and Walsingham and Clarendon over Church matters was perhaps her greatest gift to the nation. She and they wanted above all things the National Church to develop in peace, sufficiently broad and wide to hold all men. The old religion might live quietly as it liked—but woe betide risings, rebellions and intrigues on its behalf. For the sake of continuity she allowed herself to be styled the head of the Anglican Church. It is, however, generally conceded that, despite the early teaching of her godfather, she had no very deep religious sense—and here she but echoed the Nordic mind of the English. In the great controversy that the Reformation loosed on the world, as to the mystery and meaning of the Holy Communion, she wrote what may be said to sum up all the wonderings of that world, a summing-up that *should* satisfy all men:

> Christ was the Word that spake it,
> He took the bread and brake it,
> And what His Word did make it
> That I believe and take it.

Also she stood by her Bishops, being probably wise, as her successor was, to see that the Apostolic Succession was an important factor in the 'Divine right of kings.' It was James I. who actually said 'No bishops, no kings.' The Calvinists and Presbyterians might also preach and live in peace, but only so long as they did not kick up the dust of civil dissension. And all the while she was Good Queen Bess to the people, if tiresome Queen Bess to her Ministry. In the days of her beauty the visitations with which she graced the houses of the great, to their pecuniary embarrassment, brought a colour to the countryside that was popular enough. Had the old religion left Mary Stuart alone, that poor driven lady's head would not have been parted, and none was more reluctant to put an end to her than the Queen.

The Last Days

The breaking of the Armada ended the long epoch of thirty years of the Spanish shadow, although it was followed by two or three years of more forgotten, though equally serious, military dangers from Spain. But with deliverance the country forgot her. After the thirty years during which she and Burghley had watched and warded were over, England turned to other gods, and Elizabeth's popularity was gone. Perhaps thirty years of one Queen and one Prime Minister were more than any country could stand, though it was the continuity that made England. There were fifteen more years before it was to ring to evensong, but they were fifteen sad years, while Bel Phœbe turned from the handsome Tudor dame of the Tilbury review to the 'raddled old woman' that she has been described. The sinister side of her nature, a throw-back some say to a Visconti ancestor, developed. She became at times 'a fierce old hag,' and sat still when displeased, with every feather bristling. The friends of her youth were gone, had married and left Court. All the public men had changed; now came courtiers who flattered and humoured, and even feigned passion, for what it would profit them. Where she had led from verve and presence, she now led from fear, and ministers would use her name as a word of sinister power.

We need not dwell on the passion of her old age for the younger Essex. That for Leicester, despite his marriage, had dominated her for thirty years. As the old men who had upheld her and carried out her behests disappeared, it was the Raleighs and Essexes who took their place. Robert Devereux, Earl of Essex, was a very attractive young man, and she was fifty-three when he at twenty took her fancy. He was the Queen's cousin twice removed, and was no carpet-knight, having received his spurs from Leicester at the battle of Zutphen (where Philip Sidney died). His father, the more famous Earl of Essex, had married Letitia Knollys, who had, when widowed, married Leicester. It has been said that the latter helped install his stepson in Elizabeth's favour with the view of 'keeping it in the family,' a typically Elizabethan proceeding. At any rate, in her increasing age her capricious passion for the lad no doubt kept her young and interested, and the other young opportunists were kept to some extent at bay thereby. But ere long, Time's hand grew more than heavy, and the last fifteen years were those of loneliness, disfavour among her people and sorrow for the want of bairns. It was a sad ending, and had none of those joyous interludes with which we shall see that other great queen, Tseu-Hi, Dowager Empress of China, kept her youth and power far longer.

Withered, a mummy figure, still in jewelled farthingale and ruffs—fiercely bristling and dominating, now an imperious tradition whom men feared—she went slowly down the slipway to the sea of dissolution.

It had been in truth a life of sorrow, to which her bitter cry on hearing that her cousin, Mary Stuart, had a son probably supplies the key. The weakness of years came on her, but imperious as ever we hear of her saying to Burghley, who had said she must go to bed, 'Little man! Little man! the word *must* is not used to kings.'

When she was dying, Bishop Whitgift, whom she used to call 'My little black husband,' was on his aged aching knees for hours, as she prayed him to continue, feeling perhaps with Cromwell that it was 'terrible to fall into the hands of the living God.'

Those who have seen the 'Immortal Sarah,' Sarah Bernhardt, in her great part 'The Death of Elizabeth,' will have viewed what is probably a true presentation of the sad, almost unhallowed, end of a great Tudor, nay a great English lady, and would have wished it otherwise; save that it was a death in fighting trim—against Time, the enemy.

It was early morning on the 24th of March 1603, the Bishop still praying, that her inexplicable spirit was required of her.

CHAPTER V

OLIVER CROMWELL IN THE MAKING

Chronology of Oliver's Life
The Origins of Oliver
His Early Days
King Charles' Quarrel with Scotland
The Long Parliament meets
Cromwell as the Cavalry Soldier
From Troop Leader to Brigadier
Marston Moor and the Second Newbury
Naseby
Cromwell and Parliament
The King and the Army

OLIVER CROMWELL IN THE MAKING

Chronology of Oliver's Life

1599. Oliver born at Huntingdon (25, iv).
1617. Father dies, while Oliver is at Cambridge.
1628. Represents Huntingdon in Parliament.
1639. Represents Cambridge in the 'Short' Parliament.
1641. Represents Cambridge in the 'Long' Parliament.
1641. Civil War commences.
1642. Battle of Edgehill (23, x).
1642. Battle of Newbury (First) (20, vii).
1644. Battle of Marston Moor (2, vii).
1644. Battle of Newbury (Second) (27, x).
1645. Battle of Naseby (14, vi).
1646. The King surrenders to the Scots.
1647. The King handed over to the Parliament.
1649. Charles beheaded (30, i).
1649. Oliver made Protector (16, xii).
1650. Battle of Dunbar (3, ix).
1651. Battle of Worcester (3, ix).
1658. Death of Oliver (3, ix). Richard succeeds.
1659. Richard resigns (22, iv). (Lives till 17, xii.)
1660. Restoration (29, v).

The Origins of Oliver

There would on first sight seem to be no clearer exemplar of an unexpected and heaven-sent call to lead than that vouchsafed to this middle-aged country gentleman. We can do no better service to a study of leadership than probe once again the occasions, gifts and causes which called 'Old Oliver' to so prominent a position.

To gauge the causes therefor, however, it is necessary to get a better understanding of his origins, and life to middle age, than that which generally passes current as history. It will show us that Cromwell's rise to lead a majority of England, or if you prefer it a dominant minority, came to a man of forty-two who had hitherto led no public life. The false conception referred to, presents to us Oliver Cromwell as a man of sturdy humble origin, the son of a small brewer to wit, in Huntingdon, stirred eventually by the oppression of King and Great Lords, typical of that undercurrent of English thought which derives from a love of liberty and justice in those to whom the Old Testament was the salt of life.

But the plain historical facts are far different, and by stating them we put the Protector on a surer foundation, when we come to wonder what were the sources and psychology of his leadership.

Who then was Oliver Cromwell? His great-grandfather on the male side was the great Sir Richard Cromwell, *alias* Williams, of Hinchinbrooke (whose Welsh grandfather was a publican), whose father had married a sister of that Thomas Cromwell, absolutist and henchman of Henry VIII. Richard Williams became his uncle's secretary, and took his name, signing himself, when legally necessary, as 'Richard Cromwell *alias* Williams.' Thomas Cromwell bestowed on him many of those Church manors and abbey lands which he was engaged in confiscating. Richard thus became one of the millionaires of the Reformation, and, duly knighted, became the Sir Richard Cromwell of Hinchinbrooke aforesaid, who married the daughter of a wealthy Lord Mayor of London and still more added to the family fortune.

Sir Richard was succeeded by his son, Sir Henry, who married another Lord Mayor's daughter.

Henry's life was contemporary with that of Queen Elizabeth, whom he entertained at Hinchinbrooke, where he lived as a great host, entertaining all and sundry, especially the mighty, being long Sheriff of the county.

The Welsh Williams family was now emphatically Cromwell look you! and Sir Henry had ten children (besides two illegitimate daughters), of whom the daughters married into the great wealthy country or business families, Whalley, Barrington, Hampden, etc. Sir Henry was succeeded by his son, Sir Oliver, whose younger brother, Robert, was the father of 'Old Noll.' This Robert Cromwell of the Hinchinbrooke family settled a few miles off in a large house in Huntingdon, and had the then considerable income of between £4000 and £5000 a year. To the income of his estate he added the profits of the brewery business, and he married Elizabeth Steward, from another of those houses which had risen to riches on the Reformation. They had but one son who survived, our Oliver of history, and by just so much was he the brewer's son.

The young Oliver, the nephew of one of the great men of England, son of a wealthy house, closely related to a dozen or more of the wealthy country and business families of England, was brought up, to a great extent, in the grandeur of his uncle's great house, close by to his own home at Huntingdon.[1]

That is the true story of Oliver's so-called humble and sturdy English origin, sturdy no doubt, but with the independence and sturdiness of the 'Haves' rather than the 'Have-nots.' Further,

[1] The story of Oliver's origin is told sufficiently for us in Hilaire Belloc's *Cromwell.*

he married Mary Bourcher, daughter of a rich City knight.

Hinchinbrooke was sixty miles from London on the great posting road to the North, and could be reached in a day, so that its social importance in the hands of a wealthy public man can be realised. Here it was that James I. was received on his way to take up the British throne, by Oliver Cromwell the new Lord, uncle to young Oliver, and here was the scene of the perhaps mythical meeting and baby squabble between Oliver and Charles, the former four years of age, which, some folk would have it, formed an hostility complex in the former's mind.

But the Hinchinbrooke star was waning; three generations of spending and magnificence had strained the great resources of the family, and in 1628 the great house was sold to the rival house of Montague, and that was naturally a severe blow to Oliver. It was in this year that he first entered public life, in that he represented Huntingdon in the insignificant Parliament of the day, but merely as 'one of the crowd' on a dull occasion.

His Early Days

Even in the merest outline of the life of Oliver it is impossible to ignore the great prolonged religious strains of the period. It was Thomas Cromwell (great-great-grand-uncle) who had led Henry VIII. to make himself head of the English Church, when that Church reformed itself and broke from Rome in 1534, completing its task in 1547. We need not try to follow the earlier days of the Church of England. It was but the old Church purged of what were considered errors and freed from any allegiance to the Bishop of Rome, but it is well to remember how Henry, Edward VI., Queen Elizabeth and James I. had all wanted and worked for a united Church, an end for which 'The Prayer Book' was arranged. Though few in England, after the accession of Elizabeth, actually conformed to Rome, the religions in England had the tenets and thought of the old faith—that is to say, of true Catholicism—although Tudor England was not particularly devoutly minded. Charles I. was a firm believer in the value and truth of the doctrine and system of the Reformed Church.

But, apart from the reformed Episcopalianism of Martin Luther, there had come into the world the dour fierce teaching of Jean Cauvin, the Frenchman, the Cauvin which we usually write as Calvin.

What was the teaching of Jean Cauvin?

In the same year that the Crown in England was resuming and reallotting the lands held by the abbeys and other religious institutions, under the auspices of Oliver Cromwell's relatives, Cauvin had published his book. The teachings therein were to run like wildfire among many of the races that disliked the Mediterranean-born developments of the Roman teachings. It is because of the effect that Calvinism had on Cromwell that he became what he was.

Cauvin was, it is always believed, set on his course because of the misfortune of his father at the hands of the Bishop of Noyon and his Chapter, to which he was lawyer, but accused of embezzlement and refusing to submit his accounts, he was excommunicated and outcast. The father died, denied Christian burial, whatever the rights of the case. Jean was now terribly bitter. He became involved in the hatred of Catholicism and the Church of Rome, and he produced a dreary dour form of Christianity, which undoubtedly appealed to many minds as then affected. 'Predestination' was the keyword; man could not be saved by works or by faith, but only by the predestined will of God. You were 'saved' or you were not. If you were, the conviction at some time by the Grace of God came to you, not by an inherent right in baptism to be worthy and earn it, but because God chose you, or perhaps had chosen you from the beginning. We see the spirit working to this day in 'Conversions' and 'Salvation' and the old questions, still asked, 'Are you saved?' Are you 'in Grace'?

It was a sad creed, the race of man was 'accurst' not 'blessed' of God.

In English life the coming of the 'Authorised Version' of the Bible done into the English tongue, as we know in the days of James I., by the great masters of English toned the *cursus* of the Latin language, had an immeasurable effect on the English people, which lasts to this day. High and low were studying the sources of the Christian religion, generally poorly enough equipped to do so, and the Old Testament wars and analogies were over-digested. At the same time Calvin and his followers aimed at converting the world to their dour creed, and endeavoured to evolve a system of religious administration as complete and as authoritative as that of the Church of Rome. The Church of England, with its Prayer Book, aimed at the same thing, but with far wider bounds, so that its people should retain the reformed Catholicism, as the English reformers saw it, within their gates.

The teaching of Calvin and his Presbyterian system of government had spread to many of the English, both the country gentry and the commercial classes, although the party of English and Roman Catholicism was numerous.

Young Cromwell, apparently of moods and mystical preoccupation, absorbed while at Cambridge much of the Calvinistic train of thought, although his marriage at the age of twenty-two contributed a countervailing human influence. We know that before his death he was in some doubt as to whether he was still 'in Grace'—viz. destined to be saved—though at one time he knew he had been so.

During the first years of his married life, his estates, his business connection and his family affairs kept him fully occupied. During his early years there are unconfirmed stories of laxity, but from the days of his marriage, by common consent, his life was one of great rectitude, his good wife averting or softening the mystical or morose moods, whenever they threatened. His life, therefore, was that of a well-to-do country gentleman, as well as his interests, and save for his presence in a then ineffective Parliament, which rarely assembled, he seems to have had no public life. Such important qualities as he possessed were utilised in his own or purely local affairs.

King Charles' Quarrel with Scotland

We cannot follow the occasion which brought Cromwell into public life without putting before ourselves the outline of the troubles of the King, and since the Scottish imbroglio was the occasion which brought the trouble to a head it may be dwelt on at more length.

The reigns of Elizabeth, James I. and Charles I. on their religious side are one long story of the attempt to produce one uniform and acceptable Church in England. Within the Church the entirely worthy Puritan movement had been growing, and in the early days of the Stuarts, earnestness had succeeded to the laxer Tudor ways, and spread among the best classes of the people of all Great Britain. The breaking with Rome both in Great Britain and on the Continent, however, had loosed the great floodgates of opinion and controversy as well as of individual religious earnestness. Those with Puritan views that could not keep under the wide umbrella of the Church of England founded innumerable separatist bodies. Charles I. and his Archbishop Laud fought earnestly for the maintenance of the Church of England, and conformity with its teachings. The struggle and its immense literature can hardly be alluded to, but undoubtedly Charles and the apparently Romish leaning of Laud had seriously upset the Puritan side of the English nation and character. These ways were too 'Harbitrary' for the English.

The Reformation in Scotland had taken a form different from that in England. It was not, there, the maintenance of a Catholic and Apostolic Church rid of the errors of Rome, but savoured far more of the Calvinistic conception and the Calvinistic order for ministry and management—a Presbyterian *régime*, with a General Assembly, Kirk Sessions and Provincial Synod. James VI. of

Scotland and I. of England, however, understood his own people, and succeeded in grafting an Episcopal system on to a Presbyterian basis. Charles I. was not content with the endeavour to force the English system and the English Prayer Book, slightly modified, on Scotland. The old Scottish Book of Common Order used since the Reformation, unliterary and unmusical but accepted, was always supplemented by 'conceived'—viz. *extempore*—prayer. To the Scots the English Prayer Book seemed 'an evil Mass said in English,' as James VI. had once said. It was believed of the ignorant that Charles and Laud were planning the reintroduction of the Roman Obedience. They would have none of it.

Now his father had always succeeded in getting his innovations accepted by the General Assembly and confirmed by the Parliament of Scotland. Charles consulted neither, and since he had in other ways offended the Scottish nobles, the country made up its mind to resist. Resistance to the Crown meant war. The Scots appointed Alexander Leslie, a veteran of the German wars, as their commander, and could produce plenty of officers, men experienced in those wars.

The National Covenant against Popery was widely signed, and the demand for the non-insistence on the Prayer Book was increased to include the abolition of Episcopacy. Charles I. summoned a General Assembly at Glasgow. When the Royal Commissioner found that the demand was for Presbyterianism he dissolved the Assembly. That body, however, continued to sit, abolished Episcopacy and deposed the Bishops. The army moved south.

Now there was no army in England, and few

old soldiers—so long had peace endured. The only English troops were raw levies, and Charles was obliged to temporise. By the 'Pacification of Berwick' it was agreed that both armies should disband, and that a General Assembly and the Scottish Parliament should meet. The Assembly repeated its demands, and when the Parliament seemed disposed to support them, the King adjourned it. The Scottish Privy Council now authorised the Assembly to enforce its Covenant on every Scottish subject.

As war seemed inevitable, Charles, on the advice of Strafford, summoned an English Parliament, which had not met since 1629, to vote him army funds and support him.

It is here that Cromwell begins to step on to the stage of affairs. He now, in this Parliament, was sent up as Member for Cambridge. But as the Parliament, 'the Short Parliament,' clearly showed that it was sympathetic with the Scots, and in no way disposed to look on them as foes, it was dissolved. As the result, what is known as the 'Second Bishops' War' now took place, without, however, hostilities. Even when the Scottish Army crossed the Border and occupied Newcastle, in the summer of 1640, Charles met the Scottish Commissioners at Ripon, and had to agree to the occupation, until an agreement was reached.

The Long Parliament meets

While Charles had been quarrelling with his Scottish subjects, the troubles of his reign had been coming to a head. The Puritans, within the Church and out, had many demands which he was not disposed to grant, but, as has been said, Puritanism in the best sense of the word had been spreading, and even within the Church, as by law appointed, many reforms were needed. Charles' long period of governing without Parliament had in many ways been very good for the country. Both the King and his ministers were men of affairs. England was prosperous, but a country cannot be run without money, especially if it is to hold its head high abroad, and Charles was much put to it to raise money without summoning Parliament, the question of 'Ship Money' being one of his most controversial levies. The men of business and the country gentlemen were more than angry at the idea of taxation, and therefore when Charles had to summon a fresh Parliament, to deal with the Scottish question and its expenses, it was not likely to be in a pliable mood. Further, it would be none too pleased at the high-handed dismissal of the 'Short Parliament.'

In November 1640 the new Parliament met, and in it Cromwell again represented Cambridge, represented it, too, with a good deal to say about the economical and religious problems which, as a landowner and a Calvinist, touched his purse and stirred his heart.

Here now we see the double occasion which began to push this retired man of forty-two years of age to take a hand in public affairs, and at any rate put him within the grip of an unsought compelling fate. He was with all his retirement a man whose wide and important connections must have kept him *au fait* with the burning questions of the day. He had already been hot on some 'enclosures' of land by the Montague family, who had bought Hinchinbrooke, and had been coming up as the Cromwells went down, and he had had the Calvinistic experience of being 'saved' anew from the burning.

The first matter before Parliament was the incursion of the Scottish Army, which must either be fought or bought off, but it was as sympathetic with the Scottish point of view as was its predecessor. The prestige of the Crown was proportionately reduced; but the Scottish Army left Newcastle in the summer, and in September Charles followed them. In Scotland he yielded every point of controversy, making Leslie, Earl of Leven, and Argyll, the leader of the Covenant, a Marquess. But his yielding was too late, and it was pretty clear that he was hoping to find support, since, after all, he was a Scot, when his trouble with his English Parliament began.

Now began all the fierce movements within the new Parliament, with which we are so familiar, and its practical refusal to be abolished again at the King's pleasure. The road was heading for a conflict of arms, without which there was obviously no way of bringing the King—in his private life so admirable a man and a Christian, in his public life so unyielding and unaccommodating—to reason.

Cromwell had taken some part in the Parliamentary debates, both as a landowner protesting against taxation, and as a Puritan on the question of religious order and Church government. The fight for a Presbyterian system, as demanded by the Scots, had a large body of sympathisers in England, a body growing indeed since Elizabeth's time. Thus it was the Scots imbroglio that forced the break and made for the great occasion which eventually threw up 'Old Oliver.'

And in 1641 it came. The Parliament and the Crown had come to war, and Oliver, in a not very prominent way, was becoming swept up in the problems of the day, though by no means at first evident as the man of destiny. Late in 1641 had come from Ireland another shock, in the shape of a ruthless Irish rebellion in the North, the fierceness of which is the ever-living factor in the Ulster spirit of to-day. It resulted in the death from exposure of many hundreds of the English and Scottish settlers, and several hundreds more were marched out to be piked on the road, as deliberately as ever Turks piked Armenians. The lowest estimate of human beings done to death thus is 2000. The story was greatly exaggerated in England even over this total, and in Cromwell's inherently fanatical mind was set up that complex that must have guided his Irish doings in later years. The withdrawal of Royal troops for the struggle in England was the immediate cause of the trouble, and we hear of Cromwell being prominent in providing and collecting funds for the repression of the rebellion as well as the furnishing of his own troop of Horse.

In Parliament we find him proposing the Earl of Essex as Commander of all Southern Trained Bands, the sending of warships to the Tyne, the controlling of arms manufacture, and the establishing of a right of search at sea and an arms embargo—in fact in any prompt and business-like steps. We also find him supporting his two brothers-in-law in seizing, for the Parliament, the College plate which the University of Cambridge had destined for the King—evidently a man of decision, who at once realised that war meant War with a big 'W,' and not footling. We have a very colourful account of an eyewitness, one of his fellow-members, of Oliver the countryman's first appearance in the new Parliament, just before he began to lead in earnestness:

'I came into the house one morning, well clad, and perceived a gentleman speaking whom I knew not; very ordinarily apparelled; for it was a plain cloth suit which seems to have been made by an ill country tailor; his linen was plain, and not very clean; his stature was of a good size; his sword stuck close to his side; his countenance was sunken and reddish; his voice sharp and untunable, and his eloquence full of fervour.'

Soon was this gentleman of rustic appearance to become the sword-girt cavalry soldier in buff jerkin, high boots and morion.

Here was war, civil war, in a generation that knew little of it! The Parliament, knowing little enough about it, started to raise troops, in the hope of bringing their King to reason. The country gentry of Parliamentary and Puritan proclivities, and those who saw that a more constitutional and democratic rule must be obtained, armed, much as they armed when Napoleon threatened invasion. Oliver, still of the rank and file, raised a troop of yeomanry. Then came Edgehill, the confused victory of the Royalists, who knew a little about soldiering, over those who knew less, where Oliver himself, with no very effective troop of Horse behind him, showed outstanding determination. Occasion had patted him on the back, and he left the field to see that any horsed body that he was responsible for should know their job, should ride, care for their horses, handle their arms, obey their orders, and be inspired with a disciplined enthusiasm. The lore of the Old Testament gave useful metaphors, the Amalekites must be smitten hip and thigh; and the men of the bethels and conventicles, that leaven of Puritanism, Calvinism and Independency, understood the language. Occasion again had produced a dour material, and Oliver was out to use it. In many parts the English of the villages went for the King, with all the horsy element. In others it was the yeomen of Puritan ways who joined Cromwell's Horse as it grew, and the people of the bethels of the countryside and country town. The rake-helly ways of a few of the gentry were magnified to stir the Puritan zeal. Oliver, the efficient country gentleman, turns his proclivities into forming a regiment of Horse—a demon that demands efficiency of the most constant type—a system and a rotation like the best farmed land. From Edgehill his practical mind had grasped some sound tactical elementaries, which do not in themselves much differ from applied common sense. And while Oliver worked away at his own unit he was developing under occasion's spur the qualities that make a leader—a leader who takes to war as a serious business to be ended and mended, ere the world could return to its legitimate job again, as did the British in 1918.

Cromwell as the Cavalry Soldier

So in 1642 Cromwell was busy with his regiment of Ironsides. The Parliamentary authorities were anxious enough to encourage anyone who meant real soldiering, and in July 1644 came that battle in which he was to make his name and really stand out. At Marston Moor things were looking awry, when Cromwell led forth his own corps.

His first troop, the 67th, was one of a series that the country gentry, led by the Members of Parliament, had been forming all over the country. The County Military Associations, revived generations after by the threat of Napoleon's invasion in 1797, were first formed by the Royalists, an example soon followed by the Parliamentarians. Cambridgeshire and six more adjacent counties formed the Eastern Association. In Buckinghamshire Cromwell's famous cousin, Hampden, was colonel, with Oliver's son as cornet. In any of the troops that Cromwell himself could influence, discipline and drill were the keynotes, something by which the more sober country bumpkins could pit themselves against the galloping zeal of the hunt servants, the grooms and the stablemen, who joined the Cavalier Horse. But it took time, and at Marston Moor Cromwell had become a colonel and had a well-drilled double regiment, that as all the world knew had plucked the Parliament victory, that had been well-nigh lost by ineptitude, out of the fire.

The country gentleman had shown that he could organise and train and command. The noisy argumentative manner that had mitigated against him in the lesser political life of the county sobered down, as he became a competent commander, to giving clear and sharp orders in quarters and in the field, in knowing what his men and horses wanted, and, most important of all in times of stress, knowing *how far*, as a commander, he could and should go with his men.

There are writers who talk of Cromwell as a 'consummate' soldier, which is absurd. There was very little true soldiering in this war. The battles were of exceeding short duration. There was none of those prolonged fights in which the victors had fierce resistance to overcome. Both Royalist and Parliamentarian were very inferior soldiers, prone both to run away and desert, apt to mutiny if required to leave their own countryside. Among such cavalry, handled by poor commanders and most amateur staff, the troops, regiments and, eventually, brigades trained by Cromwell stood out, and where they entered the fray there they triumphed forthwith.

Cromwell had the flair of a tactical leader of Horse, and the grim determination to ride hard at the point that his flair indicated to him. His *rôle* was much that already attributed in this book to Alexander of Macedon—leading his heavy cavalry at the essential point of the enemy's lines, cavalry so drilled that they could be wheeled and re-manœuvred after a charge.

Cromwell in middle age had thus found the *rôle* that his quality most fitted him for. Because he knew his own mind and because he could think for himself he began to stand out. His counsel was worth having, and he soon began to realise that the *haute direction* on the Parliament side was bad, that no one had a mind and that very few knew how to train and discipline troops. He had discovered the secret for himself. He was coming to the front, as in our own days we have seen Haig and Allenby come to the front among professional soldiers, and as in the American Civil War we have seen that among judges, schoolmasters and planters some had the gift of leadership and of command, and the flair for training men. Thus it is obvious that at the bottom there is something, not to be obtained save at birth—but to that gift the years must build a big structure, even as the embryo must be built on, with the good food of the earth.

Money was with the Parliament, for the City was, at any rate at the beginning, much opposed to the King. Money, almost complete control of the sea, the large number of City Trained Bands, most of the Southern and Eastern counties, all constituted a very strong hand, which for a long while was to be very badly played.

Such military knowledge as there was, was with the Royalists, and except for the developing military common sense in Cromwell and a few like him, the Parliament had little to present to it. London was obviously the hub, and on the hub the Royalists were endeavouring to move three converging bodies. But a converging movement, to be successful and to synchronise, needed a better staff and better means of communication than were available, and it also needed troops that would leave their own districts when ordered.

The Parliament was equally concerned in defending its own area and in turning its rotten troops into soldiers. The Edgehill fight had been nothing very startling, and the Royalists were not yet ready to go much farther, until they too could organise. It was the North and the West of England for the King, with Oxford as his headquarters, against the South and East; and the golden guineas were in London!

From Troop Leader to Brigadier

The line of the River Trent, a river crossable only at the bridges, marked the general front in the North and Midlands. In the North, endeavouring to secure the port of the Humber, was Newcastle. He was right enough, yet during the summer of 1643 the King was planning to move on London, and let Hull go. In endeavouring to carry out this object, Newcastle was also besieging Gainsborough on the Trent, which Willoughby had seized for the Parliament. Those who had the river-crossing there could threaten the North Road as it trended south to cross the Trent at Newark, twenty-odd miles upstream. The Royalists with some perspicuity were besieging Newark also. If Gainsborough and Newark fell, the Royalist Army could sweep into Lincolnshire, and march on into the Eastern counties, where the Parliament was endeavouring to raise its Horse.

On the 25th of July, Cromwell, who had been sent forward out of Cambridgeshire to support Gainsborough, stormed Burleigh House, near Stamford, on the North Road. The instinct of Cromwell stirred him to move fast and hit hard, and he was now to burn his fingers and learn something more of war. On the 26th of July he moved on Gainsborough, fifty-five miles north on the Great Road, with 600 of that type of Horse that he had been training. With him was a convoy of food and gunpowder, and he marched as hard as his wheels would let him. On the 27th he had twenty-five miles still to go, and marched at 2 A.M. to within a dozen miles of Gainsborough. Here his technique failed him from want of practice. He ran into Newcastle's scouts, behind whom was a body of Horse covering Gainsborough, which Whalley drove back. The way to the town was clear, and Cromwell threw in his provisionment. Again had his technique failed. He had no intelligence, and long-range patrolling was not known. On the other side of the town was Newcastle in strength, and Cromwell rode into him, and very nearly lost himself.

Then he had to clear out, which he did in an orderly enough manner. He had advanced on Gainsborough with his convoy, fifty-five miles in forty-eight hours. He went back eighty miles in even shorter time. Gainsborough fell, and the convoy was a present to the enemy. A very useful lesson to the lucid mind of the burgess turned colonel. You can't be a cavalry leader, they say, till you've had a knock and learnt what's what. 'Punch, brothers, punch!' is a good cavalry motto, but 'Punch with care,' too, and Cromwell by instinct was a puncher.

When he got away, there came worse news. Lincoln had fallen also, and fallen because the Parliamentary troops would not fight. Then Cromwell sent his famous message, realising that the Crown meant business, which began: 'It is no longer disputing, but act instantly all you can. . . . Raise your bands! Hasten your horses. . . . Act lively!'—and so forth. He saw how badly the situation needed gripping by the talking-shop at Westminster. If you want to see it in modern times see Mr Bonar Law's letter on the shilly-shally folly before deciding on the evacuation of Gallipoli in 1915, 'This is not the way to make war.'

There were troubles in London town. A mob of women at Westminster, screaming for the blood of the 'dog Pym' and demanding peace—Gloucester held for the Parliament and leaguered—if it fell the King would be marching on London.

The danger, and the urgent message from Cromwell, however, were at last working. Pym was bringing in the Scots, on terms, the Scots who at any rate had an army for sale; London had got to pay; and by the end of August Essex had marched with 15,000 men, still very much 'of sorts.' The one clear and bright spot was Colonel Cromwell the wiser, whose Horse even now did not run away.

The Royalists were spreading over Lincolnshire and we come to the occasion of Winceby, that was to establish the name of Cromwell in men's mouths as one of the men of iron. It was Rupert's jest that first gave the name of 'Ironsides,' largely because of their iron breast-pieces, to the Cromwell model of trooper, who probably were put into this obsolescent equipment to give them courage and confidence. But 'Ironside' or 'Tin-belly,' as we call our Household Cavalry, or the French Cuirassiers in 1914, had the same jesting significance, before later writers thought more of it and came to use it as a term of fame.

The Eastern Counties Cavalry Association had been doing good work, and the bulk of the Parliamentary troops in Hull, under Fairfax, had come down by sea to Saltfleet on the Lincoln coast and joined up with Willoughby and Cromwell in South Lincolnshire.

Half-way between Lincoln and the coast, not more than twenty miles north of the Wash, close to the church of Winceby hamlet, Fairfax met the Royalist troops. The forces were equal, the Parliament men, largely the Eastern Horse, charged, and the resolution that made for victory came from Cromwell, who led his own troop. His horse was shot, and he had a nasty fall, but the day was won. Winnington, the Royalist commander, lost heavily in killed and prisoners, as well as in arms.

It was not a very important fight, but it put Cromwell into the picture as a man of enterprise and with the power of leading straight.

Marston Moor and the Second Newbury

By the consent of all history it was Marston Moor, fought at midsummer (2nd of July 1644), that definitely stamped Cromwell as the soldier on whom all could rely. There is no need to tell again of this battle, of which the story has been elaborated to the *n*th uncertain detail. The diplomacy of the 'dog Pym' had brought the Scots, largely bought by cash for their empty treasury and a promise of universal Presbyterianism, slowly on to the scene. The Parliament men were besieging York, the Scots with them, when Newcastle and Rupert marched to the relief. Manchester and the Fairfaxes and Lord Leven—the old David Leslie of the Bishops' wars—drew off and moved west, the Royalists following. It was evident that Manchester must fight or lose his train, and late in the afternoon he drew up on Marston Moor, five miles out of York. The two lines, as the Royalists formed, almost rubbed noses across a ditch. No one quite knows how the battle commenced. It was not till 7 P.M. on that long summer's day that the swords left their scabbards.

The Scots and Parliamentarians were the stronger, but the former's Horse were badly mounted.[1] On the Cavalier left, Goring's charge of Horse swept everything away, and had wheeled round to cut up the infantry flank in the centre. No one knew quite what was happening, but the Parliament leaders left the field, Manchester, the elder Fairfax and Leven, believing all was lost.

On their left, however, 'dogged' was doing it. Cromwell had led his 'tin-bellies' over the ditch and had attacked and driven back Rupert's Horse. Rupert had counter-attacked with some success, when a small body of the Scots rode into a gap between Rupert and Newcastle's 'white' infantry, riding down Rupert's flank in their turn.

Cromwell was down, slightly wounded, but was back in time to see, with that tactical eye of his, where some success might yet lie, despite the lugubrious account of the younger Fairfax, who had his face laid open with a sword-cut. He ordered the Horse on the left of the Parliamentarians to wheel to the right and thus outflank and sweep round in rear of Newcastle's infantry, and that, amid terrible slaughter despite the splendid spirit of the Royalist borderers, ended the day. No one quite knew what had happened in the dusk of that summer's evening, but despite the fact that the Parliamentarian leaders had gone in flight, Cromwell and his disciplined Horse had won an astounding victory—and psalms of praise rose from their re-forming ranks.

The Parliament was not much good at getting

[1] There were about 19,000 Royalists against 24,000 Scots and Parliamentarians, with 70 troops of Horse of which 22 were Scottish, the latter perhaps 1000 sabres.

on with the job, but its leaders knew now that they had a man who could soldier, and who having put his shoulder to the wheel was not among those of compromising spirit. Brigadier Cromwell was now Lieutenant-General Cromwell, not yet in any supreme command, but getting near it.

Cromwell too was now giving rein to the fierce Calvinistic side of his mind's working. More and more was he writing the letters of exaltation. It is also to be imagined that he wanted to make sure of the Puritan elements and bring them to war pitch, and so fill the Parliamentary ranks with those whose religious feelings could be stimulated to produce the same or even better results than the Royalist enthusiasm among their opponents. The fierce Old Testament wars were calling. The Maccabees—'Them old MacCabes, the sthout auld Pratestants,' as the Ulster farmer called them—were the men for the Covenanting money. Cromwell in writing and speaking in this form must at times have had his tongue in his cheek, just as an Irish squire would talk to Irish soldiers after their own manner. Hark to the O'Moore, to his Yeomanry: 'Bhoys, will ye get into the thrain, or will I take me coat off.' So thus, in the snuffling metaphor, the now inscrutable Cromwell.

Occasion was taking up all his dormant qualities and making them her own. But just as Marston Moor had shown that he was more than a good colonel, so had it shown him how futile was the higher command. He was to learn and feel it still more a little later.

Down in the West, Charles had had a notable though comparatively unfruitful success. There had been panic in London, and the King was like to advance eastwards. Manchester and Cromwell were concentrating between Oxford and London, but all was not well with the Parliamentary armies. However, some 20,000 of them now met a far smaller number of Royalists under the King himself, in what is known as the Second Battle of Newbury. The stronger Parliamentarians aimed at attacking the King in front and rear, which needed a better staff than any they had. It was an opportunity messed by the high command, and what is more, Cromwell himself did not 'come off,' for reasons many and various, and the Royal Army slipped away. The Lieutenant-General was furious, and took upon himself the difficult and dangerous task of denouncing his superiors to higher authority. There was no love lost between Cromwell and Manchester, for family reasons as well as those of State, and The Ironside had no use for half-hearted leaders and second-rate troops.

It was about now that Cromwell began to see that if he did not push his way to higher authority there was no one else man enough to grip the fighting forces.

While Marston Moor and the Second Newbury were maturing, a deputation from the Government—or what passed for such, viz.: 'The committee of both Kingdoms'—had been sounding the higher generals, English and Scots, as to not only main policy but the ethics behind it all. Almost all were for a settlement with the Crown, a reformation within the old order, and with a Presbyterian Church. It was only the implacables, of which Cromwell was becoming a leading spirit, that would have none of it. Their principle was to crush the Crown and all its works and systems, and then rebuild anew. That is a policy which sounds so easy in the debating-room. It has in our time landed Russia and China in their present plight, and it gave France Napoleon and all his works, and led at long last to the holocaust of Verdun—visited on the children to the third and fourth generation. However, those who have followed the intricate story of the Civil War know how little Charles, King by Divine Right, was like to compromise, so that the matter was working up to a struggle between two indomitable wills, far poles apart in any basis of outlook.

In November, Cromwell, in the House, made his attack on Manchester and all other footlers, with no reservation anent the Scots. Manchester could only reply, with considerable truth, that Cromwell was factious, and also a political firebrand; but the mass of the listeners knew that Cromwell was right.

The latter, however, now changed his attitude, and made on 9th December the great speech of his life. He begged Parliament not to inquire into the faults of its commanders, for all may make mistakes, but to get on with the task of ending the war, as wars should be ended, and to kill the charge, now in many men's mouths, that Members of Parliament and their generals held comfortable offices and were in no hurry to get the war over!

We need not follow this part of the story, and how by the 'Self-denying Ordnance' every Member of Parliament—save Cromwell himself—gave up their military commands, or how Parliament set about to build its 'New Model' army—a professional army of 6000 horse, 1000 dragoons, 14,000 infantry—getting its Bill passed with difficulty in the spring of 1645.

The younger Fairfax was to command, and Parliament passed a dispensation for him to remain in the Army and Parliament, notwithstanding the Self-denying Ordnance.

We may note here that the idea that it was the New Model Army which decided the war is a fallacy. The culminating battle at Naseby was fought in June 1645, a couple of months after the 'New Model' Bill had been passed. The Royalist Army, however, was already going back in efficiency from want of money and reserves.

At Naseby, as all the world knows, Cromwell commanded the Horse. The Royal Army was about half that of the Parliament, and as in other fights was the better army, but shorn of most of the good leaders of the past. It was well off in regimental officers, however, and only lacking in discipline in quarters; the infantry was professional and good. Before the King had made his move forward, Cromwell had led some long-distance and relentless raids, reducing irritating points, and clearing artillery and transport horses out of the countryside. By June, despite a good deal of muddling dispositions by Parliament, it had come again to 'push of pike,' and it was fairly obvious that the King could not afford another defeat.

Naseby

The site of the joining of battle was close to Market Harborough. Both armies, and in fact the country, knew that it might be the last battle of the war. Sir Thomas Fairfax was in command,

and his Council of War petitioned Parliament that Cromwell should be given the command of the Horse. There were several criticisms of the New Model at this beginning of its evolution, and the seniors felt that no strengthening factor should be omitted. The Commons (but not the Lords) assented, and Oliver, at Ely, was ordered to join Fairfax, and he forthwith rode hard to the West with 600 of his own men.

On the 13th of June both King and Fairfax struck their camps, the former marching on Market Harborough, followed by Fairfax—who was joined by Cromwell as he started, and all the Parliament men cheered.

By nine o' this summer morning both forces were forming their line, the Parliamentarians in front of the village of Naseby. The King had 7500 men, of whom 4000 were horse; the others perhaps 14,000, of whom 6500 were horse and dragoons. It was ten-thirty when Prince Rupert ordered the attack to commence, and himself, as usually happened, swept all before him. But he rode too far, and returned to find that Cromwell on the Parliamentarian right had swept all before him, also riding down Langdale's Horse, and having his own disciplined men sufficiently in hand to wheel left on to the flank of the Royal infantry. It is not for us to follow the fight, or even the King's attempt to lead the Horse Guards to recovery. Rupert's blue-coat infantry died where they stood, the last reserve to be drawn in. The last battle was lost; 5000 prisoners, including 500 officers, were taken, and all the King's artillery. The Parliament Army, after prayer and thanksgiving, employed itself nobly in killing the Irishwomen in the camp, and slashing the faces of all the Englishwomen, wanton or otherwise.

So ended the King's cause; numbers, plus Cromwell's 'Tins,' had brought victory if not glory. There was another sharp fight at Bridgwater, in which Cromwell as usual was to the fore, charging and breaking the Royal horse. It was noticeable that the Ironside discipline was now spreading to the 'New Model.' Several months of mopping-up now remained, to pass autumn and winter. The Scots Army was in the Midlands, unpaid and discontented, and Leslie was to take Carlisle. Cromwell, with a strong body of horse and three foot regiments, had a roving commission to mop up malignants, and in his storming of Basing House seems to have shown that fierce streak of fanaticism, which must have been inherent in his normally reasonably tolerant nature. There the Roman priests were put to the sword.

In the desire to inflame followers so as to make soldiers out of rubbish, the fanaticism of Calvinism had been aroused as a matter of policy. Cromwell, as has been said, ministered to this partly from his own fanaticism and partly of set plan and bunkum. There had always been the fear in England of a reaction to Rome, and the stories of the fires of Smithfield were not so far away. It was often the custom to talk of the Royal Army as the 'Papist' Army, in the same evil way that some of our modern Socialists strive to make bad blood. The Irish rebellion, unutterably cruel though it had been, was exaggerated, and a very genuine fear and hatred had been aroused. The astounding brutality to the women after Naseby and the atrocities of Basing were the first-fruits, and more was to follow.

When his share of the mopping-up was over, Cromwell returned to Parliament; his soldiering in the Civil War proper was over; and to arrest our impression, let it be said that Cromwell still had had no important independent command. He was as yet but a subordinate cavalry leader, famed for prompt and resolute action, for tactical flair in action, and for his gift of training soldiers. Further, his religious fanaticism, going far beyond at times the Presbyterianism that Scots and Parliament favoured, gave anxiety to such statesmen as there still were in Parliament.

It was a sad winter and spring for the King as his last strongholds fell, Exeter, Newark, Oxford. His only hope had been the Scots, and all the winter he had been trying to open substantial negotiations. There was an opportunity for an agreement, but an agreement only if the King had anything to bring to the Councils. The Scots had lost most of their regard for the English, and there was little love lost, while there was much pay owing. The Scots were monarchists, if the monarchy were limited; they had no use for republicanism, and they hated the Independents, who were now a large portion of the English Army's rank and file. So since all other courses were closed, to the Scots went the now weary King, leaving Oxford for Leven's camp on the 27th of April 1645.

Cromwell and Parliament

Cromwell the great general was not yet. Parliamentary business was difficult enough, and Cromwell had been far happier 'under orders' with the

Army, where we read of his showing greater *bonhomie* with his men than would have been expected.

There had now been four years of war. The occasion had been great enough, it had made Oliver into a cavalry leader, but not more. Fairfax, the younger Fairfax, was still head of the Army, and Cromwell was to endure the irritation of a talking-shop that talked. It had got the Crown, but did not know how to use it. Buchan tells dramatically for us the story of old Jacob Astley, prisoner after the Stow-on-the-Wold fight, sitting on a drum, with his white hair blowing in the wind, saying to his conquerors, 'You have now done your work, you may now go play, unless you will fall out among yourselves'—and fall out they did, whereby Cromwell was to become something bigger than a brigadier of horse with a fighting complex. This was 1646. Peace had practically come, but not order, and the affliction of the King had brought him much sympathy. The City of London, who were paying, were constitutional monarchists, with Presbyterian sympathy, as were most of Parliament. The Army was getting mutinous and had no intention of disbanding, and Parliament began to try to get help from the Scots against the Independents, while the Army thought of the King.

It was a situation in which the King's sense of intrigue had considerable scope, and to everyone the problem was what to do with him.

It was on the 6th of May 1646 that King Charles rode in to the Scottish headquarters. Nine months later he was handed over by the Scottish mercenary regular Army to the Parliament, in return for half the arrears for expenses and consideration that was due to them, thereby casting a stigma on themselves which is not yet forgotten, for Charles was a Scot. This was in January 1647, and early in February the King was taken from Newcastle to Holmby House, in the custody of the Parliament. All the while the intrigues of all kinds much discussed in history were taking place, and Cromwell was getting more and more disgusted at the futility of the Parliament and its various cliques. There were now three factors in play—the King, Parliament, and the Army—all hostile to each other. Cromwell, second-in-command to Fairfax, the soldiers regarded as victory personified. The Army was in the hands, however, of a semi-Soviet, known as the Council of Officers, through which alone at this stage he could act.

It is now, through these wearing intrigues of parties inside the House and out, that Cromwell the commander gradually became convinced not only that some form of dictatorship was necessary, but that he alone was the man who could handle such a weapon. But dictators are nothing without an instrument, be it Army, Nazi storm-troops, Fascists, Jew-Tartar cominterns and the like. Cromwell could see now, clearly enough, that even if he was destined to be dictator, he must have the Army to dictate for him if the country was to be saved. Nothing but grip would connect the frayed ends.

The King and the Army

It would seem that, having grasped this fact, Cromwell too entered into the struggle to get the King as pawn. But the Army being in a queer state, and almost in a Soviet condition, a phenomenon quite unknown hitherto in England, he had to sit tight and watch. It is necessary to outline the moves that pushed the King, unintentionally to all for a while, to the block, if we are to see Cromwell, by no wish of his own, forced by circumstance and his unusual character to the head. It will always be a matter for argument how far Cromwell was trying at this stage to make for peace and how far he had his tongue in his cheek; but one thing is certain, the Army was out of hand, and if there was one thing Cromwell the soldier had no use for, it was a mutinous Army and a Soviet system.

There were at this juncture, the winter of 1646-1647, conflicting overriding possibilities and problems:

(i) The condition of the Army, in which certain fanatics were already talking of killing the King.

(ii) A Scots invasion, inducing or backing up a Royalist reaction.

(iii) The management of Parliament *vis-à-vis* the Army and a reasonable system of government, and in the uncertain background of what to do with the King.

Two schools of history still dispute how far Cromwell carefully aimed at what followed and secured his aims, how far he was gripped in affairs he could not compel. His private letters and public speeches are in any case hard, nay impossible, to reconcile; he may have tried to ride two horses till they fell apart. And it will always be a matter for conjecture at what stage the killing of the King became part of his programme; whether, as some say, because it was either his life or the King's, or whether because it was finally borne in on him, that there could be no settlement with the King alive —no possible outlet in the way of constitutional monarchy.

What actually happened in brief was this. A certain Cornet Joyce was deputed by Cromwell to guard against any Scots attempt to secure the King's person, or, if you like it better, rescue him. It is said that the Army, instigated by Cromwell, determined to get him into their own hands, and that Joyce's orders were but a blind. Whichever it was, Joyce, with a strong escort, actually brought the King from his Parliamentary lodging in spacious, almost palatial, Holmby House, to lie in their midst at Newmarket, the King going joyfully. This on 4th June 1647.

Fairfax requested him to return to Holmby, but he preferred to stay at Newmarket. Meanwhile Cromwell had left Westminster and joined the Army. The Army was still out of hand and moved towards London with petitions and demands, and it sent letters signed by Fairfax to the City saying what it wanted; and at St Albans on 15th June issued 'The Federation of the Army.' This demanded a democratic system of government, denounced oligarchy, Parliamentary or otherwise, and a purging of Parliament, removing those who abused their office and cast aspersions on the Army. There was still to be a King, as no one knew a better or indeed any system that could replace him.

The Army moved on and denounced eleven members; the Commons refused to listen and the troops moved to Uxbridge. It was Oliver who kept it within bounds. Every day came rumours of a Scots' invasion; and when the Army wanted short shrift for Parliamentary Presbyterians, he kept saying that it must not be said that a settlement was extracted by force from Parliament!

Parliament appeared to give way and put Fairfax in charge of all troops, including the City militia. The City of London, however, would have none of it, and was moved by a blend of Presbyterianism and Royalism, which compelled all in the two Houses who favoured the Independents and both Speakers to flee to the Army for refuge. For the moment it seemed that the Trained Bands would defy the New Model. Then the Army came to Hounslow, and the City thought harder and capitulated on 4th August. On the 6th the Army brought back the refugees to Westminster. On the 7th Oliver rode through the City itself with his Ironsides, and Fairfax took over the Tower. Was ever there such a criss-cross situation! And Cromwell had yet to arrive. Parliament, however, had not learnt its lesson and was still largely Presbyterian. Cromwell wished to purge it. Fairfax alone stayed his hand, but through the months that had passed, as the pamphlets show us, the instinct of the nation was beginning to look to him as a politician who had hitherto been but a horse-soldier. These months had shown him, however, that if he was to be a leader, it could but be with the Army behind him. Parliament wanted they knew not what.

The Army had brought the King in their train, and its headquarters being established at Reading after the dragooning of the City, the King was lodged near by at Caversham. He was treated far better than by Parliament, having his own chaplains, his children to see him, and certain

Royalists were allowed to pass freely between him and the Army chiefs. At Caversham too, in July, Oliver met the King for the first time since the meeting at Hinchinbrooke as very small children. From then onwards, in spite of the attempts of moderate men, with whom in this connection we may at this period class Oliver, the inevitable drag downward of the King begins.

CHAPTER VI

OLIVER CROMWELL THE DICTATOR

THE BEGINNING OF THE END
THE ROYALIST RISING AND THE SCOTS INVASION
CROMWELL AND THE DEATH OF THE KING
AFTER THE KING'S DEATH
CROMWELL IN IRELAND
THE SECOND SCOTS CAMPAIGN
OLD OLIVER'S DAY
FROM DUNBAR TO WORCESTER
THE LORD PROTECTOR

OLIVER CROMWELL THE DICTATOR

THE BEGINNING OF THE END

THE occasions were now developing which were to bring Oliver straight for the top of that brink which meant Dictatorship or chaos. And it is a remarkable fact in the development of this morose and introspective country gentleman that we rarely see the least attempt to bring himself forward as a personal matter or through ambition. Always did untoward and quite unforeseen circumstances push him one rung up the ladder. The rebellious state of the New Model, and the difficulty of getting anything settled, with Parliament and the Army at cross purposes, made his position one of great difficulty, and it is not surprising if an unsuspected gift of deep intrigue was drawn out from the backwoods of his mentality.

The King was now at Hampton Court, still very well entreated, and his various advisers allowed free access. On the 28th of July the famous 'Proposals' for a constitutional monarchy were put before him. The King, alas! would have none of them, buoyed up with the idea that the Army must have him and would offer better terms. It was Ireton, Cromwell's son-in-law, who said, 'Sir! *You* have the intention to be the Arbitrator between the Parliament and us, and *we* mean to be it between your Majesty and the Parliament.'

Cromwell and Ireton were grieved, if we believe

Cromwell genuine in the matter, and the wilder men in the Army were infuriated. In October five cavalry regiments presented to the Army Council the Leveller's Bolshevist creed, and Cromwell wrestled mightily with the wild men, while prayers were hot in the air. He was also aware that the Leveller's proposal for manhood suffrage would mean a Loyalist victory in the country. Great were the discussions, and at last a practical man after Cromwell's own heart remarked, 'If we tarry long, the King will come and say who shall be hanged first,' so tired was the country of war and levies and requisitions. It wanted a settlement with a king at the head, and it wanted the old happy life back again. And Cromwell wanted one too.

Fortunately, Oliver was a master of assemblies, a gift that most great soldiers lack. He continued to wrestle with the Army, but sections therein grew fiercer, especially against the King. His speaking convinced the moderates, but not the mutinous Levellers. On 11th November 1647 Cromwell warned his cousin Whalley that there might be an attempt on the King's life.

The King that night escaped and rode for Southampton Water, where he expected to find a ship. But ship there was none, and eventually he gave himself up to Robert Hammond, military governor of Carisbrooke Castle, on the Isle of Wight. There is a view held in many quarters but insusceptible of proof, that Cromwell plotted the flight, left one way of escape open, and frightened him and his followers into going, feeling that on the island he would be safe both from Levellers and Scots. The King was undoubtedly spoiling his 'book' by intriguing with the latter for a better settlement. It may be that Cromwell did think Carisbrooke Castle a safer place for him while all was hazy and uncertain. The military governor was a son-in-law of Hampden and a cousin by marriage of Oliver. There now followed six months in which Charles, comparatively unrestrained, proceeded to put himself up to auction.

But while the King was settling down in Carisbrooke, Oliver and Fairfax were facing mutiny. Fairfax was holding a review near Ware on the 15th of November, and was anxious to assure his troops that he would attend to their interests, but must have discipline. Two of the regiments, Harrison's and Lilburne's, were not ordered to parade, but appeared with copies of 'The Agreement of the People' in their hats, having driven away their officers. Fairfax caused Harrison's to conform, but Lilburne's would not. Then Cromwell, hearing that they would seize his person, rode among them with drawn sword, and bid them tear the paper from their hats. His bright steel and grim face was too much for them, and they submitted. The ringleaders were tried, and three condemned to be shot; one only was to die, and the three drew lots.

Four days later Oliver, the man of the hour, told Parliament that the Army was at peace.

It was a very outward peace only, and during the winter and spring Cromwell's hands were full in several directions—in handling the half-mutinous Army that was daily growing more radical and might kill the King, in watching for the inevitable Royalist reaction, and studying the whole question of the status and authority of Parliament. By universal consent Cromwell handled all three problems with masterly patience, and now began to show himself a great man as well as good soldier. The facing of Lilburne's excited corps had brought him renewed fame in the disciplined portion of the forces, and this is a very important point in binding to him a Dictator's instrument.

The Royalist Rising and the Scots Invasion

We are perhaps apt to forget the length of this period of negotiation with the King, thirty-two months in all, from 5th May 1646, when he gave himself up to the Scots, to the end on the 30th January 1649.

The long course of negotiation with Charles by all parties shows how genuine was the idea for a settlement with the King at its head. By the end of December 1647 Parliament had drafted four Bills for the King to sign, which, at any rate, formed a basis on which a settlement could have been made. But the Scots had already made a similar and somewhat more attractive offer, known as 'The Engagement', which incidentally provided for England also. This Charles signed on the 26th of December, rejecting the Parliament's offer two days later.

In modern slang, that 'tore it.' Parliament refused to receive any more addresses from the King, his advisers were dismissed, and his open detention became a more rigorous confinement. Up to now his treatment either with the Scots or the Parliament and Army had been dignified;

now that he was treated as a prisoner, England grew restive.

A new spirit was apparent everywhere. Several movements and risings in his favour broke out. The 'King's Accession' was kept with enthusiasm in London, and a new war was about to ensue. A young gentleman named Burly, who proposed to rescue the King, was butchered. It was the first occasion on which Parliament had treated loyalty as a crime punishable with death.

The Governor of Carisbrooke was a Parliamentary not an Army servant, and his actions became important. In February a Royalist rebellion had broken out in South Wales. The Scottish Parliament approved, at the beginning of March, a proposal to invade England in support of the King.

Just before this, Cromwell summoned a meeting of officers at St Albans for prayer, self-examination and commune with God. The officers went into transports of emotion, and his reconciliation with the officer cadre was complete. It was well that this was so, as the Scots were about to march to release the King, South Wales was in insurrection, and the forces, except the New Model, had been cut down.

Now was Cromwell to come into his own. Early in 1648 he had been very poorly and expected death, and this was followed by a bout of melancholy introspection.

The call to arms came as a spur and a tonic. Early in May Fairfax sent him to South Wales, when the Royalists had been beaten. Even then Pembroke held out for six weeks against Oliver, whose siege artillery had been lost in the Bristol

Channel. Fairfax had marched 12,000 men into Kent. Berwick and Carlisle had been taken by Royalists, and the fleet in the Downs having mutinied at the appointment of the soldier Rainsborough to command, had put themselves under the command of Prince Charles, and were dominating the Cinque Ports.

The elder Goring had seized Colchester and prevented Fairfax moving north on 8th July, and the Scots crossed the Border, with practically nothing between them and London. Had the Scots been united they could probably have dictated terms. But Leven was against the King, and the old Scots Army had been disbanded. The army that the Duke of Hamilton led south was far inferior to that of Marston Moor. Still, with all that was on and London largely Loyalist, it was a very anxious time for the Revolution. The Duke was a poor soldier and could not realise that promptness and energy alone could give him success and rally the English Loyalists. But he marched into England by the western road, and Cromwell from Pembroke marched to Preston *via* Gloucester, Warwick, Nottingham, Doncaster and Wetherby to meet him. There he turned due west for Preston. It was a remarkable strategical march over the bad roads of the period, 369 miles in thirty-three marching days, and marked him as a commander as well as a leader of Horse. He only rested one full day in the whole march, which lasted from 14th July to 16th August inclusive—and though his force was only one-third the strength of the invaders it was first-class stuff.

Hamilton was marching with his forces much strung out, but they were something between

25,000 and 30,000 men. Cromwell's force was not more than 10,000; a sixth of Hamilton's force were English Loyalists under Langdale, who had gathered in Cumberland. The Duke's information was bad, and he could not believe that any considerable Parliamentary force could be near him. On the morning of the 17th Cromwell fell on Langdale's force (under 4000 men) at Preston and almost destroyed it, the latter and Hamilton, who had brought back a few Horse, escaped by swimming the river. Up in the north was Hamilton's rearguard, and south of Preston straggling down to Wigan like Brown's cows were 17,000 Scots.

Cromwell turned south to follow them, who had not even the courage to form front against him, and all were 'mopped up,' the Duke captured, to be tried and beheaded. The Revolution had now set up a theory, that, being successful—none too successful it would seem—all further opposition was high treason. Yet as the Duke was a Scot that argument was none too sound; *væ victis* was better Jedburgh law.

The Scots soldiery broke over the countryside that hated them, and were steadily collected by the Parliamentarians.

So ended, in the disaster it deserved, the First Scots Campaign, while the various Loyalist outbreaks that it so let down were slowly stifled. Cromwell, now becoming more and more by force of circumstance the Revolution's head, proceeded to let the lucid thorough cells of his mind take charge, with occasional incursion into Old Testament thanksgiving, especially when among his sectaries. He could breathe again, and realised that had Hamilton shown any military power and knowledge whatever, it looked like being all up with the Revolution. Although he himself knew that his actual military task had been easy enough, his own world appraised at its proper value that determined soldierly march from Wales.

The Royalist fleet in the Thames, where the Parliamentary crews were like to join them, was blown out to sea by a north-west gale. Again in their courses the stars had fought for the Revolution. Early in September Sandown Castle, in Kent, had surrendered. The Second Civil War was over, but it had been a near thing. The punishments for the so-called treasons were more than severe. After the fall of Colchester Sir Charles Lucas and Sir George Lisle were shot by court martial. Besides the Duke of Hamilton, Holland and Capel lost their heads. Regimental officers and soldiers were sold as slaves to the West Indies for a fixed period, and as conscript soldiers to Venice. Yet wherever Cromwell himself was there was less vindictiveness. The Duke of Hamilton, speaking of his trial, spoke of Cromwell's courtesy and also of his kindly treatment of his poor Scottish gentlemen. Yet Cromwell hated the Scots, and the gentle Fairfax shot Lisle and Lucas—a paradox! We shall see Oliver later in his cruel moods, as when at Basing House.

Cromwell and the Death of the King

It is a matter of unending controversy as to when Cromwell made up his mind exactly to encompass the death of the King. As has been outlined, Charles was very hard to deal with, playing a definite intrigue for better terms. But it is obvious that at any time after the Royalist rising and Scots invasion, as long as the King was alive and in custody, he must be a basis of civil war, and that no settlement, other than an agreement with him, could be final. A settlement he would not make; and further, if he had, what could he have in his heart but bitter hatred for the Revolutionary leaders! Cromwell, with his lucid mind, his growing belief that he alone could ride the Army-cum-Parliament storm, also soon came to be sure that it was his life and that of a few others, or that of Charles! We need not probe the matter further—nor all the searchings of heart which Cromwell, genuine or otherwise, went through—all the 'sword of the Lord' business.

Hammond, the military governor of the Isle of Wight, was an uncertain factor. The Scots invasion had brought Parliament and Army together for a while, and Hammond was granted stipends and donations but was still a doubtful item, especially if the Royalist risings had been more successful. He might even let Charles escape over the water.

Whatever Cromwell may have had in his mind, whatever his clear thinking had induced, Parliament was to make one more effort. Five peers and ten commoners were appointed Commissioners, and met the King at Newport in September 1648 after the final extinctions of the Second Civil War. In November, however, the Army threw down its glove and addressed what is known as 'The Remonstrance' to Parliament. It was an extensive and long-winded document, but it had one clear demand, that the author of all the trouble, *e.g.* Charles, 'should be speedily brought to justice for the treason, blood and mischief of which he had been guilty.' It was twice thrown out by a seemingly brave but otherwise quite ineffective Parliament by, to their credit, considerable majorities.

How far Cromwell was at the bottom of this does not appear, for he was in the North intending to support Argyll, leader of the anti-Royalist party in Scotland. But he was always writing to his cousin, the doubtful Hammond, to hold the King fast. Someone else was also moving to this end, for Fairfax and the Army Council summoned Hammond to Windsor. *En route* he was put under arrest, and an officer (Eyre or Ewer) came to take the King's person and keep him in sure custody. The day after the Commissioners had left the King at Newport, he was removed from the island to Hurst Castle on the mainland.

The Army was preparing a *coup d'état*. As the King arrived at Hurst Castle, it marched to Westminster, which it occupied on the 2nd of December. The notorious Hewson and his regiment occupied Whitehall.

The Parliament put a bold face on matters and remained debating all the night of the 4th, despite the threatening Army, on the terms that the King through the Commissioners had agreed to abide by. On the 5th, by 140 to 104, they decided to accept the King's proposals. That is to say, to their credit, despite their being in the hands of the Army, they refused to yield to 'The Remonstrance.' This 244 was almost all that remained of the Revolutionary House of Commons.

Cromwell had not yet arrived, but was now marching hard on London.

Before he arrived occurred 'Pride's Purge,' by

which, on the 6th, all those members who would conceivably vote for the King were forcibly excluded. On the 7th Cromwell arrives, and writes that it was all due to an inspiration of the Almighty. Next day the Army seizes the treasure in Goldsmith Hall, parades all day through the city and turns St Paul's[1] into a barrack (which it remained till the Restoration).

Cromwell holds apparently aloof, watching the way that the cat may be like to jump; for all London is in uproar!

On the 19th the King was brought to Windsor for his last Christmas on earth, and there saw the Duke of Hamilton, whose head was still on his shoulders. Cromwell had seen the Duke ten days earlier, and the latter had sealed his death by refusing to divulge the names of his English confederates. After the manner of determined men when their course is made up, Cromwell was now about to go the 'whole hog.' The Revolution must be saved, he must be safe, and only by extreme measures could England be quieted and settled.

On Twelfth Night the remnant of Parliament, forty-six commoners, debated the King's doom. They passed an Act by a majority of six only, twenty still opposing the Army dictation, that the fifteen remaining Lords did not count, and set up the Regicide Court of 135, Bradshawe presiding.

Cromwell is still playing his game of aloofness, but on the 9th of January said that if any man had dared to depose the King or disinherit his heir it would be infamous, 'But since the Providence of

[1] The old pre-Fire St Paul's.

God has cast this upon us, I cannot but submit to Providence, though I am not yet prepared to give you my advices.'

Was it comedy, strategy, Belial Machiavelli at his best?

The drama went on towards that snow-clad tragedy of 30th January—the signing by the fifty-nine, some reluctant—the order to execute signed by Cromwell himself—the protest by Lady Fairfax. It was Cromwell who saw to it that Fairfax, still the nominal commander, should not attempt a rescue, and it is of Cromwell that the story, not necessarily apocryphal, is told, of the cloaked figure that gazed on the royal corpse and the severed head and muttered 'Cruel necessity.' It was Cromwell who had spoken of the King as the most righteous (if the most impossible) of men, but from his personal point of view it was necessary enough, and we may also believe that he genuinely saw no other way.

After the King's Death

After the few bitter fanatics had dragooned England in the manner of Lenin and Trotsky, had disregarded the petition of all the important bodies, the denunciations from all the London pulpits, and had shocked all that was good and stable in the land, the future had to be faced. The King had not been executed by Parliament or people, as some in these days like to make out, but by a small over-riding Soviet, of which Cromwell may have been the deep intriguing hand behind, or may equally have been carried away by the fierce fanaticism of the Levellers, who would have disrupted the Army had he resisted them. Whatever it was, Cromwell had crashed a large part of his nature, and was now to suffer the consequences in a residue of strained neurotic temper. It was a month before he recovered and could look round on his England that hated him; but he was quite determined that government should be carried on. At the trial of the King, Bradshawe had said that 'Stronger than the Law was the author and parent of the Law,' and that is the people of England. But the people of England were to have no say whatever; a nine-year-old Parliament, and only the fag-end at that, purged of those who don't agree and quite disregarded by the Army, can hardly be called a government by the free people of England. In fact, the frying-pan of Charles' efficient, if autocratic, administration was far cooler than the fire of the so-called Republic, and taxes then demanded a tenth of the present levy.

The government was now carried out by a Council of State of forty members of which Oliver was the first President. It was in theory annually elected and worked by sub-Committees on each question. The whole of Europe was bitterly condemnatory and actively hostile, and the first Council had enough general grip of essentials to take the Navy in hand, both as to conditions and ships, adding forty-one war vessels in three years. The Council, in power only with the support of the bitterly hated Army, was a fierce autocracy, ruling by repression and spies, and abolished King and Lords.

The Army, however, had no love for their machine, the country was hostile, while countless cabals were in progress, Royalists cowed though they were, Levellers, communists, Independents, cranks *et hoc genus omne*, who are always with us in Merrie England. At the helm, so far as it could be called a helm, stood Oliver, normal again, dour, and emitting texts and Scriptural metaphor when occasion needed. Here one must give unqualified admiration to the now grim character, once a county squire, who held on, on what seemed the only course, and bided his time. The Army was the chief anxiety. An Army freed of legal ties and full of pragmatical bigots is a dangerous thing, and no wonder England with her long memory hated a standing army for over two hundred years after. A mutiny broke out, and it was Oliver who told the House 'You must break them or they will break you.' Happily Oliver and Fairfax held a review of their own regiments, and made an appeal to them to trust Parliament to settle arrears of pay, and to dissolve itself as soon as their immediate task was finished. The men took their badge of mutiny from their hats, and marched in pursuit of mutineers, of whom 400 were captured in Oxfordshire. Three executions were enough, and it was Cromwell's prestige as a soldier that did it.

But though Oliver could restore discipline by the magnetism of resolution and clear thinking, he could not square the Presbyterians, however apposite his quotations from Scripture. The spring and summer after the murder of the King were about as rough a ride as any oligarchy have had to face.

CROMWELL IN IRELAND

There was another trouble still needing settlement, and that was Ireland, torn so many ways and so many crossways, by Reformation as well as by revolution. From Parliament's point of view, there was the native Irish question, and the matter of their rebellion still not settled; there were the forces of occupation, mostly the Royal forces, many of which had come over to help the King, and indeed whose withdrawal was largely the cause of the Rebellion of 1641 already referred to; there was the old Colony and the Pale, and whereas some were for the King, some were not, some were for the Reformation and some for Rome, and that division and the former did not coincide.

The problem before Parliament was that Ireland was held for the King and his son, and with all the world against Republican England a Royalist Ireland was a very great danger and *nidus* of trouble. Between 1641 and 1649 æons of trouble of all kinds had taken place, but by the beginning of 1649 Ormonde, the Lord-Lieutenant, had welded most of the eccentric factors into one body. Monk, commanding in Ulster for the Parliament, was driven out, and only Dublin, Drogheda and Londonderry remained to the New Republic. Drogheda fell and Ormonde was besieging Dublin. By midsummer Ireland bid fair to be a compact Royalist kingdom.

The Council nominated Cromwell to the Irish Command, glad enough to see some of their mutinous army *en route* there. Cromwell hesitated and insisted on the troops being well equipped and properly cared for. This was promised but not done, and it was four months before he got what was wanted. To get his men, he called for volunteers, dwelling on the need for Britain to be supreme in the three Kingdoms. The Army, certainly the better stuff, was tired of the dog fight at Westminster and 12,000 responded. But it was not till the fourth month had passed that he was prepared to go, and forget in the field the tragedy he had seen enacted and the vexations of Parliament. Once more do we see fate calling him, and in the back of his mind, the old complex and fear of Rome and the bitter fanaticism of the Fifth Monarchy men about to gain possession. He was now irrevocably set on the road that he could not depart from. On 10th July he left London with the office of Lord-Lieutenant and Commander-in-Chief of Ireland, nominally still under Fairfax, for three years, at a salary of £13,000. He left in great pomp as a matter of policy, with many officers and a special bodyguard, and was damnably sick in the crossing like many lesser men.

He now had a more than man's task before him, and he proceeded to clear the air by proclamations. He first aimed at disciplining the Parliamentary troops under his predecessor who were out of hand, and in reassuring the population—*Bon!* A little of his Puritan stuff to Dublin on its sins did not edify them, but it would seem that he intended to carry out his task with justice and a reasonable amount of mercy. He apparently believed to the end that he had so acted, but he was not a fit man, this man of hitherto iron physique. Behind him the horror of the King's murder and his share in it preying on his subconscious mind, if not on his actual cognisance—the danger on all sides—the Scots he hated, a distinct menace—the young Prince of Wales, the man Charles on the horizon—and this Ireland that had murdered the 'saints' and been a thorn in the side of the Revolution for eight years! It must be settled forthwith, that was more important than anything else. If the Revolution was righteous, all that opposed it were of Belial.

The military situation in Ireland was serious, all the strong places were in Royalist hands, whether the last of the English cavaliers, or Scots veterans or Irish levies, Protestant or Catholic. To fight this, Cromwell was in full command, more so even than in his Preston campaign, and it is his appearance as such that clinches our opinion of his now formed character. Many a subordinate leader fails when brought to high responsibility; not so Oliver. Joined by Ireton he could dispose of 10,000 foot and 5000 horse, all good stuff. He set about in the thorough way we should expect, securing seaports and inland water-ways, which were the chief means of transport.

To Drogheda, lately taken from the Parliament, he marched, was defied on 3rd September, and storming it, put, as all the world knew, the garrison to the sword, after a stout resistance of mingled enthusiasm and fierce despair—the fury of the teeth biting at the horse's hoofs which hammer in the face. He took all responsibility for the cruelties, the breaking of faith, the murders of Catholic priests. He orders everything himself, 'being in the heat of action,' the latter his only apology. His religious phraseology is extremely nauseating and framed on falsehood, but—and it is a very essential 'but'—the treatment of Drogheda 'put the wind up' the enemy. Many places were evacuated, and it gained the vital point of time, a shortening of the duration of the campaign. From Drogheda to Wexford in the south he marches full tilt—another fierce storming and ruthless slaughter, and a butchery of friars. The anti-Papist complex was in possession and nothing was done by halves.

The lesson, however wrongfully, was read to the dying cause, and after Drogheda and Wexford came more liberal treatment. Yet to this day neither wedding nor funeral will take the roads by which Cromwell marched! Sickness now wracked the Parliament's army, including the General himself, deaths were many—Cromwell's Lieutenant-General, Michael Jones, a stout soldier, but who had great doubts in the matter of the King, died of plague. Cromwell softened, wrote a simple letter home, desired that Fairfax should impress on son Richard to mind the things of God more and more . . . 'What profit is there in the things of this world? except they be enjoyed in Christ they are snares.' Things were quietening, but by the New Year of 1650 it remained to tackle the forts of Munster. Cromwell had heard he was to be recalled and speeded up his measures. Kilkenny on the Nore, and Clonmel, gave stout resistance. At the latter Cromwell lost 2000 men, and the garrison slipped away at night.

At the end of May he was recalled to England, to be received as a hero and a conqueror. The war in Ireland lasted two more years, but its back was broken, and the Royalist generals and the folly of the Roman bishops had succeeded in detaching the Protestants and making it purely a war of the

'Papists,' a war that now could hardly be linked to any war of the Scots.

And, indeed, as a soldier had Oliver deserved the praise. Knowledge of administration and supply, prompt acting and hard marching, always on the points that mattered, were the features of his campaign. If you want to argue about the butcheries, the ruthlessness, the implacable anger against the friars, why there is a good deal to be said both ways. To him the friars, the clergy of Rome, were the main cause of all the trouble. Nevertheless Ireland is the great blot on his escutcheon. Always, save at Basing, when his ruthless mood gained the upper hand, had he been on the side of clemency. He knew apparently that he had been wrong, and that Drogheda, even if it caused the abandonment of many posts, certainly hardened into steel the defenders' hearts of the posts that held out.

Yet, again, here in Ireland do we see the well-known salient points of his character at work—efficiency, thoroughness, clear-thinking, promptness, and a great care, so far as could be, for his men. It was 1652 before Ireton and Ludlow finished the war, Limerick falling to Ireton after five months' siege, he dying of the plague that haunted the starving garrison.

After the war the Cromwellian Settlement of the land was ruthless enough; but, once over, Ireland received the same treatment as if part of England. It was a cruel business, however, and owing to other troubles but half-done. Yet lest we should fall into the snare of believing that everything done was ill done, we should realise that the cropping up of the De Valera mentality through the Irish ages must constantly have foiled and exasperated those who worked for Ireland's good.

The Second Scots Campaign

Not yet was Oliver to come to the first place. It was in June 1650 that his official welcome took place, and then for the moment he lapsed into the *rôle* of the returned pro-consul on the unemployed list. During Oliver's absence the Parliament had maintained an order and a system of a kind—but in no sense efficient—tyrannical and hated.

Scotland had finally parted with the Parliament after the execution of the King. Charles II. having been proclaimed King of Great Britain and Ireland, the Scottish envoys were sent rudely about their business. We need not enter into the story of the Scots and Charles II., but the situation bore heavily on the rule at Westminster and, together with Ireland, prevented any military retrenchment even if the Army was in the mood to be retrenched. The Council dictated, but amused itself by keeping within the bounds of submitting its doings for the approval of the fag-end of the Long Parliament. It did not dare face the people by any sort of a new election. The Scots, moreover, had a very different army from that with which the unfortunate Duke of Hamilton had essayed to rescue the King. Its old veterans were back in its ranks, and old Lord Leven was back at its head, with David Leslie as his fighting general. The death of the King had reunited most of the parties. Charles II. was at Aberdeen, but unhappy among his dour supporters, a leg of the faithful Montrose mouldering before him. Early in the summer of 1650 it was obvious that there would be a second Scots invasion, obvious as a result of the situation; yet it is of special interest to this study as one more of the series of occasions compelling Oliver up the ladder of fate.

In June, Fairfax was appointed by the Council to command against the Scots, with Cromwell as his Lieutenant. The Council contemplated an offensive campaign. Fairfax demurred, as a breach of the Solemn League. To this, Oliver, whose ideas on war and their ethics were marred by no illusions, gave the reply that all military heads give to hesitating politicians in times of crisis. Always does this question of when to strike come up. The Bismarcks of the world try to manœuvre the victim into being the aggressor. Thus Cromwell to his chief: 'Your Excellency will soon determine whether it is better to have this war in the bowels of another country or of your own, and that it will be one of these, I think it without scruple.'

Oliver was developing his own ideas of statesmanship, and he wanted to bring Presbyterians and Independents together, crush Royalism, and start the Christian State as he envisaged it, and he wrestled with prayer all night. Fairfax the Presbyterian was a better diplomatic factor than the Independents. But Oliver expected results *after* a victory and not before.

Fairfax was no longer the man of the hour or day, if ever he was. He was out of sympathy with the situation and asked to be released by reason of health and weariness, for the *coup d'état* of the King's death was still heavy on him. So Oliver, who sought it not, became the man of destiny, and on 26th June was appointed Captain-General and

Commander-in-Chief of all the Commonwealth forces.

He knew something of the Scots as warriors when properly led, and their fighting power in the Preston campaign, even when miserably handled, had warned him. Marston Moor, despite the controversy, was a useful memory of what might be before him. So he took care to take his best. It was 10,500 first-class foot and 5500 veteran horse, with Lambert and Fleetwood as his two subordinate leaders. The New Model had recovered its discipline. Monk, too, was with him, the ex-Royalist, whom Cromwell knew to be a good soldier. A special corps was raised for him—now famous as The Coldstreams. He learnt that Leslie would have 27,000 foot and 5000 horse, some good, some raw. On the other hand none knew better than he how the dead hand of the Scots Parliament and the Kirk would paralyse concentration and supreme effort, of whom he said, they were 'placing in command ministers' sons, clerks and such other sanctified creatures who hardly ever saw or heard of any sword but that of the spirit.' The soldier's tongue was here—very much in his cheek—and indeed have those intimate with Earl Haig heard him say much the same.

Cromwell therefore judged that Leslie must stay near home and that the fight would be near Edinburgh, and further if Leven and Leslie knew their business, as they undoubtedly did, however hampered, there would be little for an invader to live on between the Border and the capital.

Now Oliver knew well enough that reliance on the Lord was good business, but that man must help—not for him ravens and 'cruses of oil.'

Supply must be organised, and supply meant a port somewhere between the Tweed and the Forth, and that could only be Dunbar. He was as good a quartermaster-general as he was fighting man, and the two are not always synonymous.

Old Oliver's Day

We are now coming to that strangely persistent date, 'Old Oliver's Day,' 3rd September (O.S.), the day of the setting on at Drogheda, of the victory of Dunbar, of the 'Crowning Mercy' of Worcester, and the day on which his soul was required of him in 1658. Scotland was a very different matter from Ireland. The Irish were malignants of the worst type, die-hard cavaliers, papishry and Irishry. The Scots were in another category altogether: 'God hath a people here fearing his name, though deceived.' Oliver therefore thought he could put the case before the people of Scotland, exhorting and tempering them. If not, he was going to ding them as hard as he knew, and he did know.

He was recovering his old spirits for a while, and writing, as indeed he always did write, humanly and charmingly to his family.

On 22nd July he crossed the Border, preceded by declarations, exhortations and chidings, perhaps to hoodwink his own Parliament and Presbyters. The Scottish men had gone, leaving the women, 'pitiful sorry creatures clothed in white flannel,' fearing greatly, as well they might, for the story of the post-Naseby atrocities was well known. Filling up his wagons at Dunbar, since the land, as he expected, was bare, he lay on 28th July at Musselburgh on the outskirts of Edinburgh. Leslie was waiting for him by Leith, well entrenched, and Cromwell, seeing he must have cannon and heavy ones at that, tried to turn the position with the help of his ships in the Forth.

It was beyond him, and he fell back to Musselburgh harassed by some English cavaliers, strange bedfellows for the Scots at this period. Wind and floods delayed his ships, and he had again to fall back on 5th August to Dunbar. Thence he issued his famous manifesto to the Kirk, lashing them with their own scorpions and bombarding them with their own artillery. Isaiah is good provender for such an occasion, and he gave it them, asking 'Is it infallibly agreeable to the Word of God all that you say? I beseech you, in the bowels of Christ, think it possible that you may be mistaken.' But the Kirk was not to be shaken by such a misuse of its own stuff, though it was not happy about the young King, and there were too many of the old malignants with the Scots to please them. Still, when Cromwell fell back, the pulpits of Edinburgh gave forth, 'The wicked flee when no man pursueth.' Then we have the pleasing picture of both sides letting fly with all the invective of the Old Testament, and it would be hard to decide who took the palm. Scriptural invective was always the strong point of the termagant and turbulent ministry in both flocks.

With the enemy therefore falling back, eighty cavalier officers and 3000 men were dismissed the Scottish forces to please the Kirk, which meant a pitiful loss of good officers and a considerable disorganising of the best regiments.

Oliver recognised that the first honours were with Leslie, but by the 12th, revictualled, he was back at Musselburgh. Nevertheless, he could not find an opening to get at Leslie, who preferred to wait. The English Army had dysentery badly. Cromwell could not face the loss of prestige, his Model Army flouted, sick and wasting time, and he must get it away, let it recover and be ready to do justice to itself. A council of war agreed that to move to Dunbar was the first step. Leslie wanted nothing less, however, than that Cromwell should lie within a fortified seaport so close to Edinburgh, and he followed closely, knowing fairly well the straits that the English were in. On Saturday, 31st August, Cromwell moved back a second time nine miles to Haddington, greatly harassed by the Scots, but they could not march fast enough to intercept his line of march and compel a fight at a disadvantage. On Sunday, however, Cromwell drew up and offered battle, while the retreat continued. By the time his army drew up in mass by the town of Dunbar the Scots were but half a mile from him. Leslie marched on beyond Dunbar and drew up parallel to him on the commanding ground of the Doon Hill facing out to sea, a mile or so from the town, and had also seized the Cock'path (Cockburn's Path), a defile on the road to England eight miles on, that could not be avoided.

Leslie hoped that Cromwell would push for England in a flank march past his position, but as this did not seem to be about to mature he moved down to the Spot Burn, to offer battle should Cromwell wish to march on; if not, to attack him. The marching on meant passing within a few yards of the Scottish right.

It was a nasty position for Oliver and his army

that was none too fit. But Leslie, who had a much larger force, was a better strategist than tactician. We make a long story short by saying that on Tuesday the 3rd, 'Old Oliver's Day,' Cromwell marched his Horse close along the sands and fell on the Scottish right, while Monk, Lambert and Fleetwood attacked their front and held them to the line of the burn.

Something went wrong in the Scottish forces, who had got themselves into a position where they could not manœuvre, and they who had Oliver 'cold' were rolled up and broken beyond words . . . a sorry business . . . but an astounding victory to the Parliament, and well might psalms of praise and Old Testament texts be hurled forth by the victors. There was no doubt now as to who were the chosen people! By six in the morning all was over, and Cromwell himself led forth the psalm, 'Let God arise and let his enemies be scattered.' In Edinburgh, a minister at the daily service was promising a glorious victory, when a trooper of Leslie's, an obviously beaten trooper, half-dead with fatigue, appeared. The truth was evident.

Leslie's own statement attributed the Scots' failure to their delay in standing to arms at early dawn, being overcome with the wet night, and taken unready by the English in the grim dawn. Whatever it was, it was good soldiering, both as the tactical commander and as the leader of Horse, on Cromwell's part, and very much the reverse on that of Leslie, who should have known better. Wet nights are no real excuse when he had the situation in his own hands.

But here do we see how fate saved Oliver from,

at any rate, a great loss of prestige; indeed it may pass an idle moment not unprofitably to wonder what might have been had he lost Dunbar. As it was, the enthusiasm in London was great, among the Parliament men at any rate, and a medal with Cromwell's head thereon was struck, he deprecating.

It has been said that Dunbar killed theocracy in Britain and that the Kirk in the Scottish portion of the Island, in the modern metaphor, 'went off the gold standard.'

From Dunbar to Worcester

Dunbar was not, however, the last of the Scots. Many dissensions followed, and the young King had perforce to swallow the Presbyterian pill and accept the conditions under which he remained on the rickety throne. As remonstrance and exhortation did not produce the results that Oliver and Parliament hoped for, there was nothing for it but another dose of the sword. Argyll, to his own undoing, was with the King, little relishing his surroundings. Oliver had Leith and Edinburgh but not the castle, which did not surrender till Christmas Eve. Lambert was busy reducing Lowland castles and also repressing an outbreak of the old moss-trooping.

The Scots are every whit as obstinate as the English and far more dour at the outset of trouble. The warring parties and factions closed their ranks, the Cavaliers were again acceptable, and all the lions and the lambs, the godly and the ungodly, lay down together awhile. Charles subscribed to the two Covenants, and Argyll put the crown on his head. Leslie was amending and improving his army, and held Stirling, barring the way to the

North. Oliver was not successful in out-manœuvring him and cutting him from his supply and recruiting grounds. Also the Lord-General's health was bad, and he had few friends, save now and again he seems to have shown his soft side to some well-born hostess and established a friendship.

Things were going better with the Parliament after Dunbar. Blake, the admiral, had chased Rupert from the sea, several powers had recognised the Commonwealth, and by June Cromwell had recovered. Leslie, from Stirling, was on the move. The King and the various groups were anxious to march into England. This, Cromwell would have welcomed, since certain Royalist risings in the Eastern counties had been suppressed, and he believed that England invaded would quit King and Parliament and turn on the invaders. There were militias in England too coming into being. So now we have the interesting spectacle of Cromwell trying to get Leslie into the open, or even to march for England, and the Scots acting as he wished. Towards the end of July came the beginning of the end. Cromwell sent a force across the Forth against which Leslie sent 4000 men, who were almost wiped out at the battle of Inverkeithing, and the whole English Army now crossed the Firth of Forth. The King, insisting on a march for England, broke up the camp at Stirling and by 5th August was on the Border. The old will-of-the-wisp—that the people in England would at once rise—that was only to die at Derby a hundred years later, held the field. Charles was marching as Hamilton had done, by the west road, and Cromwell set about to follow on the east.

On the 9th of August 1651 Charles was at

Kendal, less most of his softer or more lukewarm stuff, and his original 20,000 grew less and less, while none in England of any importance came to his standard. At Warrington, whence he should have marched on London, he changed his plan. There were too many Harrisons and Lamberts in the way. So he marched to the West, which had been so true to his father. On the 22nd he reached Worcester, weary and foot-sore enough, but the net was not yet ready to close on him. When Cromwell came he was coming to make no doubt of it, and to secure every man, with 30,000 to do it with. There would be no swift march home to the Highlands for the King before the end, as there was for his grand-nephew a century later, and yet the large proportion of his men too were from the same bonnie North. It was a tragedy of tragedies, and, as Oliver had expected, the hatred of invaders was for the moment the principal passion aroused.

As Charles marched, Oliver was pelting down after him at his best marching pace, and that was no mean thing. By the 19th he was at Ferrybridge, in Yorkshire, marching as Harold of England marched with his huscarles to meet the Normans after his victory over the Danes. On the 24th he had joined Lambert and Harrison at Warwick and thence marched to Evesham. We need not follow the sad story. Oliver on both sides of the Severn, with a bridging train to save each wing from isolation, was taking his time as a cat with a mouse, yet finding a rat at bay, with five hours as fierce fighting as ever he saw before he achieved his end. Charles could play the man right enough, and tried to overwhelm the English right wing.

Oliver crossed back to oppose it, and there were several hours of stiff fighting aforesaid, Oliver apparently offering quarter in the town but only getting shot at. All was over early in the afternoon, and there was no escape. Ten thousand prisoners, who included half the nobility of Scotland, were taken. The King, alone almost, got away, happily for Cromwell. He did not need another Royal death on his soul.

And that was the end of our hero as a soldier, not a 'consummate' soldier as some would have it, since he met no conditions that could so prove him, but a first-class one in that he could drill, train, command and lead men, the latter two not necessarily the same thing. He could lead large bodies of Horse with great determination and tactical flair; he had been in sole command in all the three campaigns against the Scots; he understood the mechanisms of supply, the rock on which so many leaders split; and, above all things, he was resolute to the end. He knew the English, and it was that knowledge that enabled him to handle his men. He spoke the cant of the Puritans and often felt the genuine afflatus, and that in the peculiar times gave him added influence. Undoubtedly as a soldier among soldiers he had 'it' because of the qualities just enumerated, but they alone are not 'it,' and that must have been born to him. Without the strange circumstances of the time, however, there would have been no Lord-General, and through it all we have seen how nothing in the way of advancement did he seek or intrigue for, except perhaps when it was borne in on him that he alone had the gift or perhaps the courage to straighten out a crisis.

So much in very brief is this story of a soldier driven in middle age by a 'set of curious chances' to be one of the most dramatic personages and military leaders of our history. Cromwell as head of the State is another story, and we must for a moment glance at that.

The Lord Protector

Parliament had nothing but praise, as well probably as apprehensions, for the victor of Worcester. An extra allowance of £4000 and the Palace of Hampton Court were bestowed on him, and he soared at once into the popularity of the people. It has already been remarked that our ordinary minds do not realise the time that things take to mature—the nineteen years that Mary Queen of Scots was a *détenue* and a prisoner in England, the long years of Good Queen Bess when she had time to be loved and hated a dozen times over and by several generations. So we sometimes forget that it was close on three years after the death of Charles that Cromwell returned the victor from Worcester, still a soldier, even if the head of all the soldiers. He had had to conquer Irish and Scots, and now that war seemed over, his fierceness passed and he was the man of ruth that he had been in the early days. He wanted no more executions, but an amnesty, an act of oblivion, and would now see England and Scotland at peace and the wounds healed.

But though his victories had got rid of England's enemies and of the claimant to the throne, they had not solved the problem of government. The absurd Rump of the Parliament of 1649 still remained, and the Council of State really ruled by the sword, and the power of the Army to quell popular opinion. The country was bankrupt, the squires beggared, tramps and vagrants everywhere, the prisons full, chiefly of debtors. Only the Army was in good case, 50,000 strong, besides the Irish garrison and local companies. Its costs with that of the Navy were tearing the heart out of the country, as Charles II. was to know to his chagrin.

For eighteen months after Worcester, Cromwell 'sat very tight,' wondering, watching and gentle. He did, however, force the Rump to fix a date for its dissolution. It fixed it three years ahead, 3rd November 1654, which was absurd. Yet this he apparently accepted, and on 10th December 1651 called a meeting of officers and lawyers, and discussed the future. Some were for a monarchy, and the Duke of Gloucester, Charles' youngest brother, was even spoken of. Some, the soldiers chiefly, were for a republic. Many were the commissions set up and discussions entered on, but still the absurd rule, if rule it was, went on. The Army was getting 'fed up' with the bad law and the bad state of the country, and now demanded that grievances of religious morals and corrupt practices should be put an end to. Parliament referred the petition to a committee. Oliver was anxious that the Army and Parliament should get together, and that there should be no *coup d'état* by the former. But by January 1653 the Army had lost patience. The House was at work on a new Bill for representation, and the Army liked it not, and then prevarication brought about the famous doings of the 20th of April. Cromwell, who was apprised by Harrison of dirty doings in progress designed to 'bilk' the Army, but who had not dressed for the House that day, hurried down as he was, incredulous, but ordering a party of musketeers of his own unit to follow him. Things were rushing to the end that many had foreseen and still more hoped for. The Rump, as we know, was dissolved by Oliver, who lost his temper, finding indeed that it was proposed to remove him from command. The thoroughness in his character now emerged again. He had cast the die, and the Council of State protesting at illegality, Bradshawe of all people among them, was swept away. The Long Parliament was gone, and it could be said with Mark Antony, 'None so poor as do it reverence.'

That night some wag wrote on the door of St Stephen's 'This House to let unfurnished,' and it is Oliver himself who records that not so much as a dog barked. But the soldier had made a mistake. He had broken the routine of England, there was nothing to take its place, and he had not meant to do it.

He could have been king if he liked after Worcester, but would not pluck the fruit. He tried to find some authority that would make his power legal, he tried two forms of Parliament, abolished each as incompetent or presuming, accepted Lambert's 'Instrument of Government' and allowed himself to become Lord Protector. To this office he was duly inducted on 16th December 1654, four years after the King's death. At last, finding too many undercurrents, he had to start that rule of the major-generals that alone seemed a feasible proposition to make the machine of State run at all. The Parliament that he wanted was a body that would legalise his position and then go away for some years, while he did his best to sit on Levellers, mutinous soldiers, Fifth Monarchy men and all the wild folk that the tearing up of established order lets loose on the world. England did undoubtedly need a dictator for a while, but the government by major-generals was a horrible failure that lives in the subconscious mind of the nation to this day. Curiously enough, it will be found that even now the military headquarters of several of our commanders are still known as 'Government House.' Since government by edict provided too little money, the next Parliament was summoned a year before its due, and failed him. Then it was that he nearly became a king a second time.

So all the remaining five years of his life do we see Oliver trying to evolve a legal government, the citizen side of his mentality usually uppermost, save when a Cavalier rising, a mutiny in the Army, or a rough answer from some foreign Power occurred, when he knew exactly what to do, from the part of his mind that controlled his military habits.

But it was a sad story, and his health went from bad to worse, his mother died at ninety and she had meant much to him, and the favourite daughter died too, she whose sympathies were with the King, but he missed her terribly. As the end came, his poor mind that had so much on it was haunted by doubts. Was he 'in Grace'? He was once, he knew, and Calvinism is a sore master to serve when health be failing. Shortly before his soul was required of him he was heard to mutter several times, 'It is a fearful thing to fall into the hands of the living God.' He had hewed the enemies of the Lord to pieces, was not that enough? It was not how Charles had faced his Maker.

But to this man of iron, this great lucid clear-seeing brain, death in his disorder seemed terrible and not the passing to the Peace of God. And so he went, a righteous man in his own way of thinking, and whether he was right or whether he was wrong, a great, in some ways a typical, Englishman and—he left a navy!

And the day that his spirit was demanded of him was again the 3rd of September—'Old Oliver's Day'—the day of the trumpets at Drogheda, the day of Dunbar and of Worcester, the day of his crossing the Bar. And we who are still 'this England' or better 'this Britain' may end this outline of a leader born and led by circumstance by a saying from his own mouth:

'But if the Lord take pleasure in England, and if he will do us good, he is very able to bear us up.'

. . . .

And they tried to put in his place 'Son Dick,' whom the new Merry England dubbed 'Tumble-down Dick,' as you may see over more than one country ale-house to this day, ere the King could come to his own again.

CHAPTER VII

SOME THUMBNAIL SKETCHES

Joan of Arc
John Wesley
Napoleon Bonaparte
Field-Marshal Lord Raglan
John Nicholson

SOME THUMBNAIL SKETCHES

Joan of Arc

Explored to the depths though the drama and glory of the Maid of Orleans be, yet it is not fair to our subject to let her secret quite alone. We need not go into the corner in a white sheet as used to be the case for our share of the martyrdom, we who live in an age that has seen Edith Cavell shot for a far less weighty offence. It was the French and the French Church who condemned her to death, and the English merely the civil power who carried out the sentence — much as Pilate carried out the cruel demand of the Jewish ecclesiastics for the death of Christ. We know, and perhaps Shaw has put it clearer than any historian for us, that the maid, *tête montée*, had outstayed her welcome with the ungrateful French. Nor, since a few centuries earlier the Normans and their French knights and mercenaries had seized and parcelled England, need we admit the argument that calls our dominance of Northern and Western France unrighteous. We had plenty of right to be there, unless war and conquest be ruled out as unthinkable. Joan, by some strange mystic or at any rate psychological power, had inspired her spiritless countrymen, had reheartened the French soldiery, had stirred the French nobility. Is it to be wondered at that to the English she seemed a witch? The very terms witch and wizard were indecently used by the clergy for the women and men of the old pagan fertility cult prevalent in Lorraine till the fourteenth and perhaps the fifteenth century. Its existing as an organised business in Cumberland well into the eighteenth century [1] may give much of the clue to her success as a leader and to the Church's fierce hatred of her.

Joan, a simple village lass living in a part of the country in which the dying paganism (pagan = peasant) was intermingled with the new Christianity, stirred as pagan or Christian might be with a lively patriotism and a horror of the rule of a stranger, hears the mysterious voices. Virgin and goddess both call to her in her untutored mind. To the French soldiery perhaps she called in both names, for the gods and saints of the countryside had great appeal. The *riposte* and hatred of the Church called the followers or dabblers therein witches and warlocks, and invented stories of their doings, and they were days when ruth had left men's hearts even in their own land.

Whatever the truth of her 'voices,' and the real reason of the hatred of her own people, the phenomenon is more than astounding, and the causes—the occasion of changing from a patriotic maid with a bee in her bonnet to be the great mainspring of survival—more than ample. The British Atkins, then much the same as now, in every keep, and in every castle and village of Northern and Western France, whether their right to be there was good or bad, for generation on generation, was more than any true French spirit could stand for ever. There must have been plenty of stout hearts wait-

[1] *Vide* the Cumberland Witch Trials of 1720, the devil in black being sometimes the squire in his dress as master of the lodge or coven.

ing for some galvanising portent, plenty to rally round this lass who brought a charm, and several to see that here was a card worth betting on and a horse worth backing. As the British Conservatives backed David Lloyd George and saw him through for the sake of their country in its crisis, and Reichwehr and Junker support the portent Hitler, so did all that was worth while in France support the miracle of Heaven, whether moved by the living God of the Christian faith, or the same Almighty viewed more mistily through the older legends.

The physical courage of the maid, her simplicity, even if spoilt by her growing boorishness as the afflatus grew weaker, is a sign for all time of the power of mind and imagination over matter in times of dire crisis. That the Church of Rome did well to repent and canonise her, all the world admits. Whether the voices were of God and the Virgin, or whether they were born of an introspective mind worked on by the old legends, the results were the same. If we believe, as we should do, that all religions strive after the one Almighty, even through a glass darkly, the portent remains. Since we accept the divine leading and direction of Moses, it should be equally possible to accept the divine mission of the Maid, however engendered, to convince the English that it was not intended that they should hold France, burn they the intervener never so fiercely. Providence so obviously has guided England and given her so much, that she has done well to accept the slap in the face that the Maid was destined to give her. Seen as men then saw, however, the crime of executing the Church's decree, which so suited

England's book, was not so heinous as it seems to us in our armchair. Incidentally it may be remarked that the death of 'Blue Beard,' her ardent follower Gilles de Rais, in the years to follow, and his joyful going to his heretic's death as a vicarious offering, gives some colour to the legend of paganism.[1] When all is said and done, however, we come back to the two facts, the dire occasion of France working on Joan's honest pure brain and on those who looked for a portent, and the sudden inspiration that came to her; the entering into her soul, as the old belief had it, of the Kings of Orion.

John Wesley (1703–1791)

I. *The Incubation*

Hitherto we have looked on those whose careers have led them to the path of the might and dominion of the world, or on courses of progress whose end has been bloodshed. Now we may relieve our eyes from the strain of a film that dazzles and flickers, to watch the emergence of John Wesley as a fisher of men—the struggle to come through the maze and to grip a call that had haunted him. It was no less a man than Lord Macaulay who considered that it was Wesley's sweeping call to higher thoughts among the humble and lowly that saved England from some turmoil like unto the French Revolution. It has been urged herein that 'no occasion, no hero.' But here we are to have an instance of something different, the occasion of the religious indifference in which the men of

[1] For some light on the subject, see Dr Murray's *God of the Witches* (Sampson Low).

England were sunk. The decaying and empty churches, the poverty-stricken countryside, born of our civil war, our religious struggles, and, above all, our struggles against the might of France and the greed of Holland, furnished the dire but not emergent occasion. These had left all purses bare, for it has well been said that what makes the rich poor, makes the poor poorer.

This epic of Wesley, for epic the later half of his life truly was, begins ordinarily enough, and for some years the internal struggles of mind and soul, seeing but darkly and searching long for the true course to the haven, produced what can but be called something of a prig.

John Wesley, as all the world should know, was born in 1703, and destined to live on to peace and glory to the age of eighty-eight. He was one of nineteen children of whom ten grew up, of a mother of character and a father of worth, who, born Dissenters, had come back to the mother church of England, the father being eventually Vicar of Epworth, in Lincolnshire. The mother was a staunch Jacobite and the father a Whig, which indeed resulted in a separation till the accession of Anne removed the source of quarrel. John was the first-fruits of the reunion, and the lad, whose character had been developed by a long tussle between his own will and that of his mother's, entered the Charterhouse for six years, going to Christ Church in 1720 at the age of seventeen.

To see him in his blossoming we must follow the outline of his earlier days. The years of his youth are marked by study, by a considerable number of friendships and love episodes with high-grade and stimulating young women, notably 'Varanese'

Kirkham, 'Aspana' Grenville, and later Sophy Hopkey. The two former were women whose influence tended to uplift, and who discussed with him eagerly the religious working of life that puzzled him. Had he had any possible means of matrimony one or other would doubtless have shared his life. Ordained first in 1725, he was 'priested' in 1728. His relations with the Vicar of Epworth were not always harmonious, but from 1728 to 1729 he was his father's assistant curate. There, of small stature, he was the dapper little country parson, who took part eagerly enough in country life and country jollity. But the great doubts and causes of religion which had now disturbed the growing world so long were stirring and rending him, while the philosophy of life was equally perplexing. Jean Calvin, Thomas à Kempis, Jeremy Taylor, all changed piquets in his mind. Salvation by works was a Popish doctrine, he must seek for a rule of life, for 'The Way' that so many of all colours and creeds have sought. In 1726 he had been elected a Fellow of Lincoln, a very different Wesley from him of the parish side, a grave and brilliant young Don, a good classic admittedly, a shattering logician, but quite uncompanionable. His habit of weekly Communion was making a toil of a pleasure! and folk began to laugh at him, which he hated. The serious and Spartan side of his nature had come to him as an undergraduate, when he and his brother and several others had formed a coterie, which his fellows called 'The Holy Club,' those who had hoped to find salvation, among other ways, by mortifying the flesh and living hard, to the grave injury of some of them. He had left Epworth in

1729 and would not think of his father's living. Keeping apart from the other Dons, he followed the 'method' of the 'Holy Club,' with definite fastings, austerities, rescue work, exorcising of spirits; and all the time searching for the true 'Way,' often by methods that seem trivial enough.

In 1736 John and his brother Charles accepted service under Colonel Oglethorpe proceeding as Governor to Georgia, as Chaplain and Indian Secretary. We read of John in some difficulties, ministering to his fellow-passengers. There were troubles and bickerings, and to his surprise a Moravian confrère inquired if he really knew Jesus Christ, a question he rather liked to put to others himself. But it set his mind thinking again and again 'Where was the true "Way"?' 'How could he find it?'

The two years in Georgia were a nightmare. There were many troubles and the Governor's light-o'-loves were an embarrassment and responsible for terrible scenes; but he loved his flock and strove mightily for them. He now found some personal appeasement with Miss Sophy Hopkey, niece of the chief magistrate of Savannah, then recovering from an unhappy love affair. Taking her by ship to Savannah, the susceptible evangelical, who was personable and attractive enough, proposed marriage, which happily was not accepted, but for a while he was torn, now by celebacy, now by thoughts of Sophy. The young lady came to him a good deal, now pressing for a proposal which she had at first rejected. With the help of his bungalow mate and friend, the older Delamotte, three slips were put in a hat: '*Marry*,' '*Think not of it this year,' 'Think of it no more.'* He drew the last. A final effort in fresh questions of fate drew the slip, '*Converse with her only in the prescence of Mr Delamotte.*'

Wesley, who had a bent for sortilege, now felt that the Almighty had signified His will. He very nearly succumbed again a little later, however, to the charm and wiles of Sophy. But Wesley saved himself—if salvation it was—but quite forgot what it might all mean to Sophy. She married a man named Williamson; there were more troubles, Sophy neglected her religious duties, Wesley refused her Communion and he was apprehended for defamation and refusing the Sacrament. A grand jury of forty-four persons found against him, and he was charged with much neglect of religious duties. None were pressed, but Wesley now very wisely decided to leave Georgia, and escape from so involved a situation. The troubles, born largely of his wide sympathy and of a nature that was obviously at this stage more enthusiastic than wise, show us the very human stress and strain through which he was passing before he got into the fairway of purpose. They are makings of experience as essential in throwing out the dross and eliciting the true man as were ever the workings of Cromwell's spirit or the inferiorities of Moses, or her disappointments to Tseu Hi.

The voyage home brought great misery and uncertainty to his mind, accentuated no doubt by bad weather. His doubts of everything increased. Could the Gospel be true? And on his return to Oxford all was still unstable and controversial. He officiated in Anglican churches too rebelliously and vigorously to men's liking, and as yet he had no lesson and no message to deliver. On a second visit to Oxford he met his old friend Delamotte, who 'put it across' him. 'You have a simplicity . . . but you trust in your own works. You do not believe in Christ.'

II. *The Great Call*

However true old Delamotte's thrust might have been, it was soon to be over. Again he consulted the Bible by lots, looking for guidance. As he worked away, preaching he knew not what, there came to his hand 'conversions' among those in his audiences, as well as for himself. He himself put it on the 24th of May 1738. There followed the days of brotherhood, companionship, discussions with his friend, and later opponent, Whitfield, and he saw more and more of his Moravian friends. His preachings and communings started him founding his brotherhood of those who sought God, and he initiated his tours and his helpers, his lay expounders, and the teaching of his 'method' of chastening the body and awakening the spirit. It was not till 1744, six years after his return, when already he had his chapels, that his 'United Society of Methodists' took shape. Wesley himself passionately repudiated dissent, he planned but a 'ginger group' within the apathetic Church—to enliven it, to make truths live, to get the Gospel into the hearts of the neglected and also some amelioration of their conditions. His chapels had clocks for many years, to tell the congregation when to leave their extra devotions and go to their parish church; the Prayer Book was their guide. But to others, the Church of England being what it is, dissent and opposition were unavoidable. Wesley claimed that his dissenters, those who followed the 'method' as he preached it, were more truly the sound part of the Church of England. And while he so preached and traversed the whole land, the sun had come out from behind the clouds, he now saw clearly and his doubts were gone. He knew and felt that he was 'in Grace,' as Old Oliver would have said, and with the knowledge thereof, his influence and confidence and his strength of magnetism increased a hundredfold. Thousands of followers, swelling to tens and hundreds of thousands, listened and joined his body. It was not a new religion or a new doctrine; it was but the spreading of the old gospel, in what was often virgin untilled soil. Up and down the length and breadth of the land rode and tramped John Wesley, and those he had enlisted in his cause, and finally 'illegally' ordained.

Branches of the societies opened everywhere, and while it was to those lost pockets of early mining and industrial communities, the jails, the lazarettos, that his mission forced themselves, thousands joined his societies from the educated and better to do. To the latter it was a religion revitalised and a way of life refound.

Wesley, after his early troubles and as the good looks of his youth passed and his auburn locks greyed, was becoming more and more attractive to men, his charm of manner greatly developed. His dominion over women was marked, and his letters to his adorers always tender. His brother, in 1748, prevented him marrying an attractive young widow, almost forcibly joining her to one of his preachers, leaving John beside himself with anger. But evangels travel the fastest who travel alone. Alas! in 1751 he married a Mrs Vazeille, a stout well-ordered widow of forty. The great treks of Wesley, four to five thousand miles a year in all weathers over all roads, were too much for her, and it has been said that she harried the life out of him. It was no sort of success and in no way conduced to his happiness. This was another stone in the character trials which were making the man through the long years of energy. The physical endurance, the mortification of the body which he submitted to, caring naught for bed and board, were stupendous. Penniless himself, he was fortunate in finding some followers, notably the Countess of Huntingdon, who could help the essential finances. With it all, the troubles of organisation were heavy. To prevent back-sliding, more and more preachers were necessary, and this soon meant a system of government. There were schisms and rebellions that were heart-breaking, there were schools and orphanages that succeeded, training colleges that failed.

In every circumstance that favoured him, even to a fine day, Wesley saw the special blessing of God; in every untoward event, even a stone from an angry mob to an impeding snow-storm, the machination of the Prince of Darkness. Still, in Wesley's own mind he was but a priest of the Church of England, preaching the gospel as that Church knew it and could have preached it. But the educated Christians often seemed his special enemies; perhaps those who were not indifferent preferred their own 'method,' for within the 'many mansions' there can be many genuine methods. The number of ordained clergy among his preachers were not very many. In America, where he had many adherents, he had none, and the Sacrament was the difficulty. So late as 1786 Wesley prayed the Bishop of London to ordain a priest to go to the colonies, but it was not possible. Wisely or foolishly, the Church could not take Wesley to its heart, and the great act of separation came about; the apostolic succession was broken. Wesley persuaded himself that a presbyter and a bishop were the same, and that *he* could ordain. He did. Because he did so he was able to start a ministry eventually as the years rolled on, dignified, organised and controlled. Since the Wesleyan method is but the neglected method of the Church, which has seen countless variants of the religious disciplining and development of its members through the ages, and since Wesleyanism is not far from Anglicanism, many of its ministers pass on to the Church of England, famous and welcomed.

The years of the schism, the quarrels, the growing opposition of his brother Charles are but the 'bellying of the curtain.' The leader went on through the years, nearly half a century, of his apotheosis from strength to strength. A quarter of a million miles did he ride in the Kingdom, rain blow and snow, or shine, his personality being more and more revered, his personal charm becoming more and more compelling, his 'Society,' that was now almost a Church, becoming yearly wider and greater, the chapel clock to tell its members when to go to Church still the outward sign of his own intention. But even evangels are human. From Ireland, in 1789, where he was conducting a pastoral tour he then being eighty-six, he writes, 'I now find that I grow old.' A little later, on New Year's Day

1790, 'I am now an old man decayed from head to foot. My eyes are dim'—as well they might be. 'However, blessed be God, I do not slack my labour, I can preach and write still.' Next year the great spirit passed away quietly, he then being in his eighty-eighth year, and the mighty compelling force and magnetic personality returned to the God who gave it.

A writer has said, 'How beautiful was the old age of Wesley! It was a great sunset, full of peace and prophecy, aglow with that mellow old experience of things eternal—like the oncoming evening and the star-crowned night.'

Where was the secret? How came this unsettled spirit to the calm that enabled him to see the Way, and whence his great power and influence? The occasion was there right enough, but not so obvious, not so immediately insistent as in those of the worldly leaders. The dynamic spirit was there waiting to free itself, forged by those anvils hot with pain that have been indicated. There was the astounding control of will over his physical weakness that made possible his lifelong journeys by eighteenth-century road and bog. When all is said and done, the great man was born not made, and perhaps hardly even developed, merely evolved from the maelstrom of his own nature answering the Call and receiving the Blessing. We may leave it at that. Alexander of Macedon is clay and dust and no man even knows where his ashes lie. Napoleon has left but his Code. It is nearly a century and a half since the quiet passing of John Wesley, yet his 'body goes marching along' with unabated blessing, a peculiarly British development of 'The Way.'

Napoleon Bonaparte (1769–1821)

'How far is St Helena from a little child at play?'
A St Helena Lullaby (R. K.).

No figure in history perhaps has been the subject of more literature, more biography and more complex study from every side of his character and life than this astounding Emperor of the French. But, again, to write essays on leadership without saying something, however trite, on his character and career would be absurd. He, like Alexander of Macedon, is one of the leading examples of leadership with a very big 'L' since history came to emerge from legend. His story also serves to further the thesis of these essays—the occasion, the equipment, the use thereof.

It but needs to outline the state of France—the Revolution dead of its own canker; the leaders removing each other; a vast army, half-disciplined, with officers and soldiers of the *ancien régime* ready to lead and anxious to rise to heights of fame, but none fit to do so; the country crying out for reconstruction; Paris in an orgy of the new fashionables, and no one to direct, scarcely anyone left to say 'I will' or 'I won't.' The occasion and then the man!

What was this man's equipment to avail himself of the occasion? It was not very far to seek in the first place, because all the world knows that the lad cherished ambitions. Here was not the citizen drawn unexpectedly to war as was Cromwell, nor the king brought up in purple and suckled on super-nationalism as was Alexander, nor called on late in life as Lord Raglan, nor searching for 'The Way' like John Wesley. Here was the professional cadet, entered in a military academy at ten, commissioned in 1785, when sixteen years of age, in the Royal Artillery, fed on the great traditions of the Grand Monarque, of Turenne and Villars, as the British subaltern on Blenheim and Dettingen, and the tradition of Churchill—repining at his birth in the piping days of peace! Then the tragedies and excitements of the Revolution. The young artilleryman, then twenty-three, actually saw the mob invade the Tuileries and the extinction of the Crown in the same year, after the constitutional attempts to make a popular monarchy. From a Royal officer he became a Republican one, in the great uprising to resist the dictation of Europe. Following his prominent part in the following year (1794) in the siege of Toulon against the English, he then being twenty-five, the callow youth, for such he still was, became the fiery general of artillery in the war with Italy. In 1795 fate took him from his own corps and started him on his real career. Paris was in rebellion, someone prompt, shrewd and heedless of consequences was needed. General Bonaparte is given by Barras the task of suppressing the movement. The 'whiff of grape' at the right moment becomes the passport for his return to Italy, not only as a real general of all arms but as a commander-in-chief, and he but twenty-six.

After this, anything might be possible were he man enough to bear a great part, to suppress and dominate his far older subordinates, to lead men to the cannon's mouth, to try daring map strategy and be successful. He could do it all, and he did. The four years of profound excitement and the few years' boyish study could not have taught him. The born flair for war was there, the fierce Italian spirit, and also for silent intrigue. Born! Born!! Born!!! Born indomitable, snatched by fate to opportunity, endowed by nature too with a brain, in which the flair for organisation, administration, justice and economics far exceeded even the flair for tactics and the intuition that was strategy. The army of Napoleon has not lasted to this day, the Code of Napoleon has, and it still carries the admiration of the world. An adventurer? Yes! An impostor? Never! A genius, perhaps even a patriot, but certainly one who understood the people he led and ruled. The people, intoxicated, stunned and rejuvenated, reacted to La Gloire for a full decade before they had time to mourn their dead and lick their wounds. But that he could have become Emperor or ever dreamed of such was only possible, as it was to Cromwell, when it became evident that the men who could destroy a system could not replace it. The Napoleons and the Cromwells brook not babbling politicians, nor the Mussolini who eagerly claims the 'Little Corporal' as his compatriot, and the Hitler who copies his attitude and combs his few hairs in the same manner.

Opportunity and occasion let the obscure lieutenant push through the crowd, nature gave him his 'brain' and bred within him the flair for victory. 'Would you be a Napoleon, my son? Not likely!' Here in our England we can still keep the coach in the middle of the road, and keep the roadway fit to drive on, without great leaders, without great occasions, since Tumble-down Dick went back to his manor and the simple life. Perhaps it is because we give the loser leave to prate, and still send our naughty lads to sea, or its equivalent.

That the end of Napoleon was tragedy many still deplore.

FIELD-MARSHAL LORD RAGLAN

One summer's day in 1855,[1] in the whitewashed farmhouse on the Crimean Chersonese which was the British headquarters, there passed away a character which to those who know of it, more fully illustrated the 'it' that we are trying to estimate and separate than almost any that we can throw upon the screen.

Fitzroy Somerset[2] was the youngest son of the First Duke of Beaufort and at the time of the Crimean War was Master-General of the Ordnance, at that period a minister of Parliament distinct from the Secretary at War or the General Commanding-in-Chief at the Horse Guards. His early career had been full of incident, and then to outward appearance had lapsed into one of dignity and peace if not of leisure, and he had none of the practical training in the more active sides of warfare that we are familiar with to-day. Born in 1788, he had been, as a young man, A.D.C. to the Duke of Wellington in the Peninsula, and had there imbibed that intense reverence for the Duke's character and first principles which so marked all those of his entourage. On the coming of the peace of 1814 he went as Secretary to the Embassy in Paris, only to rejoin his master for the 'Hundred Days' as Military Secretary, losing his right arm at Waterloo. From there he returned to the Embassy, eventually becoming Military Secretary

[1] 28th June.
[2] Lord James Henry Fitzroy Somerset, First Lord Raglan.

at the Horse Guards, which post he held for twenty-five years until appointed Master-General of the Ordnance.

It does not sound a career of any great importance, yet it was one that had emphasised all the qualities innate in the man. In the first place he had become the repository of all the wisdom and tradition of the Duke, which to the Army was, for over a generation, the law and the prophets. He had imbibed from his master an instinct for first principles, a remarkable knowledge of the arbitrary politics of continental Europe, and had developed a dignity and fascination of manner and a knowledge of the world of his time that is hard in these days even to imagine. Neither he nor his master had been able to stand up against the Manchester School and the belief that there could be no more wars. Thus the Army was entirely unorganised for war when England began to talk to the Tsar, much as our unthinking folk would have us talk to Japan or Mussolini. But the Department of the Master-General of the Ordnance was responsible for the Royal Artillery and the Royal Engineers. These two services went to the Crimea far more efficient in their ethics and conception than the rest of the Army.

When the British and French forces went on their somewhat nebulous mission to the Bosphorus, Lord Fitzroy Somerset, as he was best known, was marked out as the only commander fit to carry out the semi-political mission that the command involved. To his many qualities he added a most lively sense of loyalty to the Government that employed him, a considerable understanding of the French, and the knowledge that in both Armies the seniors had served in the Napoleonic Wars, and that old antagonisms might well up, especially in more impressionable French breasts.

So much for the outward story. Now let us premise that the Army, which first landed in Bulgaria to support the Turks on the Danube against Russian attacks, was condemned to inactivity, because the British Government had failed, had indeed refused, to provide transport. We must also remember that what brought the Allies into a state of active hostilities was the destruction and massacre, by the Russian Black Sea Fleet based on Sebastopol, of the whole of a weak Turkish fleet at Sinope on the Asiatic shores of the Black Sea. The failure to take surrender and save life had stirred all Europe.

When the Turks, assisted by a few British officers, mostly of the East India Company's Service, had repulsed the Russians on the Danube, the British Government directed Lord Raglan to capture Sebastopol if he thought it feasible, telling him that the French Commander-in-Chief had orders to follow his lead. September was the perfect month to land in, winter was not due till Christmas. Lord Raglan considered that he could disembark, storm the fortress from the practically undefended land side, destroy fleet and harbour and re-embark before winter set in—a winter, however, which all reports said to be by no means excessive. As he could land on an open beach, march over well-watered grass downs, and be supplied from the fleet, the shortness of land transport was not now of paramount importance.

There was never the slightest idea of a winter campaign. A *coup de main* was intended, followed by prompt departure. How the force was compelled to stay two winters does not matter here, but this outline is given because of the misconception as to Lord Raglan's efficiency and success. The story of the winter troubles and the troops' misery was followed by eighteen months of efficiency which is forgotten.

The further salient points before we turn to the mysterious qualities innate in Lord Raglan are that the dying French Commander-in-Chief would not pursue after the victory of the Alma or agree to the immediate *coup de main.* Three weeks later two siege trains, by heroic and astounding endeavour, opened fire on the fortress as a prelude to another *coup de main* only baulked by a *contretemps* which again upset the new French chief. Even then an assault and escape before winter still held the field. When, after the costly victory of Inkerman, there occurred the blizzard followed by snow, that had not been known for a hundred years, which wrecked twenty-one British store-ships full of supplies and the largest steamer then in the world crammed with hospital stores and warm clothing, assault was no longer possible. These details are given to combat popular conceptions of the peculiar story, so that Lord Raglan's share of the troubles, so rarely understood, may be followed before outlining his special power and domination as part of our study of leadership.

That power, by general consent, was quite remarkable. No one came to him without going away strengthened and refreshed, without seeing his burden lightened and his troubles melt away. Marshal St Arnaud, vain, tricky, presuming, immediately gave way before him, dropped his presumption, abandoned his pretensions, showed the better side of his character. Officers, generals, doctors, all felt the comfort and calm that emanated from him. At the Alma a strange freak, almost an escapade on his part, had taken him into an unoccupied knoll in the Russian front line. An excited French officer rushed up to him and implored aid. His Lordship, in frock-coat, cocked hat and feathers, and empty sleeve, on a great calm English hunter, sat unperturbed, spy-glass in hand and reins on his horse's neck. He spoke much as a mother would give the breast to a fretful child. 'There! There! I can spare you a battalion,' and the excited one metaphorically snuggled up against the ample breast and took heart of grace. It was typical of all he did. Nor were his battle tactics anything but based on the first principle of military common sense. That he carried the great burden of Napoleon III.'s intrigues is both well known and yet forgotten. But he also carried everyone's burdens, including the Secretary at War's neglect in not providing proper hospitals to which sick and wounded could be evacuated.

Kinglake wrote of him:

'He was gifted with a diction very apt for public business, and of a kind rarely found in Englishmen—whether he spoke or whether he wrote, whether he used the French tongue or his own clear graceful English, it seemed that there came from him the very words that were the best and no more. He had the subtle power to draw men along with him . . . without pressure or argument, his mind by its own mere impact broke down resistance. This dominion, however, was in a great degree dependent on his actual personal presence. . . . Young men going to him in diffidence came back radiant with joy. A British Prime Minister once said of him "that he could lead the State."'

Again just before the Alma:

> 'M. St Arnaud, mounting his horse, was elate, but he was elate not with elation of having achieved a purpose, but rather, it would seem, from the sense of that singular comfort which anxious men always drew from the mere power of Lord Raglan's presence.'

When nine months of the burden of the French, the inadequacy of his own army, the tragedies of the post-blizzard months, and the failure of his own troops to storm the Redan had worn him to a frazzle, he succumbed, as did Stanley Maude in Bagdad, to a bout of Asiatic cholera, which his frame was too worn to resist. Deep was the mourning of all who had been in touch with him. The electric Pelissier, who had succeeded the less effective Canrobert in the high command of the French Army, stood weeping for an hour by the side of his death-bed.

What was it, this strange influence, so forgotten in all that followed, so insistent at the time? It was, of course, helped by dignity of birth and stateliness of upbringing. It was enhanced by righteous outlook on the world. It was developed by the inspiration of the Duke of Wellington's companionship and tuition. But when all is said and done, there have been plenty such in our wonderful history, but there was here an inherent gift of magnetism which cannot be explained, least of all by those who came within its orbit. Had fate and fortune been different, and had not the grave closed on him before success came, hugely would he have bulked among England's great men. It is a sad story, and the weeping Pelissier by his side is the ending thereof.

John Nicholson

There is a name among soldiers, nay, among English people, still to conjure with, and it is that of John Nicholson, the captain of the Indian Army with the temporary rank of brigadier-general, who died in glory and in failure. From his glory and his sacrifice there is always much to learn. Who was John Nicholson?—and the information is, for the generations who in the natural order of things do not know, set forth in brief. He was an officer of the Army of the East India Company, born of the Protestant colony in Ireland, who had come to India in 1839 at the age of seventeen, and having a good reputation as a useful energetic subaltern, acquired in the First Afghan War, was selected for what is known in India as 'Political service.' That meant service among the wilder and unsettled borders and states, and comprised magistracy, administration, policy, organisation, rough-and-tumble soldiering and the like. To John Nicholson it meant also service under the great Sir Henry Lawrence, who, as Resident at Lahore, was endeavouring to restrain the wild Punjab during the minority of the little Maharajah Dhulip Singh, after the tragedy of the First Sikh War.

As a man of tireless days and sleepness nights he brought the lawless Moslem tribes in the broken hills between Rawalpindi and the Indus to order, they who from time immemorial had preyed on the traders' routes. In the Second Sikh War he had guided the Army on countless difficult occasions. After the annexation of the Punjab it was he who settled the frontier districts of the Derajat and of Bannu, whence the Sikhs had driven the Afghans.

Righteous, generous, sympathetic, fierce and masterful, the tribesmen not only adored but worshipped him.[1] Tall and hard, fierce of eye and dominating, he looked the part, and to the ambitious young officers of the Army his name was a talisman.

Prompt to improvise, the coming of codes and rules irked him, and his superiors were constantly girding at some of his more arbitrary actions, yet knowing that no one else could hold the fort one-tenth as well.

His spirit and prominent nature were born within, deepened by the bitter experience, when a lad in Afghanistan, of being with a post handed to the enemy. Ghuzni, besieged by the rebel Afghans, rebelling against their own Government, eventually surrendered, the survivors of the garrison, the 27th Bengal Native Infantry, becoming prisoners in no gentle hands.

When the Indian Mutiny broke out, the safety of the Punjab, the country of the hardy and lawless, was of untold importance; while available forces marched to Delhi, a movable column traversed that province, and Nicholson, then the civil administrator at Peshawur under Edwardes, rode day and night, like a lambent flame, against all disturbers of the peace on his border. The command of the movable column fell vacant, and Captain Nicholson, to the huge delight of the younger men, was appointed to command, with the rank of brigadier-general. The seniority-mongers were aghast, but a man who could march day and night, and stay forty-eight hours in the saddle, was what the

[1] A religious sectlet, the *Nikalseyns*, was formed of some of his worshippers.

country needed, and thanks to John Lawrence [1] they got it. Presently came the call to the still-untaken Delhi, the mutineer centre, and there, as the last available reinforcement, Nicholson marched his column, after several lightning blows against mutineers or possible mutineers in the Punjab. Wherever there was danger, resolute, silent, hawk-eyed was the Brigadier, and as he marched into the stagnant atmosphere of the camp behind the Ridge the cry went round, 'John Nicholson has come'—the man of action and decision, whose name was in every man's mouth. With the accession of strength that the column brought, and with the stimulant, to stout hearts, of his name, the General in command, Archdale Wilson, was able to stage the long-deferred assault, for, covered by Nicholson, was also marching the heavy siege train. Before the storming he led out his column to destroy a large body of sepoys from the rebel city who threatened the road from the north and the lumbering siege train. Over them, despite the intense heat and heavy rain of the dying monsoon, he effected a complete victory.

His commanding figure, visiting the outposts, had stressed the tired besiegers. The men had seen the electric figure, had answered short pithy questions, and the coming of the heavy guns obviously indicated the approaching climax. On 13th September 1857 four exiguous columns of British, Gurkhas and Punjabis were to storm the breach and bastions around the Kashmir Gate. Nicholson was to lead the principal column up the breach in the Kashmir Bastion. As all the world knows, the storming of the breaches was successful

[1] Then Chief Commissioner of the Punjab, brother of Henry.

in the early dawn, and then Nicholson led his own column along the walls and parapets to secure the Lahore Gate and the great bastion that commanded it.

Alas! once more, the race is not always to the swift nor the battle to the strong. The men were worn with effort in the heavy heat. They would not follow farther, not even Nicholson! For their moral and physical petrol was for the moment exhausted. To the hardened leader more effort was possible, and he demanded it; human nature refused for the moment; no leading can overcome heat exhaustion, and the General fell in the attempt to call them on, by exhortation and even jibe, a failure that that irresistible, insistent nature must have felt bitterly as he lay mortally wounded for several days.

Apart from the brilliant services that he rendered to his country, what was the secret that he possessed in thus being able to so dominate the Asiatic that they worshipped him, and that founded a sect of his fervent admirers; and what enabled him to stand out equally among his fellow-Britons? That there was an undoubted 'it' all the world agrees; there was, of course, character born of ancestry and upbringing. There was the outward appearance that does justice to the inward fire. That was a chassis strong enough physically to support the high-powered engine. No skirts urged or impeded the lambent flame of his energy. The 'it' lay in the spirit that drove him, nor was the occasion necessarily more than the particular platform on which he was asked to appear. Before the drama of 1857 was announced there were far-seeing men who said: 'If there is great work to be done in India, John Nicholson is the man to do it.'

He was mad, the lesser men said! 'Let him bite my Generals!' If he drank, which he emphatically never did, the whisky would have been needed in barrels for others. What was the secret? No man knows; his was just one of those spirits that happily well up among us in times of action in stress. In quieter times they are neither to hold nor to bind, as the letter books of his master, John Lawrence, testify for us. He was one of those 'Sons of Thunder' at whom all lesser men must marvel. And we who love a man, and watch, in misunderstanding, God's purposes, may dwell sorrowfully at that death-blow by the Lahore Bastion in a moment of failure—failure to spark the plug to a battery that was run down. *Sic transit gloria mundi.*

CHAPTER VIII

TSEU-HI (1835–1908): THE DOWAGER EMPRESS OF CHINA

THE TRAGEDY OF A MANCHU MAIDEN
FAREWELL, ROMANCE
THE PRESENCE
IN THE SADDLE
THE COMING OF THE BARBARIANS
THE EMPRESS TSEU-HI
THE SECOND REGENCY
REST IN THE SUMMER PALACE
THE JAPANESE WAR OF 1894 AND THE FINAL COUP
THE BOXER REBELLION
THE RINGING TO EVENSONG

Chronology

1825–1850. Emperor Tao-Kuang.
1850–1861. Emperor Hien-Fung (whose concubine was Ye-Ho-No-La).
1861–1875. Emperor Toung-Tchi (son of Ye-Ho).
1875–1908. Emperor Kuang-Siu (nephew of Ye-Ho).
1908–1911. Emperor Pu-Yi (grandson of Tao-Kuang) now Emperor of Manchukuo.

TSEU-HI (1835–1908): THE DOWAGER EMPRESS OF CHINA

THE TRAGEDY OF A MANCHU MAIDEN

ONE of the most remarkable stories of history is that of the little Manchu maiden, Ye-Ho-No-La, taken by her mother from her young Manchu sweetheart to be an Imperial concubine of the third class, with a hundred-to-one chance of sharing the Imperial bed. It parallels in many ways the long life and tragedies of Harry's Daughter done into Chinese. Majesty and dominion mingle with power, pique, prejudice, patriotism, *pudor* and panders.

Known to the modern world as the 'Dowager Empress of China' and to China as Tseu-Hi, she upheld with iron, invisible, almost legendary, hand the system and China of her ancestors, when the centrifugal force of Westernism and modernism was hammering on the ancient fabric. She had seen the allies of Europe driven in 1860 to stand up for some rights of courtesy and fair treatment to foreigners, and finally take Peking, and take and loot the Summer Palace itself. In 1901 she still sat behind the scenes, the live yet almost mummied despot within the screen, to see once again the *foreign devils* invade Sacred China—and pass away—and still the Manchu *façade* remained.

How did it all come to pass? What was her secret? With a life that was lived behind the veil, guarded by a host of eunuchs, the inner story of the development of such a character is not easy to follow. But we do know a good deal, and we can see many sides to a character, one side not unlike that of 'The Widow at Windsor,' without a tenth of the happy memories, the other stern and ruthless, as a Semiramis or a Catharine de Medici.

If we think of the beginning, we can but wonder at the possibilities of development for good or evil that lie within the simplest human character, under varied stress and strain and incitement.

Little Ye-Ho-No-La was a pretty little cuddly Manchu maiden, demure and well brought up in Tartar manner and etiquette. Her father was a commander of one of the eight Manchu banners, much what we should call a Territorial Divisional command, a man of status and worth, hard put to it to keep up his status on his inadequate pay. He died young, leaving a widow and three small children to be brought up, on straightened means but plenty of honour and traditions that buttered no parsnips, even as are so many of our own officers' widows. Ye-Ho-No-La, the eldest, grew out of babyhood, well educated in the lore and culture of her class. From early days the lass had imposed her will on her playmates and adopted a queenly air on the village green. At an early age she was affianced to one of her circle of young people, a young Manchu of equally good descent named Yong-Lu. The affections of the pair followed the designs of their parents; the young Manchu was intoxicated with the beauty and charm that the passing years unfolded.

But etiquette now demanded that Ye-Ho-No-La should be snatched from the freedom of the playground that was becoming unseemly for her growing nubility, and Yong-Lu was now only allowed to see his sweetheart from afar, while she, poor lass, was being set down to the blackboard and the various finishing graces that a well-born maid must acquire. But all the while, behind her decorously lowered eyelids with the Mongol fold, she looked back longingly to the days of romps and freedom, and forward to the marriage that was arranged, making faces all the while at the solemn Chinese histories that were read to her, but perforce absorbing some of their lore. She was thus but a typical Manchu maiden, of whom it might be sung, as they used to sing in the West:

> 'What are young girls made of, made of?
> What are young girls made of?
> Ribbons and laces and sweet pretty faces
> That's what young girls are made of.'

And with it all, the little Manchu rotundity was blossoming into a being of such charm and beauty that, added to her ancient class and famous family, set the Manchu ladies a-gossiping, while Yong-Lu was only allowed to look from afar.

Then came the great epoch of fifteen years of age, when marriage should be made, and the mothers pressed forward the arrangements, while Yong-Lu waited eagerly for his hopes and joys to mature, and Ye-Ho-No-La squinted through her fingers at that choice young man and goodly who hovered round the garden. And then there occurred one of those catastrophic strokes, which changed the whole world of two young people. And here let us remember, in dealing with the character development of a maiden whom fate is to draw to great heights and stresses, the influence of the womb on character; how the sublimation for good or for evil of the gift of life, carries mind and body to far greater heights and depths than the sex influence does for men; they are born for action, but women to be the temples of life.

Farewell, Romance

In 1850 Tao-Kuang, the Emperor of China, the Holy Son of Heaven and Lord of Ten Thousand Years of Precious Past, was gathered to his fathers—summoned to leave the Dragon Throne to mount the Dragon Chariot. Since that great throne must not be empty a moment, the heir, Hien-Fung, at once ascended the throne. But, however much China might call, 'The King is Dead! Long Live the King!,' the period of mourning and the rites of funeral were long. For twenty-seven months did the Court mourn, and since the family of Ye-Ho-No-La and Yong-Lu were what in India would be called '*Năzdīk*,' akin to the blood royal, all thought of marriage was out of the question, and the ardent young pair were doomed to possess their souls and bodies in patience for two and a quarter years. There was nothing for it but for the maid to return to her studies. Her zeal and zest were turned from thoughts of her lover to a prolonged study of that Chinese history and glory at which she had turned up her nose, and it gradually became an obsession, the enthusiasm of a young soul and a body that should have cuddled a caboose. And then, too, ambition had come on Manchu mammas; the new Blessed Man of Heaven would want an Imperial outfit of women. Already was he married and widowed; a wife and concubines of honour would be needed. The honourable households were agog, and to Ye-Ho-No-La suddenly came the idea that she might be swept into the great and glorious weft of Imperial power and carry on that history which she now counted so high. Alas, poor Yong-Lu!

And then came the announcement from *Madame Mère*. The Dowager Empress was seeking thirty Imperial concubines from among whom she would choose an Empress, the others would take their place as concubines of honour graded as *Fei*, as *Pin*, as *Kouei-jen*, or as *Tchang-sei*, according to merit.

The famed beauty of Ye-Ho-No-La caused her to be summoned to the Purple Palace by the Dowager Empress. And we must imagine the lass, well trained in all Manchu etiquette and courtesy, being carried in a lacquered curtained chair, escorted by guards and palace eunuchs, her heart all a-twitter, mingled with ambition and the glory of China. Hey la! What girlish heart of noble birth could be anything but excited? But as she went, the bride-to-be of seventeen peeping out from the silken curtains, she saw, and her heart sank for a moment, the disconsolate Yong-Lu, from whom the whole world had fallen away. For on her the palace gates closed for all time, or so it seemed.

The Dowager Empress was searching in her examination—beauty, grace, and also knowledge of the past greatness of China were her concern. Many were rejected, but Ye-Ho-No-La's manner and knowledge earned great approval, as well as her beauty. She found herself among the thirty winners of this Imperial beauty competition.

The details of this gambit in a great life are elaborated somewhat so that we may see something of the making of a queen-bee; as indeed we have seen it in Elizabeth, in Tudor England.

Now the Empress made no *Fei*, as that is a matter of experience and promotion. The sister of the childless young Emperor's dead wife was declared *Pin*, and likely to become consort. Ye-Ho-No-La became *Kouei-jen*, or 'honourable person,' a concubine of the third class, which was no bad start for a *débutante*!

And then we learn of the next stage, which was well calculated to shock the mind of a virtuous if ardent well-brought-up maiden of family.

Having been declared and accepted in an honourable grade, the maid was conducted with ceremony by the eunuchs to the beautiful prison apartment where she must live her life, in some hope that she might be summoned ere long to the presence of the Son of Heaven. But—the pathetic but, that must often bring gloom to the concubines of even the most virile of owners—the maid waited the summons that should lead through the portals by which she would be one with the destinies of China, and she waited long and lonely, this burning peach-blossom, whose love, Yong-Lu, wandered disconsolately far away. What was the price she had paid for ambition? We can see the seeds of disappointment being sown, and the crop of power and sternness being prepared.

Twenty months thus passed for the poor little Manchu peach-blossom, but it was relieved to some extent by, so the story goes, one of the most strange of semi-scandals that courts have ever heard. One day soon after her internment Ye-Ho-No-La found standing by her a young-looking man, and on her demanding who he was, he explained that he was the Grand Eunuch, at which the girl was overcome, since her parents had often spoken of this functionary with awe. He called on her to divest herself of her clothes while he carried out his duty of seeing that she was fit in body, in temperament and in health for her rôle of Imperial 'Stepney.' But the frustrated Ngan-Te-Hai was terribly overcome with her beauty. The ordeal which the maiden was to undergo was a considerable shock to a modest and well-brought-up Manchu maiden of family, and the eunuch must have exceeded his duty.

For twenty months this growing uncanny liaison continued, of which in the years to come all the Court whispered cognisance, and all the while came no summons to the Imperial bed, no life of love and cherishing save at Ngan-Te-Hai's incompetent hands, and Yong-Lu was inaccessibly distant. Far away too, and apparently equally inaccessible, was the Son of Heaven for whom her distant reverence and awe appreciably increased.

The intimacy with the eunuch extended to her becoming his confidante and to her hearing how he, a fine young Manchu like Yong-Lu, came to be chosen for and submit to his position. The maid had undoubtedly a deep regard for him, her only solace, but had soon learnt enough to see that she must take her fate into her own hands. She divined that Ngan-Te-Hai had no wish to see her in the Emperor's arms, and that further there was some mystery. If she was to take a part in China's greatness, she must be stirring. Twenty months had elapsed since she had entered the Palace.

So one day she demanded very forcibly that the Chief Eunuch should see that she was brought to the Emperor: 'He is childless still; I will be mother to an heir to the throne.' And the story says that jealous Ngan-Te-Hai promised to make it so.

The Presence

The long period of sickening waiting was over. The crimson lamp burned over her apartment, the green jade plaque had come. The Son of Heaven had chosen her! Moment of moments! Holy China!

The Dowager Empress had been scolding her son for not giving the throne an heir, the Grand Eunuch had been suggestful, the summons had arrived. Ngan-Te-Hai had come to fetch her and say that the sun had sunk and the Emperor was in his bed-chamber. She entered the chamber through the heavy embroidered hanging that the eunuch held up for her, as with trembling knees she tottered towards the Son of Heaven and prostrated herself before the couch of gold—and there she lay for what seemed hours. Gradually her youth overcame her sense of fear—all was silent, and she dared to peep through her hands that covered her face. She could not believe her eyes. There before her lay the Emperor. Did he sleep? Would he not speak to her? Poor little *Kouei-jen*! Poor little honourable person! She peeped again, and saw by the couch a bottle and glasses, to which now and again the Imperial hand ineffectively reached. The truth came to her—the Son of Heaven was as 'drunk as a lord'—the great semi-deity, the head of the Celestial Empire, he round whom all her worship centred, was a sot! In the twinkling of an eye the quick little brain grasped the position; no more worship and reverence, but a heaven-sent opportunity for influence. She watched the Emperor, whose eyes opened in a drunken stare. Audacity seized her. Once again the hand endeavoured to reach the glass. Rising to her feet she gave it, with the caressing air that a mother gives her breast to her child, and cradled his head as he drank. He revived, and then the puss drank with him.

We need not follow the rest of the story, which is easy. Little Ye-Ho-No-La—cunning little Ye-Ho-No-La—had lost reverence and found opportunity, and to the extreme surprise of the Palace had become first favourite—a sordid enough story too, when we think of the deterioration of innocence involved. But it served a purpose. There was to be an heir, not by the Empress it was true, but under the difficult circumstances more than acceptable.

So we can now see how the train was laid and how the little peach-blossom with the gift of dominating her child companions, love stifled in her heart, strange half-passions given to the eunuch, bears a child to a sot, who is, however, the head of that Empire she worships, and there we see occasion and circumstance rough-hewing the ends and destroying a woman to make a despot.

The Dowager Empress herself promotes the 'honourable person' to the degree of '*Pin.*' Curiously enough, at the same time the Empress-wife is also declared *enceinte*, and it seemed that Ye-Ho had really roused the Emperor to a sense of his duties. She had certainly restrained his excessive drinking.

To the excitement of the Interior, the Empress

and the concubine '*Pin*' were running a race, not for priority of place, but for superiority of issue. Both lay agonising for a son. Everybody recognised that Ye-Ho was first favourite of the Son of Heaven, but the Imperial Spouse must have official pride of place. Nevertheless, if she failed of a son and Ye-Ho succeeded, what then? Never was Court so intrigued.

The Empress, not unnaturally, was furious with the Chief Eunuch, who had introduced this lump of fertility to the Emperor; but after all that was duty. Then came a day when in due course the latter gave birth to a son, and the Emperor publicly announced him as heir-presumptive, although of a concubine mother. Ye-Ho was forthwith advanced in rank to *Fei*.

The Empress redoubled her prayers and—gave birth to a daughter. Ye-Ho fainted with joy and pride as the faithful Ngan-Te-Hai brought the news.

The Emperor had shot his bolt, he had for the moment satisfied the demand of his mother, and now gave way to his besetting sin without let or hindrance. It was generally known that this rendered Ye-Ho's position as mother of the heir-presumptive quite secure. Evil whispers said that she now let him follow his bent, and filled his cup. In the bee world he would have been stung to death rather than drink himself helpless. His work was done, and it might be said of him:

> 'You played and lost the game,
> Perhaps your share
> Lay in the hour you laughed and kissed,
> Your son may bear the honours that his father missed.'

And all this was happening when Good Queen Victoria was leading us in England by other means and the Crimean War was in progress.

In the Saddle

Once in the saddle, Ye-Ho gave rein to her inherent power of influence and was soon to show herself competent to grasp the nettle danger, and to that end she prepared the way. With a *roi fainéant* on the throne, there were forces of rebellion that might arise. Prince Kuong, younger brother of the Man of Heaven, became her close ally, and she married her sister to him. Mindful of her earlier love, she now saw to it that Yong-Lu was created, by Kuong, Commander of the Manchu Guards, and her mother was created a duchess, which gave her access to the Palace at all times. Ye-Ho even began to sit behind the screens at the Council of State.

Thus do we see how the wheel of fate was spinning a dictator out of a day-dream.

Even now were her actions beginning to bolster up her China, a bolstering that lasted as long as she did—and that was to be half-a-century. Rumours of the feebleness of the Emperor were prevalent enough, and in South China 'King' Hong was leading a revolution that had already seized Nanking, the Southern capital. For years the 'Celestial King,' as he styled himself, and his followers the Taipings had been gathering strength, and it was high time someone did something. Here was little Ye-Ho's gift, she was one of those who knew when 'something ought to be done about it,' and since the Emperor was worth nothing, and

14

had paralysed his executive, it was Ye-Ho who insisted that the best General should be sent south. The cruelty of the Taipings had paralysed southern authority. In the north, where the movement was spreading, Yong-Lu would put it right—and he did. The Council of State was beginning to look to this determined little lady who could grasp the nettle. She was already far from the cherry-blossom days when she began to lead in the playground and say what game should be played. Opportunity was turning the piece of goods born to lead a household into a *Führer* behind the curtains. And all the while the Imperial Spouse, nursing her contemptible daughter, bit her disappointed lips, and specially longed for vengeance against Ngan-Te-Hai, who had intrigued to bring his own favourite to male motherdom!

Further, the Emperor's younger brothers, Hsai-Yuen and Touan-Houn, far different from the good Prince Kuong, with their foster-brother Sen-Chuen, were engaged in constant intrigue to undermine her influence.

Now it is to be remembered that Ye-Ho was but twenty-two and by rumour the most beautiful woman in the Kingdom and made by nature for love. Neither the rare and futile embraces of the Emperor nor the sentiments of Ngan-Te-Hai could help her forget the ardent memories of her youth. The Chief Eunuch, fearful of the vengeance of the Empress, was wholly hers, be he never so jealous. Yong-Lu was her support and counseller by day—at night the Chief Eunuch alone could advise and help her.

Ye-Ho felt that she could not sustain an empire on such cold comfort. She decided to move into the greater freedom of the Summer Palace, connected with the Forbidden City by the private Imperial canal. Such was the extent of her influence that there she went, taking in her train Emperor and Empress. In these beautiful surroundings she sent for the Commander of the Manchu Guards, whose prancing Tartar horsemen had protected the Imperial route. Drawing the curtains of her private reception room, she threw herself into the arms of the also twenty-two-year-old Yong-Lu, and thus began a real partnership of love and confidence which worked both for the content of the '*Fei*' and the permanence of the old order of China. Secure, with a brave general and a clever chief eunuch as lovers, great things were possible. Clever Ye-Ho knew what was wanted to preserve her own balance in the appalling task that she saw before her of saving China. Had Harry's Daughter thought as hard, her life might have been greater and happier.

The Coming of the Barbarians

And indeed the first great shock to the Empire of Heaven was about to arrive; it was 1860; Chinese custom, Chinese supreme conceit had exasperated the white-faced barbarians beyond bearing. British and French were marching on Peking to get that satisfaction at the cannons' mouths—nay, only a civil hearing—which Chinese diplomacy refused them.

The Council of State were in despair, the brave little Tartar Horse were being swept aside by British and Indian soldiery, and Jean Baptiste was marching on Peking. The Emperor, despite the withering scowl of Ye-Ho, announced his intention of starting at once to hunt in distant Jehol. Then Ye-Ho took the step that acclaimed her a man among men and placed her at the head of Chinese affairs for life. She took the Imperial barge and rowed back to Peking from the Summer Palace, which lay fifteen miles from the Tartar city.

In that palace she had found beauty and love, had painted hard to amuse herself, had known her intimate and illicit hours, with her pseudo-lover also conniving, and now hard cruel facts of Empire came to her who loved the tradition of China even more than Yong-Lu. It is a sad, stirring story that we follow as we watch the enthusiastic young life developing into the 'Old Buddha.'[1] She left her loves, her paint-box and her son, to sit with her little hand clenched and her chin firm behind the curtain, so that she might '*ginger*'—and no more orthodox expression will convey the meaning—the haughty, frightened, incompetent ministry.

It was a bad time even for an efficient *haute direction*. Ancient guns and brave horsemen made no barrier, the Manchu armies fell back on Peking, the barbarian columns tramped on, and down in the south King Hong gained new life. He was able to say that Peking could not save the country. And it was true. Prince Kuong had realised that he had no troops to defend the city. The Emperor had taken the last-formed bodies to guard his route to Jehol.

Then the Prince spoke up to Ye-Ho and told her that they must accept terms, and that she, the mother

[1] See hereafter. The affectionate name by which she was so long known in China.

of the only hope of the Empire, must go too, and that she must not, as she declared she would, die at the head of her Tartar Horse. The barbarians could not be kept at bay till King Winter came to the rescue. The mother of the heir-apparent must run no risks. Indeed were the 'scornful Chinese cats eating horrid mice.'

The shrewdness of Ye-Ho came to her rescue, so back she went to the Summer Palace. All was in confusion. The Emperor drunk in his litter, everyone trying to save his hidden wealth, everything contemptible—where was her son? Then wonder of wonders! She learnt that the Empress, burying jealousy in her care for the dynasty, had carried off the boy with great care and safety. This was the beginning of an alliance between the two for the sake of China as they conceived it.

The rest of this epoch does not matter. The barbarians occupied Peking; they sacked the Summer Palace—indeed, had the Emperor been responsible, it was a not unsuitable revenge for ill-treatment of a mission which had, at Chinese invitation, ridden forward in the hope of arranging a solution. It had been seized, most cruelly entreated, and several members executed; China's first attendance at a Western school had not been propitious. The terms extracted from the Celestial Empire were in reality the key to China's entry into the modern world had she but chosen to make it so, or rather had Ye-Ho but learnt the lesson. Alas! Furious at the incompetence of the Son of Heaven, bursting with indignation that Sacred China of the North should have been violated, softened by no true domesticity, this beautiful woman was being driven within her own soul, the simple soul that had become drunk—in those twenty-seven months of Imperial mourning and love delayed—with the history of Imperial China. But to save her idol from breaking into a hundred thousand crinkum-crankums, power and more power, to lead those who could not lead themselves, was necessary. Can we not imagine the working within that beautiful little head, that had been happiest painting in the Summer Palace and thinking of those meetings with her Manchu general, that alone compensated for the dry dust of the Imperial couch!

The 'Old Buddha' was born of the Allied victories, victories that they had no course but to win; and the sacking and the burning of the Summer Palace—an uncontemplated accidental vengeance—turned Ye-Ho's heart to stone.

But the ineffective Imperial Spouse and the masterful first concubine had formed an alliance of hearts and duty. They would live for the glory and protection of the Dragon Throne. Far had Ye-Ho travelled in those short years from the gardens of her childhood—and now—barbarians had burnt her Summer Palace!

Yong-Lu, ordered by the Emperor himself to remain and protect him, had not been on the walls of the Tartar city. Reproached by Ye-Ho, he explained his orders, and how he could, at any rate, save her and the heir, not from the barbarians, but from the enemies at home.

While the *Fei* followed the Imperial pair and her infant to far Jehol on the timorous tiger shoot, Prince Kuong in China's eyes had worked wonders. He had appeased and bought off the barbarians by an indemnity, executed lesser folk for the murder of the white mission, and had saved his face by, of all things, hiring (for so it seemed to Chinese eyes) these very barbarians to deal with the dangerous Taipings on the Yang-tse and rid them of King Hong.

Then as the Allies returned to their ships, and the Court was about to return to Peking, to the joy of the cart-shaken concubines, the Holy Son of Heaven died.

Here was opportunity to get rid of Ye-Ho; and the two evil princes and their foster-brother issued a decree proclaiming themselves Regents for the five-year-old son of Ye-Ho. But the Ye-Ho's of history are not so easily got rid of. Ye-Ho had long held the Imperial seal, without which no edict was effective, affixing it, when necessary, at the Emperor's command. That seal she would not surrender. But nevertheless she seemingly acquiesced in the decree, and the Regents bided their time to get the seal.

During the long march back to Peking with the Imperial coffin at their head, Ye-Ho's caravan was marching ahead. The situation had been communicated to Yong-Lu now away in the north. The Regents, the story runs, had arranged that robbers should attack Ye-Ho's cortège and that the seal should be happily found on the body of the murdered *Fei*. But now, just as this attack is opening and her small escort of Imperial Guards have been massacred, Yong-Lu and his Tartar Horse arrive, the cortège is saved and proceeds to Peking, followed in due course by the child Emperor, the Regents, the Empress and the Imperial coffin. Long and interminable are the obsequies, and at a suitable occasion therein Ye-Ho plays her trump card. A decree is read, 'coming from the five-year-old, and stamped with the Imperial Seal,' declares Prince Kuong. The Empress, under the name of Tseu-Ngan, 'The Maternal and Peaceable,' is proclaimed Guardian and Empress of the Western Palace, and Ye-Ho-No-La, as joint and equal Empress and Guardian, under that of Tseu-Hi, 'The Maternal and Propitious,' Empress of the Eastern Palace. Prince Kuong and the Council had agreed to this, knowing that the false Regents would have their lives without scruple. Then as the infant Emperor is shown to the people, the enthusiasm knows no bounds. All the world knew too that Ye-Ho alone had faced the music of the barbarians, that Prince Kuong had saved the face of China, and that the real Empress had buried all jealousy and joined forces with Ye-Ho to save the heir and the throne of China.

Then it was that Yong-Lu, his Tartars at his back, touched the shoulders of the false Regents, and bore them off to the prison that they had earned.

That is the story of the chain of circumstances and the house that fate built, on the germ of leadership that lay in a maiden who could take the lead in games—she who should have developed in the happier rôle of cuddling Manchu babies and the management of a household. And we may again notice how, in those twenty-seven months of disappointed love and Imperial mourning, the history and greatness of China had penetrated the little soul and become a fierce religion on which her frustrated heart fed.

The rest of her life in bare detail may be given, although the story of the making of the leader is over. We shall see how the woman, thus made, is to comport herself through the generations and what came of it. From 1861 to 1908 is a long time.

THE EMPRESS TSEU-HI

The Empress Tseu-Hi, that was once Ye-Ho, now sits on the Imperial throne by the side of the other good maternal and peaceable one, and all the world knew and rejoiced to know that power would be in the hands of one who would use it. Prince Kuong too realised on which side the Chinese bread was buttered, and he was ready to support Tseu-Hi as the national *Führer*—Tseu-Hi, in outward looks a lump of Manchu delight in her prime. That, however, was but known to her soldier Yong-Lu and her supporter and admirer Ngan-Te-Hai, who overflowed in adoration.

The wicked Regents were tried by the Grand Council of State, and sentenced to death by the 'Thousand Cuts.' The merciful Tseu-Hi, however, decreed that the foster-brother should be simply beheaded, and the two princes permitted to hang themselves, for with such men to deal with, 'stone dead,' as humanely as possible, 'hath no fellow.' Their families she pardoned, and by this wise act gained many friends. Sentences on State functionaries who had been privy to the usurpation she also remitted. This unexpected clemency was much applauded, and it was from this early date that the woman of but six-and-twenty received the affectionate nickname of the 'Old Buddha' already referred to.

The Taiping rebellion was more serious than ever. Li-Hung-Chang, the Viceroy of the province of Kiang-Su, could not restrain them, and the

Empress, repressing her hatred of the white barbarians, employed them to suppress the rebellion. To us it is the epic of 'Chinese' Gordon; to China, as related, it seemed the height of astuteness. At first an army of adventurers made no headway, and the 'ever victorious army' was a gigantic jest till Tseu-Hi made Gordon commander-in-chief of a hundred thousand men, equipped in some sort by Li-Hung-Chang. The history of his breaking his sword in fury and resigning when the Viceroy butchered the Taipings who had surrendered on his parole is well known. He had already brought the rebellion to an end.

It did not worry Tseu-Hi, who covered her Viceroy with her own authority. Taipings were best dead anyway, and as Gordon had done most of the work, the sooner he was out of the way the better. Li-Hung-Chang and his generals were able to finish the remainder of the Taipings and capture their strongholds, to an accompaniment of astounding massacres of prisoners and all who had sympathised. The leaders were brought in cages to Peking to die of the 'Thousand Cuts' in public, to the huge delight of vast crowds, and Tseu-Hi, ex-Manchu peach-blossom, was now absolute mistress of China.

The 'Old Buddha' was developing uncanny wisdom, and, realising the effect of mystery, never showed herself to her people, and was even heavily veiled before the Council of State. To Yong-Lu alone were the features of the most beautiful woman in China known, some said to a few more, for gossip will not let women alone. She was also of extraordinary robustness, and while gossip—and indeed something more than gossip—attributed to her, as the years rolled on, days of work and nights of love and sometimes of orgy, yet never was she tired or dull. Ngan-Te-Hai was not only the arranger of such relaxation, but also her constant confidant.

As the years rolled on, he, as might be expected, became dishonest and arrogant, and at last was executed by a distant governor, as an act to save China, by the intrigue, it was said, of the other two Regents. Tseu-Hi bit her lips, mourned deeply, and bided her furious time. China had recovered herself under the 'Old Buddha's' wise despotism and Prince Kuong's wise control, but it was an old Manchu-ruled China, with no new ways of the West and of the United States—where many Chinese were going—to guide her in a modern world.

The years still rolled on. Tseu-Hi, seeing that Prince Kuong was necessary, smothered her anger over the execution of Ngan-Te-Hai, appointed Li-Hien-Yu Chief Eunuch, and carried on. But one more phase had passed in the hardening of the heart that once belonged to a Manchu maiden. For Ngan-Te-Hai had been greater almost than Yong-Lu in her deep affections.

It was now 1872. Tung-Tchi, her son, was seventeen years of age, and must now be Emperor in fact. But how could this youth of seventeen handle the China that was yearly growing more complicated! Tseu-Hi dreaded the future, and married him to a young princess whom she expected to be wax in her hands. But the young Imperial pair showed a lamentable independence. Tseu-Hi bided her time and abdicated from her position of power, but had secured that Li-Hung-Chang, who had finished off the Taipings, should be Viceroy of Pi-Chi-Li.

Then comes a story of great sadness, if popular belief be true. Her son had inherited his mother's ardent sex nature and his father's craving for drink. Tseu-Hi, whether to secure her return to power or to save China from the feeble hands and Court intrigues she saw arising, determined to get rid of him. To encourage his vices seemed the shortest way, and in this the new Chief Eunuch was already coadjutor. The brave little Empress confronts her mother-in-law—she is *enceinte*; if she bears a son, *she* will be the Regent by Imperial immemorial custom. Tseu-Hi listened grimly. The boy Emperor, deep in debauchery, contracts smallpox and dies before the Empress can be delivered. She demands that the throne await that event in vacancy. Tseu-Hi declares the throne of China must never be vacant, calls on Li-Hung-Chang and Yong-Lu to surround the Palace with their troops, and summons the Council of State. Then she announces that her nephew, the son of her sister and her brother-in-law, would be Emperor under the name of Kuang-Siu, and flourishes the Imperial Seal, soon to be affixed to this decree. The Council vote accordingly—Prince Kuong alone dissenting. Tseu-Hi is once more proclaimed Regent and once more she chooses Prince Kuong, who has opposed her, but who she knows lives only for China, as coadjutor in the Regency. A sordid story. Yet—the country breathed again. Another Regency of the 'Old Buddha' meant peace and order—of the old kind. Yet was China turning in her sleep.

The Second Regency

Tseu-Hi was now recognised as indomitable and unassailable, although the senior of the Court of Censors protested at the election of the new four-year-old Emperor and then committed suicide, which was an annoying and untoward fly in the balm. The birth of a son to the widow of the dead Emperor would be an embarrassment, and it now happened fortunately that this brave little princess died mysteriously before her delivery. The path of the Dowager Empress was now clear, and we see the character of our original Manchu maiden now hardening from decision, to fierce ruthlessness in removing all barriers to China's prosperity—as emblemised in her!—for we need have no doubt that the subconscious mind fused the two conceptions.

The years now rolled on peacefully. Each day the veiled Empress presided at the Grand Council and astonished the wisest by her acumen. Even those who gossiped most could but admit her strength, her wisdom, and her nationalism, while the charm of her hidden voice was said to be so great that those who stood in her way would gladly be beheaded rather than affect its tones! And all the while gossip said that in the interior there was no pleasure and no vice that was not sampled—but always with the moderation that kept her body in its splendid beauty and health. And faithful Marshal Yong-Lu, the boy of her girlhood, was always the strong support to whom she returned.

And while Tseu-Hi reigned, and ruled, and lived, the Empress of the West devoted herself to the infant Emperor Kuang-Siu, as she had to Tseu-Hi's son.

The day arrived when Yong-Lu fell to a Tartar maid of honour of the Twin Empress, the result perhaps of an intrigue to entrap him. Tseu-Hi spared him, but her heart hardened with the shock, and he was deprived of his honours. Yet all the while, in retreat, he watched for her safety. But Tseu-Hi, believing that the Empress of the West had encompassed the death of Ngan-Te-Hai and seduced her Marshal, warned her ancient rival to prepare for the long journey, and it is said now commissioned the Chief Eunuch to that end. Soon was it announced that the Dowager Empress Tseu-Ngan had died of the same mysterious disease as the widow of the late Emperor, little Ha-Lou-To. Tseu-Hi saw that the Empress was buried with due and ancient splendour; and thus it came about that she sat on the all-alone-stone of China.

Rest in the Summer Palace

The 1880's were now drawing to a close, Japan had Westernised, while China dozed on in the Manchu ways, kept on the prosperous track of her ancestors by the 'Old Buddha' behind the arras. Yong-Lu was still banished; Li-Hung-Chang in Pi-Chi-Li wanted Western arms and he got them, but he forgot Western discipline. In the south, from Tonquin, France pressed on the Celestial Empire, and the 'Old Buddha' had not learned the lesson of 1860. The French admiral in the south could not be met without railways or ironclads. China provoked her neighbours without the wherewithal to talk. Tseu-Hi was furious at the indignities suffered. By a stroke of the pen and the magic seal Prince Kuong and Council were removed.

She and Li-Hung-Chang alone could save China. Kuong's younger brother—Prince Tchuen—and a new Council were installed, useless but at least obedient to a dictator whose parallel the world had never seen. No Burghley or Cecils hampered and intrigued; alone did this determined lump of delight—for so in lighter moods she still was, beauty and health defying time even as with Ninon de l'Enclos—rule China, using the Viceroy of Pi-Chi-Li as her servant to face the urge of the West.

But time was marching in other ways. The Emperor was now (1887) eighteen, and his aunt had to face the question again; that which in modern slang is written 'What about it?' For two years more she ignored his existence, save to marry him to her niece, the daughter of her elder brother. She had taken care that this little Empress should not defy her as had the last, but would, she hoped, dominate the Emperor on her aunt's behalf. Tseu-Hi then could retire to the happy hunting-grounds of her youth, the now restored Summer Palace, and there dream of her early love. But this Ninon of the East felt and looked no more than forty. She was still determined, the story goes, to retaste some of the glamours of youth. But alas! the principal source thereof, the Marshal, was in exile, and she bitterly regretted her jealous action therein. Already had she restored him to honours in a distant province. It was the story of Essex. But since her Marshal was not here, rumour said that the Grand Eunuch had to find her some solace from various sources. Young men, introduced to some outlying palace under promise of the favours of a maid of honour, perished in the morning at the hands of the Grand Eunuch, lulled by a drugged, if refreshing, cup of tea, and disappearing in the ditch of the Tartar city with a stone round their necks. Of such is the female of the praying mantis. Ere long Tseu-Hi sent for the Marshal, to find that youth reigned with him still. She recovered a lover and a faithful soldier, and was mentally at rest again.

The Japanese War of 1894 and the Final Coup

Thus in some peace passed a few more years in the Summer Palace, years of an Indian summer, and then came ominously her sixtieth birthday. The Emperor Kuang-Siu made great preparations to celebrate it in due and ancient form, when bad diplomacy resulted in war with the 'Japanese Dwarfs.' In vain did Li-Hung-Chang's half-modernised troops and navies contend. Humiliation followed, and though the Powers interfered to prevent Japan retaining all her gains, Tseu-Hi was furious. She seized the power from the ineffective Emperor, cancelled all festivities, dismissed Li-Hung-Chang, recalled the good Prince Kuong; and once more, to the relief of all, the 'Old Buddha' was openly at the helm. She had staged a dramatic and successful 'come back,' but only for a while; with Kuong at the helm, Yong-Lu as Governor of Pi-Chi-Li, and her dutiful niece by the Emperor's side, Tseu-Hi withdrew once more to the Summer Palace, to paint, to read, to write poetry; she even appeared on a private stage. It was not for long.

In 1890 the young Emperor had lost his father and in 1898 his mother, the sister of Tseu-Hi. Then, without their guidance, he actually ventured to intrigue against the influence of his aunt and neglect the advice of his wife. He was falling under the influence of the Chinese reformers and agitators from the States! A big intrigue was developing.

Tseu-Hi was pretty well informed of what was in progress, and one fine day descended on the Emperor, determined to arrest the leading associates of her nephew. Forewarned they fled. Tseu-Hi stormed, Kuang-Siu grovelled. Believing the situation restored, the Dowager returned to the Summer Palace.

Grovel the Emperor never so humbly, he girded and fumed at the yoke which he knew to be intolerable, and planned a *coup d'état.*

Yuan Shi-Kai and the reformed troops were to seize the Marshal Yong-Lu, and behead him, surround Tseu-Hi and imprison her for ever, and decapitate the Grand Eunuch and all her supporters. Yuan departed from the Palace on his mission. But he and Yong-Lu were sworn brothers of a secret guild. Yuan informed the Marshal, the Marshal rode for the Summer Palace to apprise Tseu-Hi. The latter, prompt as ever, summoned all conservative ministers and supporters. A Council of State prayed her to take the throne, Yong-Lu rode to arrest the Emperor, rebellious and progressive heads flew in all directions. Then the Dowager proceeded to deal faithfully with the miserable Son of Heaven: reviling him in bitter fury, she told him his fate—to live alone in solitary confinement till she decreed his death. His favourite concubine was also interned, and Long-Yu, his little Empress, who hated him, was made his gaoler by her aunt. Miserable Kuang-Siu! . . . Again had the 'Old Buddha' her hand firmly on the helm,

15

this time for keeps. She was now sixty-five, and throughout China a revulsion had arisen—a fierce anger against the West, and it has been said that it was here that Tseu-Hi took the fatal turning for, at any rate, a Manchu China. On the other hand, despite her Tudor-cum-Chinese peremptoriness, she was probably right in feeling that none of the reformers had characters or prestige sufficient for their aspirations, and that Kuang-Siu was quite unfit to control and direct the spirits that he was like to summon.

The Boxer Rebellion

The impingement of Western enterprise on China and the coming of modern methods of business, and modern inventions often at the point of a not unrighteous bayonet, had for fifty years been stirring the hearts of conservative China. The 'Old Buddha' hated foreigners, and so did yet the bulk of her people. This well-known attitude, and all the foreign pressure combined, resulted in a widespread anti-foreign movement, known to the world as the 'Boxer' Rebellion. The name came from the Europeans owing to the pugnacious attitude of figures on the 'Boxer' posters. And it was heartily stimulated by the Dowager Empress, whose acumen was now groping through realism unknown to her. She was yet the impervious Chinese. An heir-presumptive was needed to the Emperor, who was at a propitious moment to be done to death. Her choice and that of the obedient Grand Council fell on the lad Pou-Tsiun, a cadet of the Imperial family.

In the meantime the seeds of the Boxer movement burst into bloom. Everywhere were Europeans, including the missionaries, murdered or otherwise injured and attacked, and these culminated in the attack on the European Legations in Peking and the famous 'Defence of the Legations.' Then, as in 1860, did the French and English, accompanied this time by Russians, Germans, Americans and Japanese, march to Peking and rescue the Legations. Once more Chinese troops failed to prevent them.

Much against her will, the Dowager Empress agreed for the second time in her life to leave the Forbidden City for Mongolian Jehol, taking with her the wretched Emperor. Li-Hung-Chang was recalled, though over eighty, to make the best bargain he could with the 'Foreign Devils,' while Tseu-Hi fiercely turned on all who had failed her, especially those who had massacred foreigners at her instigation. But Li-Hung-Chang made an exceedingly good bargain with the invaders, and once more China lost far fewer tail-feathers than might have been expected. Tseu-Hi was advised to return, and return she did, for she had learnt her lesson, cleverly realising the game that was now to be played. She, the all-powerful, all-merciful, all-progressive, came smiling and frowning, receiving diplomats, Kuang-Siu on a small throne beside her, entertaining the ladies of the Legations and the mercantile community.

'Fancy,' as the ridiculous British burlesque at Shanghai had it,

> 'You and I in the all-together
> Prancing alone across the heather,
> At our time of life.'

But so it was; despite all her predilections she had to eat the 'horrid mice' of progress and foreigners, and she was voted a 'wonderful old girl.'

But it was certainly not a situation for Kuang-Siu, and so he died, and she very prudently married the changing situation, to paraphrase another famous commentary. Pou-Tsiun's succession, he having shown lively and imprudent tendencies, had already been declared void by edict, and Tseu-Hi's choice had fallen on Pu-Yi, a three-year-old, promising a long minority! Now Pu-Yi was grandson of Marshal Yong-Lu, Tseu-Hi having married his daughter to one of her brothers-in-law. The present Emperor of Manchuria[1] is the same Pu-Yi, then aged three, that Tseu-Hi had insisted, in spite of other advice, in nominating Son of Heaven, being grandson of the Emperor who died in 1850.

As the 'Foreign Devils,' before they went, demanded the execution of the Boxer leaders and supporters responsible for the murders of Europeans, this was a heaven-sent opportunity to get rid of many of her enemies and opponents, which she used freely, so that her readiness to produce offenders was looked on as evidence of her desire to be just and friendly.

The 'Foreign Devils' gone and not much harm done, Tseu-Hi sat down to restore the prosperity and peace of her country, with Yuan-Shi-Kai as Viceroy of Pi-Chi-Li. But she also was clever enough to scent the change, and numerous edicts regarding reforms on modern and more representative lines were issued.

[1] Or Manchukuo.

The Ringing to Evensong

Wonderful as was her constitution, Tseu-Hi, that once was maiden and peach-blossom, was near the end of her tether. She had contracted dysentery, which would not leave her, and though manfully she fought, yet the brave, ruthless, loving, patriotic Manchu lady knew she was destined soon for the Yellow Fountains. In 1903, to her great grief, the Marshal had died. Li-Hung-Chang had hardly survived the peace with the foreigners. She was now in that sad state of loneliness that age brings. At first she carried on well enough, China prospered and democracy stirred. An edict appointed Long-Yu, her niece, as Empress Dowager, on the assumption that Pu-Yi was the adopted son of Kuang-Siu, and Tseu-Hi declared herself 'Grand Dowager,' as indeed she was.

Disease was wearing her down, assiduously though she attended to detail. But then came a day when she appointed Pu-Yi's father, Prince Tchuen, and the new Dowager Empress as Regents, put on the funeral robes and lay down, in quiet dignity and frail though still obvious beauty, to await the summons—wondering, as so many arch-concentrators have done before, how her country would fare without her.

The world has said that, whatever her faults, she had saved the China she knew times and again, and she, dying, had said that never must China be ruled by a woman! The grip of that five hundred million and their vast lands needed a superman. Yet Tseu-Hi, who once was Ye-Ho and loved love and beauty, had been forced to build on that small basis of a child who could lead her playfellows, the most astounding life of mastery that history has yet seen, and had done so for more than half a century. Occasion on occasion had called for leadership, and ever the Manchu maiden rose to it. History had given her the Chinese and Tartar complex deep down in her heart and soul. Occasions, complexes, patriotism, impinging on a grain of inborn character, of such are leaders made. 'Oh! well batted, little Ye-Ho! in the only kind of cricket you knew.'

CHAPTER IX

ABRAHAM LINCOLN, I

Abe Lincoln
His Earlier Days
The Boiling of the Slavery Controversy
The Road to the White House
The Secession of the South
Lincoln at the Helm

ABRAHAM LINCOLN, I

Abe Lincoln

Among the most remarkable—nay, astounding—careers and glories of modern times is that of the ramshackle Abe Lincoln, squatter and handyman of Illinois, who not only became President of the United States but led that great country with conspicuous success through the terrible times of their Civil War. We shall first find this man of humble origin, endowed with all the qualities of the greatest, called by a series of chances, added to his own strange qualities, to be the first man of the State. We see that, unlike most leaders, no particular occasion led him to that high estate, but that, once there, a national disaster, which would have submerged most men, found him competent, a simple, strong-minded citizen, rising to a remarkable occasion, *after* he had achieved his high position. For all time, citizens, it will be hats off to this man of the people, this man of righteous thought, of direct aim and untold courage, and ramshackle appearance!

This is the period of his life:

Born 1809.

First sat in Legislature of Illinois, 1834.

First seat in Congress (two years), 1847.

Elected President of the U.S., 6th November 1860. Took seat 4th March 1861.

Secession of the Southern States, 20th December 1860. (South Carolina.)

Outbreak of the Civil War, 12th April 1861. (Bombardment of Fort Sumter.)

End of the Civil War, 9th April 1864. (Richmond falls, Lee surrenders.)

Assassination, 14th April 1864.

His Earlier Days

The descent and early days of Abraham were most uninteresting save as showing how hard times develop grit in the stronger nature. He used to attribute any of his finer parts to an unknown Virginian gentleman, whose illegitimate daughter his mother, Nancy Hanks, was. She died when he was eight years old, but he had always a grateful remembrance of a stepmother's care. His father, little more than a squatter, was in the habit of moving farther 'west' from time to time, in search of a better holding, and the family lived a rough precarious existence, never gathering moss. Abraham had but twelve months' non-consecutive schooling in his life, but enough to enable him to teach himself to read and write, and he early developed a love of reading. His stock of books, read and re-read, consisted of *Æsop's Fables*, *Robinson Crusoe*, *Pilgrim's Progress*, a *History of the United States*, and Weem's *Life of Washington*. Now if you know the first three by heart, you will have acquired an astounding, accurate, wise and simple 'rule of life.' The wisdom of the late Mr Æsop was just the common-sense way of tackling problems which Abraham was to exhibit in later life. By nineteen years of age the lad was six-feet-four, and, if stirred, a prodigious worker as a labourer, handyman, or at anything else that would keep body and soul together.

In the small and now vanished township of New Salem, Abraham made his contacts with his fellow-men, now and again standing up to a bully with plenty of courage, wrestling, listening to fierce and gloomy preachers. Singing popular hymns, speaking himself on any subject to his workmen friends, becoming a raconteur, usually of Rabelaisian stories, he finally found himself attracted by law, and a book on the laws of Illinois fell into his hands, to be eagerly absorbed, as had been *Æsop's Fables*. The Rabelaisian story habit remained with him all his life, not for the Rabelaisian side, but because wit and antithesis are more often contained therein than in more decorous ones. Wit, humour and, in his younger days, fun appealed to this rather outlandish son of nature. There is an apocryphal story of a wedding of two sisters in the countryside, when after the customs of the countryside the happy pairs retired from the merry-making to their own apartments, since there was nowhere else to go to. It pleased young Abraham to mix up the brides, and it was the brides' mother who rescued her daughters. 'Here, you're in bed with the wrong man.' It was at least typical of the humour of a whimsical untutored mind, and is quoted here as giving some hint of the popularity and ascendancy that he was to have over simple folk. Ere long Lincoln becomes a storekeeper, and adds *Kirkham's Grammar* to his literary treasure; floors in a wrestling match the leader of a local gang of bullies and store-wreckers, and begins to emerge among his contemporaries as a man of parts. In 1832, then aged twenty-three, he announces that he will stand at the next election for the Illinois Legislature. There was now trouble with Black Hawke, chief of the local Red Indians. Abraham turns soldier and is elected captain of a company. He saw no fighting, but his little experience at any rate kept him for five months, and gave him enough experience to find military aphorisms when dealing with 'Boy' M'Clellan in the Civil War.

A great affection for animals and all living things surged within him, and having by chance seen an unusually callous slave sale and a fine Mulatto girl shown to purchasers like a prize sow, his mind not unnaturally took on strong colour on the slave question. His first election manifesto has been preserved. A model for all time! 'Fellow-citizens, I presume you all know who I am. I am humble Abraham Lincoln. I have been solicited by my friends to become a candidate for the Legislature. My politics are short and sweet like an old woman's dance. I am in favour of a national bank. I am in favour of an internal improvement system and a high protective tariff. These are my sentiments and political principles. If elected, I shall be thankful; if not, it will be all the same.' Bravo, Abe! . . . Though not elected, he obtained nearly all the votes in his own neighbourhood. In other words, his character and personality were acceptable to all who knew them. To be six-feet-four, ramshackle, ill-dressed, eloquent and witty was to attract attention, and that is half the battle.

He now wanted to be a lawyer or perhaps a blacksmith. He, however, went into a small business, was swindled and failed. Eschewing the protection of bankruptcy, he screwed for fifteen years, and paid his debts. Abraham now had to fall back on jobs for farmers, and eventually became an assistant surveyor. He now read Gibbon, and then turned to such unsettling fare as Voltaire. In 1834 he stood again for the Legislature, made speeches bristling with sound sense and simple humour, and was elected, being then twenty-five years of age. He had, it would seem, the gift of putting the comether over his fellow-men. Not so over women. His attitude to them was one of respect and great shyness, and two attempts to marry failed. He served in the Legislature for eight years, being elected four times in succession. During this time the State capital was moved to Springfield, and there he made his home. It was a large town with fashion and culture and various uplift societies. Local politics gave him an insight into the management of men, and he was great at bringing about agreement among rival schools of thought, his store of a thousand anecdotes, often, as has been said, with Rabelaisian savour, enabling him to drive home his points by some convincing analogy. At Springfield a third attempt at matrimony was successful in that Miss Mary Todd joined her life to his. The union was never very satisfactory and did not give him that peace at home that public men should have. His high-tempered wife developed insanity after his tragic death.

Life was now rolling on. Lincoln, after practising in courts that admitted an untrained and unlicensed advocate, at last became a full-fledged lawyer of the American variety. After his eight years in the Illinois Legislature his ambition turned to Congress, but it was not till 1847, when thirty-eight years of age, that he was sent to the House of Representatives at Washington, thirteen years after he had entered the local Legislature, and during these years his power of bargaining and combining, his shrewd interpretation of life, and his attitude of common sense increased and developed. His lawyer's business developed steadily but undramatically, and his two years at Washington were uneventful; only in the Mexican War question was he at all prominent.

Mexico had seceded from Spain as recently as 1826. Seven years later the huge territory of Texas had seceded from Mexico and declared itself a republic. In 1839 Texas, in which a good many slave-owning migrants from the Southern States had settled, sought annexation to the United States.

This in itself raised the question that eventually brought about the Civil War, not that of the abolition of slavery, but whether any new slave States should be permitted or created. President Tyler, at the close of his term of office, though what is now known as a Republican, had got the annexation approved. It involved a frontier dispute with Mexico which eventually developed into the questionable Mexican War in which, of course, the United States were victorious. A speech of Lincoln's, made at the time of a vote on war supplies, had recited the whole of the unpopular case for condemning the war. There was a good deal of humour and licence in it, but it contained an extremely lucid outline of the case against the whole proceeding and it attracted attention. So far so good. Lincoln had achieved, to some extent, a public career, but one supremely far removed from the Presidency and still farther from any appearance of a great national hero and leader.

During his two years in Congress he had introduced a moderate little Bill for the abolition of slavery within the United States enclave of Washington. It was prompted by neither abolitionists nor the slave supporters, but of his own ideas of fitness, and it, of course, met with no success.

His period as a representative now came to an end and he was not re-elected; nor did he stand again, and his party even lost the seat. His attitude on the Mexican War made him enemies. There was an election for the Presidency, and he spoke in several places in favour of General Taylor, a straightforward soldier, who had done well in the war and owned a few slaves. Then he retired into private life, a tired and perhaps a disgruntled man. He was but forty years of age.

The Boiling of the Slavery Controversy

While Lincoln sits in retirement we may watch the growth of the occasion which was to bring him to fame in a little more than ten years. The railways had come, and the great treeless prairie States could now get timber and material and begin to grow. The march to the West was in full swing, and first came the rough-and-ready 'territories,' and then territories began to come to the Union as full-fledged States. The slave question thus became acute, apart from the frenzy of the impractical abolitionists. The matter of the original and sanctioned additions to the old slave-owning States was not in dispute. Lincoln himself, with his abhorrence of the slave principle growing within him, was quite sane on this point. The slavery in the old States must be left to time, progress and gradual liquidation, with laws of amelioration in the meantime. The creation of new slave States, so late as the fifties of the nineteenth century, was quite another matter. Yet so many of the new 'squatters' in the southern territories had been slave-owners, whose slaves had accompanied them; and indeed in many cases negro labour alone could work in the heat. The 'Wilmot Proviso,' voted down in Congress, had proposed that there should be no new slave States. This Lincoln had sturdily supported. General Carr had proposed that each new State should decide the matter for themselves. In 1849 California, a then lawless cosmopolitan diggers' territory outside, it seemed, the United States jurisdiction, set up a definite constitution of its own in which slavery was prohibited. This soon raised the question of whether this upstart territory should be admitted to the Union with a constitution 'on its own' or conform to the rules and laws of the United States on Federal matters. The South wanted to have none of them and to force slavery on California, the theory being that it was a beneficent institution. President General Zachary Taylor, though a Southerner, saw how arrogant such a position was, and advised the admission of California with her own Constitution. No statesman, but a straight man with character, he died in 1850 before the question was settled. His deputy succeeded as a matter of routine, and the question was compromised. The South were bought off by accepting California but allowing two new slave Territories in the South (New Mexico and Utah). A Federal law was also passed dealing with the return of runaway slaves to Northern States.

For the time the question grew less acute, and it may be remarked here that for many years the Southern States had taken much more care to send good men to Congress than had the Northern States, where politicians were in some disrepute. Lincoln during the first four or five years in retirement had sunk the politician in the lawyer. The Bible and Shakespeare apparently were now his chief literary studies, with fiction as lighter food. Politics appeared forgotten. He was now middle-aged, his clothes his wife's despair, and his profession as a lawyer his interest. In fact to him, as to Cromwell, a call to action seemed the last thing likely.

But all the while his mind was clearing; an unusual study, that of Euclid, was still further improving his lucidity of reason. His children were a delight to him, but he appeared outwardly a gloomy disappointed man, though he pushed his way through the crowd of life with his rough and genial jest. Yet many loved and trusted him, and noted his anger before wrong and injustice. His legal practice improved, and he achieved some notoriety in throwing up cases if he did not like the justice and rights of them. He rubbed shoulders now with first-class lawyers, and attracted their attention.

Then in 1854 the slavery question came to the fore again, chiefly owing to the action of a lawyer, Stephen Douglas, chairman of the Territories Commission, by whom a Bill for the Government of Kansas and Nebraska was altered to allow these territories to decide, whenever they liked, whether they would be 'slave' or 'free.' The Bill was passed, and migrants from the South and also the North poured in. We must for the moment turn back to the 'Missouri Compromise.' For long, American statesmen had aimed at keeping the slave question from becoming a burning one and perhaps disrupting the whole Union. In the earlier days it had even been the custom to create new

States in pairs, a 'free' State and a 'slave' State together, lest the 'free' States should become too numerous and swamp the South—Louisiana, bought from Napoleon, had been by treaty a 'slave' State. But in Missouri, also formed from French territory, a fierce discussion arose as to its status, and eventually a compromise was enacted in 1820, by which, in territory acquired from the French, slave-holding north of latitude 36° 30′ was illegal. Originally regarded as a defeat by the North, it eventually came to be regarded as an Anti-Slavery Charter, and so it remained till 1857, when, just as the Supreme Court has recently ruled out (1935) Mr Roosevelt's New Deal as unconstitutional and illegal, so did the Supreme Court of the United States declare that the exclusion of slavery from any portion of the territories was illegal. The 'Missouri Compromise' was therefore illegal and void. We need not here go into the story of Dred Scott, the negro slave who had become free under the 'Compromise,' and now sued his master in a Federal Court. But his case and the decision of the Supreme Court put the whole of the slavery fat into the fire. Four Presidents of the United States, all who had been alive when the Constitution was formed, had believed that the United States could prohibit slavery in the territories; the fifth had actually signed acts based on this conception.

Let us now hark back a year or so. In 1854 circumstances of which we know very little brought Lincoln back to public life, far better known locally, and far more loved and respected than in the days of his first emergence. He was taking, as he had already taken, a great interest, a human yet moderate and understanding interest, in the slave politics, in the excitement roused by the ruling of the Supreme Court and the Dred Scott case. When in Congress before, he had always supported the Wilmot Proviso. There was now to arise the new orientation in American politics of the Republican and Democratic parties. The former at that time meant those who stood for the Union and a gradual extension of Federal authority, the latter believed in the sovereign right of each of the States, which had but given up a few of their rights to the Union for the sake of general convenience, secession being at all times a right inherent in their federation. The politics of each side soon took up a hundred other divergent issues, but State *v.* Federal Right was then the main line of cleavage.

In 1855 we find Lincoln writing moderate views (almost the only private letter of the period extant) to his friend Joshua Speed, in which he combats the latter's adhesion to slave rights in a reasoning and accommodating manner. No doubt he spoke in the same manner in public, yet always with consideration of the rights of the real slave States. There is an amusing, not very creditable story come to us worth repeating, of a very conservative Southern paper which had published an article justifying all slavery, black *and* white. It was a paper that had too much influence, and the unsuspecting editor gave leave to Lincoln's friends to reproduce it. They did so. That was practically the end of the conservative organ! It was as if *The Times* and *The Morning Post* published some of the more imaginative of Sir Stafford Cripps' views as gospel, quoting the source. No doubt a fair political 'leg-pull.'

In 1856 there was a vacancy for an Illinois Senator in Congress. His supporters were very anxious for Lincoln to fill it. For various reasons, in the wire-pulling methods of elections, he was not sent up. In 1858 he again contested the vacancy, against Douglas the Democrat, he being now very definitely Republican. The two candidates disputed on many platforms together, Douglas being successful, but Lincoln gained great regard as a man who could hold wise and sound ideas, and could express them with remarkable clarity. The gloves were not yet off on the great issue, for all moderate men cared more for the Union than the slave question; men who, hating slavery, while accepting the old States, wanted no new ones, held their hands. Some of his sayings show Lincoln's attitude. 'We allow slavery to exist in the slave States not because it is right, but from the necessities of the Union. We grant a fugitive slave law because it is so "nominated in the bond."' He was ready to give the slave States any possible guarantee that the Constitution should not be altered so as to take away their existing right of self-government in the matter. Abolitionist frenzy of the old Exeter Hall type he would have nothing to do with, largely because it dealt in bitter exaggeration. Moderate abolition was, of course, his principle. Nor was he at all in sympathy with the 'equality of man' theory said to underlie the Constitution so far as negroes were concerned—justice and humanity, yes; but not entire equality, because nature had not so arranged. This came up very much in the matter of miscegenation, in which public opinion in the United States to this day is as equally uncompromising as ever. In fact, for those who marvel at the Indian caste system, whereby the old white races protected themselves from being swamped by half-breeds, that system can be seen in the making in the United States. Lincoln said, 'I protest against the counterfeit logic which says that since I do not want a negro woman for my slave, I must necessarily want her for my wife. I may want her for neither. I simply let her alone. In some respects she is certainly not my equal. But in her natural right to eat the bread which she has earned by the sweat of her brow she is my equal, and the equal of any man.'

So it came about that Lincoln began to appear as the most courageous, and yet the sanest and most moderate, exponent of duty and right in the matter. He wanted to put slavery back where their fathers had put it, a system due for gradual extinction, and not, as recent legislation and legal decisions seemed to put it, one to glory in and perpetuate.

So now we begin to see fate working, and bringing forward this really obscure citizen to, at any rate, a public position for which his great character and his sanity were fitting him, and doing it at an age when most men who had not come forward earlier would slip into the ease of less ambitious old age. He was at this time moving towards the sixties.

The Road to the White House

We can now see still more clearly the stresses and strains that were making for leadership, and the effect of a full diet of *Pilgrim's Progress*, the Old Testament, and the six books of Euclid in righteousness, sanity, simplicity and clarity.

From 1855 to 1858 Lincoln and his principles

fought long against Douglas and his opportunism. His Republicanism in the form of the sacredness and paramountcy of the United States Federalism grew also deeper and firmer, and as a doctrine it has been called his, and that of his party. Now Douglas was a United States personage. Lincoln was but a man of Illinois, and the factor of Douglas' notoriety brought his opponent into the limelight. Feeling in Congress between North and South was growing pitifully bitter. In the South a great many people agreed in principle to abolition, and were prepared to support steps in that direction, but they were d——d if they were going to be dictated to by the North; all the old Norman principles bristled. The North were largely newcomers and upstarts; *they* were the old original folk. It was *they* who had fought their parents for freedom, *they* would call their own tune in their own time.

To make the work of goodwill more impossible came the tragedy of John Brown, the fantastical zealot, who led a party of abolitionists and negroes into a slave State and seized the United States arsenal. He had, of course, to deal with the United States troops and Robert E. Lee. With two dead sons by his side, he was captured, badly wounded, and rightfully hanged as a conscience gone mad and turned to murder. 'Yet his soul goes marching along.' There were great men in the South who would have liked to have seen him saved, 'Stonewall' Jackson among them.

Lincoln remarked of Brown's raid: 'It corresponds with the many attempts related in history of the assassination of kings and emperors. An enthusiast broods over the oppression of a people, till he fancies himself commissioned by Heaven to liberate them.' Longfellow wrote deploring the execution 'as sowing the wind to reap the whirlwind.' Yet John Brown in his madness had taken the lives of many innocent people.

In 1859 Lincoln was still out of Congress, and Douglas was in, but he was speaking in many places. Early in 1860, at the Cowper Institute in New York, a typical New York audience of the day had come to hear his Western fun and his rumoured Rabelaisian wit; and instead they heard a speech of United States policy and economics of singular simpleness and clarity, whose only beauty was its truth and the sincerity of the speaker. Abraham Lincoln had arrived. For an hour and a half his fire held his audience in his hand.

Already there was a movement among his friends to secure his nomination, with the Republican ticket, for the Presidency, a position for which in 1859 he 'did not think himself fit,' but, to cut a long story short, he did at the convention next year in Chicago receive that ticket. As someone then said: 'Well we might have chosen a handsomer article, but I doubt whether a better.' It was, however, a remarkable choice.

Humble presidents there had been before, but none who showed so outwardly the signs of poverty and ramshackledom. But the united North had used its numbers to outvote the democratic South. Here was their anti-slavery man, determined, reliable, yet an apostle of moderation. It was believed that he might solve the insoluble—settle the slavery question yet preserve the Union. Alas and alack! In the South the election was greeted with a howl of derision, but for no very good reason. It is just possible that the leaders of the North had seen what was coming, and felt it better that a stranger of no name and credit should fall into the maelstrom ahead. If so, they were justified enough in their planning, but also they had builded better than they knew.

The Secession of the South

When Lincoln stood for the Presidency, the last thing that he had looked for was to put duress on the Southern States. Reason, humanity, compromise within the Constitution were the weapons he meant to use. But before he was in the saddle, or had even put his foot in the stirrup, the fatal steps had been taken. The 6th of November 1860 had been the date of the election, and the Southern States had, wrongly enough, looked upon Lincoln's election as the sign of a determination to enforce illegal coercion. On 10th November the South Carolina Legislature discussed secession, but it was not till nearly six weeks later, on 20th December, that it passed its formal 'Ordinance of Secession.' For some weeks now important personages had been trying to find a formula that would postpone or even avoid a break, but without success. On 4th February 1861 Mississippi, Florida, Alabama, Georgia and Louisiana followed South Carolina in passing ordinances of secession. Virginia, less involved either way, assembled on 6th February 'a Peace Convention,' attended by delegates of twenty-one States. But to no avail. On 4th February, also, representatives of the seceding States met to form a Southern Confederacy.

It was not till 11th February 1861 that Lincoln

left his home at Springfield to grip an impossible situation that was none of his making, with all the would-be presidents in the land thanking their stars that it was not *their* job! It was a pathetic little parting speech that he made, commending himself to the Divine help and blessing in the task before him. It was a task greater than that of Washington. He was very sensible of his own incompetence, and very anxious to get the help of the right men, yet entirely courageous in the task before him. *En route* he stopped at several provincial capitals, and upset New York, not quite sure of its own gentility, by going to the Opera in black kid gloves! His speeches were simple: he referred to his own inadequacy, but asked for the support of the people. At Philadelphia he made a speech that was criticised, but at this distance seems more than statesmanlike in its main point. 'There will be no bloodshed unless it is forced on the Government. The Government will not use force unless force is used against it.' To avoid threatened assassination he changed his route, and arrived quietly at Washington. It was on 4th March that old President Buchanan came in his carriage to escort him to the inaugural ceremony, where his former antagonist for the Legislature, Douglas, seeing that he did not know what to do with his new top hat and his preposterous gold-knobbed cane, took charge of them for him—a kindly act.

We have now seen how occasion and opportunity had forced this simple man of the people to high office almost by chance, and we have seen how that man had been developing his own character, without, however, the spur of ambition. We have now to see how he was to comport himself on this almost insupportable occasion to which he was so unexpectedly called.

Lincoln at the Helm

We need not here follow Lincoln's selection of Ministers. Seward the old republican, Chase the newer one, were among the principal. To Seward he had submitted his draft of his speech known as his 'First Inaugural.' This, with Seward's suggestions, has been preserved. Several the President adopted, others he firmly set aside. Many in the North were looking for some gesture of defiance; this, save in words of quiet dignity, Lincoln would not give. He described the situation and controversy calmly, but asserted that the Union was indissoluble. But his remarks were very unprovocative. 'The power confided to me will be used to hold, occupy and possess the property and places belonging to the Government, and to collect the duties on imports, but beyond what may be necessary for these objects there will be no invasion, no using of force among or against the people anywhere. The mails, unless repelled, will continue to be furnished to all parts of the Union. . . . In your hands, my dissatisfied fellow-countrymen, is the momentous issue of Civil War. The Government will not assail you. I am loath to close. We are not enemies but friends. We must not be enemies . . .'; and he ended by an appeal to 'the better angels of our nature.'

The outgoing President had not made the situation easier, but his errors may be excused by the inherent difficulty of the hour. There was in the North considerable opinion that would even have preferred the acceptance of secession to war. The right to secede was in many ways recognised, and it had been accepted at the time of Union. It was the impetuous action of South Carolina that made war unavoidable. There were in the Southern States certain United States forts and garrisons. Fort Sumter in South Carolina was one.

South Carolina now claimed it, as part of the recognition of that right of secession. The Southern Confederacy had sent Beauregard to watch and threaten it. President Buchanan had refused for the moment to acquiesce in any such claim. Lincoln had already declared that United States property would be held. Commissioners from the Southern Confederacy had already come to Washington to treat for the surrender of this and other similar points. There was a considerable opinion in favour of evacuating Fort Sumter for the moment, pending negotiation for the return of the seceders. Seward favoured this, and was strained and excited over the position and only anxious to reconcile his country. He wrote some minutes on 1st April for 'The President's consideration.' Now Seward was one of the ablest men of the day. Lincoln at once intimated that he alone must make the decision, on the advice of all his Cabinet, and Seward, the disappointed candidate for the Presidency, wrote to his wife: 'Executive force and vigour are rare qualities; the President is the best of us.'

Major Anderson, the commandant of Fort Sumter, had reported that he could hold out only a few weeks unless reinforced and provisioned. General Scott, the head of the United States Army, said that it would now take 20,000 men to relieve the fort by land. The naval chiefs thought it could be revictualled and reinforced by sea; but the soldiers thought the Southern batteries too powerful. The Governor of South Carolina was informed that provisions but no troops would be sent. That was Lincoln's decision. He had been firm as to no abandonment, but he was not going to precipitate war. Indeed, though he perhaps did not realise it, the North was quite unprepared for war. There were some in the South who thought bloodshed was necessary, or pacific intention would return. An Alabama gentleman had written to Jefferson Davis that the struggle must be hastened, 'Unless you sprinkle blood in the face of the people of Alabama, they will be back in the Union, in ten days'—a crude but probably sagacious statement. Davis sent orders to Beauregard to reduce Fort Sumter. By that act he fastened the war guilt on his own head. On a small scale a similar geographical situation exists in South Ireland to this day. For the purpose of the defence of the British Empire Imperial troops hold certain sea forts in the south by treaty.

Beauregard sent a summons to Anderson, both hitherto officers of the United States Army. Anderson, who was starving, replied that if not revictualled by 15th April he would surrender. By some misunderstanding, perhaps by Beauregard's orders, Confederate batteries opened fire on Fort Sumter on 12th April. The fort became untenable. Anderson had to surrender just as the food-ships appeared in the offing.

Now it is quite probable that but for this occurrence the Civil War would not have taken place, and that the right of secession would have been, at any rate for the time, acquiesced in. But

Beauregard had torn it! Uncle Sam, hitherto perhaps in disrepute, came by his own. He, the great American Union, had been insulted. The fat *was* in the fire this time, and the unfortunate Lincoln, with no knowledge of war or war politics, who had never had to bestow a thought on such abstruse matters, found himself at war, with few troops and fewer trained officers. Why fewer trained officers? We must look at the facts of armies. Only the 'gentry' will accept for its glamour so unlucrative a life as that of the army officer. The commercial classes will so serve only on emergency. The majority of the United States permanent cadre officers came from the South. A few to whom Uncle Sam bulked greater than their own State remained, the bulk, some great men, resigned their commissions to join the Confederate forces. Incidentally there grew up between the Northern and Southern forces the feeling which an imaginary inferiority complex produces, and at times a bitterness.

CHAPTER X

ABRAHAM LINCOLN, II

Lincoln as the War Head
The Second Bull Run and the Antietam
The Emancipation Coup
The Bad Days of the North
The Steam-roller of the West
The End and the Sacrifice

ABRAHAM LINCOLN, II

Lincoln as the War Head

Indeed were the backwoodsman President's difficulties now to become apparent. The South had made an appalling mistake in firing on the Stars and Stripes. The many in the North who had been prepared to acquiesce in secession were now brought to a different frame of mind. Artemus Ward has summed it up for all time in his account of an interview with Jefferson Davis, anent the confiscation of his show in the South. He makes Davis say: 'Even now we have frens in the North.' And the reply comes: 'J. Davis, there's your grate mistaik. Many of us was your sincere frens, and thought certain parties amung us was fussin' about you, and meddlin with your consarns intirely too much. But, J. Davis, the minit you fire a gun at the piece of dry goods called the Star-spangled Banner, the North gits up and rises en massy, in defence of that banner. . . . The gentle-hearted mother hates to take her naughty child across her knee, but she know it is her dooty to do it. So we shall hate to whip the naughty South, but we shall do it if you don't make back tracks at onst, and we shall wallup you out of your boots.'

But that course, however righteous, was going to prove an extremely difficult proceeding.

In the first place neither North nor South had any real army, or any extensive retired cadre to do the training, as had Britain, say, in 1914. The United

States Army totalled perhaps 16,000 men scattered over an immense area in compulsory garrisons and on the border of Indian reservation. It had had its Mexican War a few years earlier, but that was a small war. The last real war had been with Britain fifty years before, when the latter had occupied Washington and burnt the Senate House. It had no navy, and the seceding States had a large seaboard. Its capital was in a slave State and close to the South.

The first step taken by the President was to issue a proclamation calling out 75,000 men from the obsolete and rusty militias of the Northern States, who could be embodied only for a maximum of three months, and who had no officers' cadre of serious value. This proclamation was issued a day after the attack on Fort Sumter, and it certainly reassured the North. Two or three days later, when Lincoln and his Cabinet realised how broken was the military reed, it was decided to raise an unlimited force from volunteers. This was in the third week in April. By June perhaps 300,000 men of all kinds were enrolled, a far greater number than it was possible to arm, clothe, equip and make cannon for for a very long time, in the then state of the world's productive powers.

The South had all the immediate advantage on their side, especially that of being concentrated on interior lines, comparatively easy to bring together. Their President was a man of experience and affairs. He had commanded a regiment creditably in the Mexican War. He had been Secretary of State for War in a United States administration. To Lincoln all such matters were Greek. He was quite unversed in any affairs of State, and the all-important matters of foreign affairs were quite new and unfathomed. Ere long the commanding question was whether the States of Europe would recognise the Confederacy, and, should they do so, exercise the neutral right to supply, or deny, war material to both sides. England to a great extent sympathised with the South, for the North had never troubled to make itself popular there. Lincoln had competent secretaries, but had of course difficulty in knowing enough to choose his Cabinet. He was quite man enough to be no puppet in clever Ministers' hands, and it may be said that he knew enough of Jethro's great advice to Moses not to try to do their work. He soon was able to direct without interfering with their detail. They soon realised that their backwoodsman had grit and 'guts,' and public opinion, while wondering, was reassured at his attitude, firmer than most, after the Sumter aggression.

He and his Cabinet had appalling difficulties of military command to face. General Scott, the military head of the United States Army, was an old man of some knowledge of main principles and how to set to work. It was at first proposed that the one great card of the United States Army, General Robert E. Lee, should take command of the main United States forces, but Lee was a Virginian. Virginia too, after some hesitation, threw in her lot with the seceding States, and General Lee, although he denied the right of a State to secede, conceived that his prior duty lay there too. The North had no one. Captain M'Clellan, 'Boy' M'Clellan as he was called, a young engineer officer who had taken himself to see the war in the Crimea, became a general and actually encompassed the resignation of Scott, and to a great extent took his place. Scott, Admiral Faraday and several other Virginians remained true to the North.

The Southern States had equally no army and few officers, save the seceders from the United States Army, but they had a fine outdoor population of soldierly instincts, especially men of the horse, and the situation of their railways aided their operations. Jefferson Davis had established his capital at Richmond, in Virginia, on the James River. The situation of Washington, close to Virginia, and surrounded by slave-owning Maryland, was precarious at all times. Had the Southerners wished to be quite so resolute, and taken an offensive, they could in all human probability have taken it. Indeed the defence of the capital was the first anxiety, and Lincoln's satisfaction when a real regiment, the 6th Massachusetts, came in was almost laughable. Military opinion favoured the defence of the capital for some months, while the Northern forces were being trained and equipped. Public opinion shouted for a blow against the rival Richmond, and Lincoln and his military advisers thought it prudent to acquiesce. General M'Dowell, a competent Northern commander of the troops on the Potomac covering Washington, was to advance south, while another force in the west was to deter Southern forces from uniting. The Northern combined movement failed. M'Dowell was fallen on at Bull Run (first battle) by Beauregard and Joseph Johnston, and very badly defeated, the new Northern levies fleeing in great disorder. The raw Confederate forces, however, were seriously disorganised by their first effort, although the South gathered confidence, while the determination of the North was stimulated.

We cannot follow the President through his trials, absurdities and mistakes. He slowly learnt what clothes to wear, and thus avoid the loss of dignity which social mistakes engender. He learnt something of war and war organisation, and his innate soundness of judgment—one of the greatest qualities required in leadership—which we have seen, served him always. In no case was this more evident than in his settlement of the '*Trent* affair,' when over-zealous sea officers stopped the British ship *Trent* and took off two Southern emissaries bound for Europe. This was hopelessly illegal, though had the British vessel suffered the far more serious delay of being brought into an American port for judgment it would have passed muster. Lincoln, in defiance of Northern fierceness, saw that this was where England 'got off,' and made suitable apologies.

It is more than interesting to watch the attitude of public men, American and others, towards their backwoodsman, and how, steadily, as able Secretary Seward had so promptly done, opinion began to recognise the kernel within the strange husk, and those qualities which have been indicated in the study of his earlier days. *Pilgrim's Progress* and the six books of Euclid do make a background. Many misjudged him for some time. Senators, journalists, men of affairs, for long could not see the stern determination that shone behind his ignorances and incongruity. Yet to the simple unaffected folk of the Northern State this plain, this very plain, man gave confidence. But gradually, as might be expected, the stern occasion opened him out. Foreign affairs were no longer a Chinese puzzle, many of his generals knew less than he did, for clarity of vision is the key to all professions. From ignorance and groping he came to knowledge and decision. His decision and his simplicity enabled him to skate over the bad places that his rawness so often made. Motley, the writer and historian, records: 'I went and had an hour's talk with Mr Lincoln. I am very glad of it, for had I not done so I should have left Washington with a very inaccurate impression of the President. I am now satisfied that he is a man of very considerable native sagacity, and that he has an ingenuous, unsophisticated and noble character. I believe him to be true as steel, and as courageous as true.' Several years later he wrote: 'His mental abilities were large, and they became more robust as more weight was impressed on them.'

In fact ere long we see Lincoln assuming that the powers conferred by the Constitution on the President personally were unlimited in times of danger. He did what he thought right, and expected Congress to back him later, which it usually did.

The military course of the crisis is more than well known, and the faintest outline will suffice here. How, under Lee and other Confederate leaders, the Northern forces were beaten time after time. How the North faced the South on the Potomac and also on the Mississippi on the west, how Lincoln could find no God-given commanders, how the hearts of the North and their President were broken again and again, and year after year, by defeat and disaster, how they slowly arose stronger and more defiant. How both sides became nations in arms, how the resources of the North in men, in mighty armaments, and in the manufactures of the world, slowly wore down the fierce determined patriots of the South, are all written in the Great Book of Life and Fate as well as in the pages of man. On the sea the Southern flag, at first bold enough, was extirpated. Blockade runnings became too dangerous a job for even the venturesome English, and slowly the stranglehold spread. For a while 'Boy' M'Clellan, able, optimistic and an organiser, held the field as Lincoln's soldier-in-chief, and the sea-fed advance upon Richmond seemed to promise reward. The First Battle of Bull Run was fought on 21st July 1861. Till March 1862 the main Southern army was perfecting itself at Manassas. Johnston had 47,000, M'Clellan 147,000, and the two armies south of the Potomac were but twenty-five miles apart. Then, early in March, Johnston, feeling that the situation was too dangerous, marched away behind the Rapidan. The North was getting more than restive. It wanted something done. The inactivity of M'Clellan infuriated public opinion. Lincoln screened his commander, allowed him to develop his plans and train his levies unmolested, but applied quietly a little ginger. He drew up a plan of his own. It was the one plan that Johnston dreaded. M'Clellan would not accept it, and demanded more men and more material. Lincoln remarked that it was 'like shifting fleas across a barn with a shovel, half of them never got there.' M'Clellan complained of civil ignorance, but he was also personally rude to the President. In the spring M'Clellan, who had been ill, was still full of the inadequacy of his force, although it was three times as large as his opponent's. On 27th January the President ordered a forward move of the Eastern and Western Armies to commence four weeks later, on 22nd February. M'Clellan brightened and undertook on his side 'to be in Richmond in ten days.' But 22nd February passed and he had not moved. Lincoln, to the annoyance of his Cabinet, still protected the General, and allowed him to carry out a plan of his own to move his army to the peninsula between the James and York Rivers as an easier road to Richmond. Lincoln, however, put a series of exceedingly shrewd and searching questions to M'Clellan before he sanctioned the move. The latter was a gigantic business, and it was not till the end of April 1862 that M'Clellan found himself at his new base of Fort Munro, seventy-five miles from Richmond. His advance, however, was still, at any rate to the anxious Government, extremely slow. After some weeks the advance commenced, and, attacked by Johnston, the Northerners won a successful action on 31st May. It was not followed up, and it was still many days before M'Clellan advanced to fight the serious series of actions known as the Seven Days, which went on from 26th June to 2nd July. These brought him, after many casualties, close to Richmond, but severely shaken. The President in Washington, constantly threatened by the clever Southerners, had naturally had to prevent M'Clellan drawing the force protecting the capital to him, and the Southern commander now hoped to chase M'Clellan back to Fort Munro. A masterly move, however, by the latter sixty miles up the James River brought sufficient of the Northern base to Harrison to enable M'Clellan to refit his troops without withdrawal, and the President himself came to Harrison. He found that M'Clellan still held his army's confidence. A good organiser, careful of his men, imposing, and surrounded by a brilliant staff, riding a fine horse, he undoubtedly filled the bill as a fine regular officer, yet was, it appeared, wanting in the characteristics that could command success. Nevertheless, Lincoln saw that for the present he had none better. Before he came he had written to M'Clellan a generous letter, promising all reinforcements, and reassuring the crestfallen commander, who had reported despairingly.

During this period Lincoln and his Cabinet were under great difficulties in the matter of commanders. Although the dramatic side of the war was represented by the force near the two capitals, away on the western frontier of the seceding States increasing Northern forces were endeavouring to advance into the Southern States. The governing factor here was the Mississippi, of which the North had secured the navigation and were endeavouring to use its two navigable tributaries as a line of advance eastwards. From among the leaders here Lincoln had summoned Pope to be in command of all the detached troops in the north not under M'Clellan, and Halleck (on Scott's advice) to act as his own adviser, and later as commander-in-chief. Halleck arrived shortly after Lincoln's visit to M'Clellan to settle whether the latter should stay where he was, and be given the reinforcements he was demanding, or whether he had better withdraw to the Potomac.

Eventually this was decided on, and M'Clellan, who excelled in this form of staff-work, carried out the return move effectively enough.

The Second Bull Run and the Antietam

Now was to begin that terrible series of Northern reverses at the hands of the daring Lee, and the other active and brilliant Confederate leaders, which was to try Lincoln in a manner in which few men have been tried, and to show both his weakness and his strength. His popularity with the people had been steadily rising. He was no longer Abe Lincoln, or Uncle Abe. He was now 'Father Abraham'—a term of belief and enthusiasm, and often no doubt of mockers in the clear senatorial atmosphere of Washington.

We need not speculate on the military wisdom or otherwise of the withdrawal from Harrison. Lee always confidently remarked, and no doubt correctly, that if Richmond fell, which did not mean much, he would have merely 'swapped Queens'—viz. taken Washington—since Richmond could not have fallen unless Washington had been denuded of troops. In view of the situation, Lincoln and his advisers decided to operate from the Potomac southwards, thus covering the capital, as a boxer covers his body by hitting to his front.

While M'Clellan was completing his moves—and while doing so his troops as they came across were to be put at Pope's disposal for a while to move south — Pope was ordered to advance against Lee, who had 55,000 men. Had M'Clellan acted promptly there should have been 150,000 Northerners to do it. Lee took upon himself to try to cut Pope from Washington, running risks but knowing his man. It ended in the Second Battle of Bull Run, when, on 29th and 30th August 1862, the Southerners again achieved as striking a victory as they had done the previous year. It was but the story of the Parliamentary and Royalist forces at the commencement of our Civil War, outlined in these pages. Pope, alleging that his men were demoralised, begged to be withdrawn behind the defences of Washington. His own nerves were badly shaken and it was obviously necessary to relieve him. Lincoln, while considering that M'Clellan, who had arrived in Washington at the height of Pope's trouble, had not displayed adequate alacrity, further, did not like his attitude towards Pope's difficulties. But since no one else was available, and as M'Clellan still had the confidence of his troops—a most essential point in an army raised as the North was—and also since Lee was believed to be on the point of invading Maryland, Lincoln, disregarding his Cabinet's views, ordered M'Clellan, by word of mouth, to take command of all troops at Washington. He gave him few instructions and a free hand, saying to his private secretaries that even if M'Clellan could not fight himself he excelled in making others ready to fight. No other steps could have succeeded so quickly in restoring order and confidence to the army. And we may here well remark on the greatness of character of Father Abraham. M'Clellan had been personally rude and discourteous to him, he had given what in the army is known as 'back-chat' to his pastors and masters, he had abused the Government immoderately, as soldier to politician—a step not permissible in high command, even when a true bill—he had failed to deliver the goods, in spite of every support. He had many enemies and detractors. Yet with it all he had qualities the State required for a while, and Lincoln used him, treating him with confidence and distinction for the sake of the United States.

Lee was to act up to the plans attributed to him. Washington was too strong for him now, but into slave-owning Maryland he marched, over the Potomac between Washington and the sea. Lee treated his enemy cavalierly, leaving Jackson behind to capture the Northern port at Harper's Ferry, which he did. He gave M'Clellan several opportunities, but the result, free of detail, is that on the 17th of September he finally fought the latter on the Antietam, a creek on the north bank of the Potomac, some sixty miles north-east of Washington, and received a reverse. The Northern attacks were unco-ordinated, and might have been much more effective. It was the first serious Northern success, and Lincoln telegraphed: 'Please do not let him get off without being hurt.' To get back there was the Potomac for him to cross, but Lee got back unmolested, and M'Clellan with twice the number of troops lay for a fortnight on the field of Antietam. The President went to him after the victory, and came back in the belief that his commander would advance, and he and Halleck thought that Lee could be cut off from Richmond. When M'Clellan complained of the fatigue of his horses, he telegraphed: 'Will you pardon me for asking what your horses have done since the battle of Antietam that tires anything.'

That sort of thing is an old story. What had probably happened was that the Confederate cavalry, 'making rings' round the Northerners, had worn the latter to a frazzle in ineffective movements. Whatever the cause, it was not till five weeks after the battle that M'Clellan crossed the Potomac, and then took a week in doing so.

An idea had slowly been taking shape in Lincoln's mind that M'Clellan, a democrat in politics, did not want to hurt the South. He wanted, perhaps, to bring the war to an end without a crushing defeat. There is no doubt that, rightly or wrongly, Lincoln thought so, and at any rate, eighteen months after the outbreak of war, he and all his people wanted something effective. Perhaps he did not realise that some of the Northerners were very chary of getting too close to the ubiquitous Lee and Jackson. At any rate the President now withdrew his support of M'Clellan, despite the difficulty of replacing him, and on 5th November the latter was removed, and General Burnside appointed to the command.

Apart from the position in America, the recognition of the seceded States by Europe was now getting imminent, and its occurrence would change the whole aspect of the struggle. No wonder Father Abraham was harassed, and yet we see him in greater matters always dignified, always raising discussion and policy to a higher plane.

The Emancipation Coup

While the battle of Antietam was in progress, Lincoln and his advisers were about to launch a *coup* which would bring matters in many ways to a head. All his life, as we have seen, while hating slavery, he had considered abolition as possible only by stages; now, by a set of reasons we need not here enumerate, but for military more than politically necessary reasons, it was decided to issue the famous illegal, save as an act of war, Proclamation, liberating slaves in the seceding States. It was largely conceived in its actual form and period of launching by Lincoln himself. The resources of the South were largely based on their slave labour. There was no doubt that the war was now a fight to the finish. The Antietam did deprive Lee of a victory that would bring Europe to the Southern side, and made men see that the war was to the side that could last. It was patent that the North had all the cards in their hands, but had they the heart? We have seen in our own share of the World War how necessary it was to make men angry to get final efforts. The kindly citizen must be taught for his own and the world's civilisation to drive his bayonet into the dummy with a savage grunt. Something was necessary to bring the North to boiling-point, so there were inner reasons at work, more patent possibly to Lincoln than even his advisers. On the day of the news of the Antietam he took his draft proclamation from his drawer, saw M'Clellan, drew certain conclusions, and, on the fifth day after, summoned his Cabinet. Then, *more suo*, he read them Artemus Ward's 'High-handed Outrage at Utica,' to compose himself and them, and then put the draft, which he had shown them before, before them. It declared all slaves free, save in the slave States which had not seceded (for whom provision was to be made). That meant that all run-away slaves in Northern territory became American citizens. Controversy and annoyance there was. It brought him much support, though not, as he had expected, more recruits. It turned the South to hectic fury, especially as negro regiments were raised in the

North, at first for guard duty, but later as fighting units, which eventually totalled 140,000 more men.

To the world it was the expression of the President's and Cabinet's confidence in their power to beat down the 'Rebellion.' But it put into opposition most of the democrats of the North, who did not want the war to develop into a 'Slave War.' In any case it was a stateman's act, and showed the grimness which Lincoln was developing; and one result was the recruiting song, 'We are coming, Father Abraham.' But, though it was noticed how much Lincoln was developing an appearance of self-reliance, and becoming the rock and the man on whom all could place their burden, yet always was it his practice to place his own troubles in God's hands and ask for guidance. History has said that it was vouchsafed him, as perhaps at times it was to Cromwell.

Before he could win through, that new-found confidence was to be sorely tried, his popularity to wane and rise again, and the North was to find that the period of military disaster presaged in the two battles of Bull Run was to continue till the iron entered into their souls.

Lincoln alone stood four-square to the storm, looking all the while for the soldier who could win battles that mattered, till the Star-bespangled Banner should be carried to the sea, over the corpses of their heroic, and perhaps misguided, countrymen of the South. It was a form of that anti-Norman conquest which is to be referred to hereafter.

The Bad Days of the North

But whether it was to be M'Clellan, whether it was to be Burnside, the formula of victory had not yet been found. Father Abraham, however wise and unperturbed, however faltering and perplexed, was to come on a new series of vexations, and with it, as just said, to lose for a while that support and popularity that had sustained him.

Burnside, the senior soldier among M'Clellan's corps commanders, was an oldish man and not particularly notable, though he had had some successes. He advanced on Richmond and attacked Lee, who was strongly posted at Fredericksburg, where he was impregnable. The result was a bitter costly defeat with sadly heavy losses. Burnside's corps commanders were loud in their complaints. Hooker was especially vociferous. Now Lincoln, as we have seen, was by no means eager to remove a commander because of one failure, although Burnside offered his resignation. Lincoln refused to accept it, but Burnside would not withdraw it unless all his corps commanders were removed—an impossible demand.

Lincoln's Cabinet was hard put to it to find another, and at last, at Chase's recommendation, Lincoln agreed to try 'Fighting Joe Hooker.'

But he first wrote him a letter, which is worth quoting since it shows not only his quaint wise outlook, but the growth of authority and determination. To the imposing M'Clellan he had been too courteously deferential.

'I have placed you at the head of the army of the Potomac. Of course, I have done this upon what appears to me sufficient reasons, yet I think it is best for you to know that there are some things in regard to which I am not quite satisfied with you. I believe you to be a brave and skillful soldier, which of course I like. I also believe that you do not mix politics with your profession, which of course I like too. You have confidence in yourself, which is a valuable if not indispensable quality . . . but I think that during General Burnside's command of the army, you have taken counsel of your ambition and thwarted him as much as you could, in which you did a great wrong to the country and to a most meritorious and honourable brother officer. I have heard, in such a way as to believe it, that you have said that both the army and the Government needed a dictator; of course, it was not for this, but in spite of this, that I gave you the command; only those generals who gain successes can set up dictators. What I now ask of you is military success; and I will risk the dictatorship. . . . I much fear that the spirit which you have aided to infuse into the army, of criticising their commanders and withholding their confidence in them, will now turn upon you. Neither you nor Napoleon could get any good out of an army while such a spirit prevails in it; and now beware of rashness. Beware of rashness, but with energy and vigilance go forward and give us victory.'

Hooker, a fine soldier and a fine figure of a man, took it in good part, and in fact was enchanted with a rebuke such as this. He could organise, and he was aghast at the spirit of collective inertia instilled by M'Clellan among men who were really daring enough. At the end of April Hooker crossed the Rappahannock and the Rapidan, which now divided the Northerners from Lee who still covered Richmond.

In the first week of May 1863, more than two years after the outbreak, the Northern Army for the fifth time advanced against the enemy capital. Crossing both rivers, the brief but stirring campaign ended in the three days' battle of Chancellorsville. It ended in a complete and astounding victory for the South. But the race is not always to the swift nor the victory to the strong. Hooker, dazed with pain, lost his nerve and with heavy losses drew back across both rivers. One satisfactory point however emerged, the Northern armies were full of brave men and officers whose fighting efficiency had greatly increased. The South suffered the supreme loss of 'Stonewall' Jackson—of Bull Run and Shenandoah fame.

In nine months now had Father Abraham seen three armies suffer crushing defeat. Lee was preparing to invade Maryland again. More than ever did Europe seem likely to recognise the Confederacy. But the immense resources of the North and the steam-roller of the West were eventually to trample out the brave.

Before that could come to pass, Lee, whose trump card was always invasion of the immediate North and pressure on Washington, had once more crossed the Potomac, making for industrial towns, and largely living on the country, and had passed the Capital some way to the west. Hooker followed, though overstrained and at loggerheads with Halleck, a situation which Lincoln laboured to ease, but in vain. On 27th June 1863 Hooker, feeling himself 'done,' resigned, and Lincoln made the unexpected selection of General George Meade to take his place.

Meade, marching parallel to cover Washington, encountered unexpectedly some Confederate troops at Gettysburg. On 1st July an encounter took place which developed into a general engagement lasting three days, when each side suffered some 23,000 casualties, the North remaining on the field as victors and Lee withdrawing across the Potomac.

Here was the first great Northern victory, that Lincoln wanted so badly to justify himself, his Cabinet, and his generals, before their countrymen and the world, and it sounded the death-knell of the South.

But in this year and in the next, Lincoln, after all the harassment of finding generals who could deliver victory from the custody of the military South, was sitting on a volcano of his own. He regarded himself, being the constitutional head of the army, as legally entitled to be a dictator, since practically the country was now administered under a martial-law system of which he was the head. It was administered by his Cabinet, and his measures for conscription, essential though they were, were resented and misrepresented. The Emancipation Proclamation had been gathering a crop of fury. There had now arisen an opposition, which, however good in peace-time, was disastrous in war. Agitators who tried to make soldiers desert got short shrift. As Lincoln said: 'Can I shoot a boy soldier who deserts, and leave alone the pamphleteer who has corrupted his mind?' His enemies now began to talk of 'King Abraham I', all of which would have been more than disastrous had not success begun to steady men's minds. Through it all our backwoodsman with all his lesser failings was standing square to the storm. The 'Old Man' was justifying himself, and the fourteen cardinal points of his early readings kept his head and mind sane in such a storm of troubles as our British statesmen, even in 1918, had never to face. Every time let us recognise and bow our heads to the innate staunchness of this man of Illinois!

The Steam-roller of the West

The importance of the operations near the brain centres of Washington and Richmond has always in modern days eclipsed those of the west and on the Mississippi, of which mention has already been made. The conduct of operations there, however, and the difficulties of finding commanders occupied the attention of Lincoln's War Department equally though not so insistently as those on the Potomac. From the spring of 1862 to the end of that year there had been no great movement, both sides resting, and the Northerners naturally gathering the more strength. The story of Confederate daring and the slow-growing Federal activities are outside the province of this brief memoir, but it was from here that the war was to end, and it was here that Lincoln was to find that born leader who could give him victory—find him, too, as a reward for his own loyalty to a decried commander, which we have already noticed as so sterling a feature in his character.

That commander was Major Ulysses S. Grant, ex-West-Pointer, ex-United States Officer, failed business man with a taste for the potheen, the out-at-elbows old officer, with neither hope nor prospects, yet full of fighting character and grit, that we in our army know well. We read of Lincoln, who could not be in touch with the U.S. generals in the west as in the north, trying hard to understand their personalities and equations. Under the stress of service Ulysses Grant was coming to what he was meant for. He was, after a little, made a major-general in the Illinois Militia, then under Halleck, who helped him little enough. He had taken Fort Donelson on the Ohio with 10,000 Confederate soldiers, but after this, with a few more successes, activities had to a great extent lapsed. Lincoln, who had been pleased with what he heard of Grant, when told that he was drinking paraphrased King George's remark on Wolfe: 'I wish I knew what whisky he drank, that I might send some barrels of it to my other generals.'

The spring of 1863 saw the forces on the Northern Mississippi fairly stationary, but that under Grant was endeavouring to capture the Confederate fortress of Vicksburg, which maintained the Confederate control of the lower portion of that river.

As George Meade was winning his battle of the giants at Gettysburg, Grant had taken Vicksburg, after earlier failures had produced disappointment, and freed the river. To use Lincoln's great phrase: 'The father of rivers goes unvexed to the sea.' He was now in supreme command in the west. This victory was followed by another, that of Chickamanga, farther up near the Ohio. On 19th November Father Abraham, at the opening of the National Valhalla on the Gettysburg battlefield, made that short famous speech for which his memory in the United States is ever green. On the 1st of March 1864 Grant was directed to hand over his command to his staunch and loyal second, Sherman, and come to Washington to succeed Halleck in supreme command with the substantive rank of Lieutenant-General in the Regular Army, never yet conferred on any United States officer (Scott was a Lieutenant-General by brevet). Sherman was fearful for his chief entering the entirely new political turmoil of the Capital, and was afraid for him of mistaken dictation by the President. But Lincoln's earlier dictation had been but due to the pressure of Northern opinions at the slow results of his generals. He was only too weary of it, too anxious to leave all sheer soldiering in the hands of a soldier, who could and would 'deliver the goods.' Grant began warily with him, but soon found he was with a kindred soul, and the two gave each other their confidence.

When at the end of April Grant left Washington, he and the President thoroughly understood one another. Lincoln wrote: 'Not expecting to see you again before the spring campaign begins, I wish to express in every way my entire satisfaction with what you have done up to this time so far as I understand it. . . . You are vigilant and self-reliant, and pleased with this, I wish not to obtrude any constraints or restraints on you. The particulars of your plans I neither know nor seek to know. . . . If there is anything wanting which is within my power to give, do not fail to let me know, and now with a brave army and a just cause may God sustain you.' Grant's reply was in terms of satisfaction with all that had been done at his request.

Between 5th and 13th May the fighting had been severe. Grant had lost 35,000 men; Lee, whose resources could not be augmented, perhaps half as many, and fighting wisely his defensive campaign he was back on a line but ten miles from Richmond.

Grant now led the army of the Potomac towards Richmond, or rather Lee's army that had to cover it, in that difficult country known as 'The Wilderness.' From 12th June to 3rd July Grant, in pursuit of his firm plans, fought the battles that were his most disastrous enterprise, losing 14,000 men to Lee's 1700, and Lincoln, though thoroughly trustful, wrote to him of the effect on men's minds of such heavy losses. Once more Lee played his strong card of a threat to Washington. Thrice in July did General Early in what is known as 'Early's Raid' defeat Federal generals, and actually attacked one of the forts in the Washington *enceinte*, to which the 'Old Man' himself, to the horror of his entourage, went. But it was too late for a dozen Earlys to save the Southern cause. Grant was directing the whole operation, and his trusted Sherman was in command with 100,000 men marching from the Tennessee River into the heart of the Confederate country.

There was, moreover, for the first time real co-ordination of effort in all the forces. Sherman set out from Chattanooga on the same day as Grant crossed the Rapidan, moving on Atlanta, the manufacturing centre in Georgia, capturing that place on 2nd September. Early's raid on Washington was followed by none too brilliant a series of operations in the Shenandoah, till at last Grant sent General Sheridan to take command, with very imperative orders. Lincoln highly approved the terms thereof, but warned Grant that giving high-termed orders at this stage was not sufficient. 'I repeat to you it will neither be done nor attempted unless you watch it every day and hour and force it.' He had realised how the moral petrol was nearing exhaustion, for it was the fourth year.

Then came the great surge of the Western roller. Sherman now proposed his great march to the sea, bringing the weight of war to Georgia. Grant somewhat reluctantly concurred. Lincoln watched, apprehensive but mute. The song 'As we go marching through Georgia' is famous all the world over still, though Sherman hated it, but it was the other one we know best, reminiscent of that terrible gambit of the anti-slave fanatic, John Brown, that was the popular equivalent of Tipperary:

> John Brown's body lies mouldering in the dust,
> But his soul goes marching along.

It was a fierce rollicking promenade. Rich Georgia was devastated, and foraging was free and lawless enough. Starting in November, Sherman emerged at Savannah, on the Atlantic, just before Christmas, having destroyed the Southern railways and ravaged their great sources of supply. In the North, Richmond and Petersburg were one vast fortress, against which Grant was steadily pressing.

Despair was showing its grim head in the councils of the thrice-gallant, hitherto victorious South. This time, dogged was not to do it, opposed to that other doggedness of which Lincoln was the centre. Supplies were running short in Richmond, recruits were not forthcoming.

THE END AND THE SACRIFICE

With leaders he could trust and a military machine that could supply them, Lincoln was freer. A Presidential election was due in the autumn of 1864. M'Clellan was standing for the Democratic ticket, and we have the strange issue that, being on the point of victory, was the North 'to forgo it or finish it'? There was much to do also in organising the occupied Southern territories. But Lincoln's Government had to face a supreme matter of policy. Peace by negotiation was not possible. Lincoln saw the issue more than clearly. Jefferson was not the head of an enemy State, he was a rebel; complete surrender was the only end, and here Lincoln was adamant. If the United States were to continue, there was to be no yielding on this point. The people saw that clearly, and Lincoln was again elected.

There has been no opportunity here to speak of the President's complicated, trifling, earnest, generous dealings with his Ministers. He cared not what they said so long as they did their job, so long as their hearts were in their work. The eager, impatient Stanton was allowed to disobey and flout him openly. Indeed Lincoln's position and prestige could only have allowed him to interfere on serious occasions. His good temper and sense of humour made him make these sort of comments:

'Did Stanton tell you I was a d——d fool? Then I expect I must be one, for he is almost always right, and generally says what he means.' Now and again Stanton and other objectors saw the man in his wrath and strength, and were wise.

The human — the over-human — story of the

Presidential election and of how some of his Ministers behaved and acted is strange reading. But with Lincoln re-elected, the war rolled on to its inevitable ruthless end. And all the while Lincoln was strangely accessible to all and sundry, giving great satisfaction to quaint and humble people, who spread the story far and wide. The accumulation of personal misery and despair and the sad petitions turned down moved him terribly, and he was one of those men who at times could take a man's heart from his breast, look at it, and put it back again, intensely uplifted thereby—the gift of God to few kings.

We need not dwell on the last super-gallant struggle of Jeff Davis and his superb Lee, now in supreme control of the Southern armies. The roll from the west, with Sherman on a sea-base south of Richmond, was the end.

It was on the 4th of March 1865 that Father Abraham took up his second term of office. His 'Second Inaugural,' like his speech at Gettysburg, will live for ever. This speech was largely religious in its fervour and probably uncalculated. 'The judgments of the Lord are true and righteous altogether . . . with malice towards none, with charity for all, with firmness in the right as God gives us to see the right. Let us strive on to finish the work we are in . . . to bind up the nation's wounds, to care for him who has borne the battle, and for his widow and his orphan . . . to all which may achieve and cherish a just and lasting peace among ourselves and with all nations.'

Within a month the end had begun. Between 2nd and 9th April 1865 Richmond had fallen and Lee had surrendered. The end soon followed.

But alas and alack! on 14th April Lincoln fell to the pistol of one of a group of young fanatics from the South, at the theatre in Washington.

That Lincoln's death was an intense loss to the State and to the unfortunate South goes without saying. The troubles and tragedies are now buried in the mists of time, but before we leave them let us glance once again at the qualities and reasons that brought this simple character to such stress and strain. Occasion of course there was, occasion thrice intensified, yet in its dénouement unexpected; almost too can we say that fate, chance, put this local lawyer, who was hardly a politician, into the Presidential chair, to find, as he went there bewildered, that his kingdom had fallen in two. There were no precedents to guide him; opinions were widely divided.

The clarity of mind that saw the true issue to be the majesty and dignity of the United States, the gift of mental courage, the clear simple courses of the mind due to his repeated restricted early reading, almost memorizing, a few great books, all combined to produce a character to ride the storm.

We can almost see his Ministers uniting to give the 'Old Boy' a run, as a quaint figurehead, to discover that when it came to difficult matters and dangers he was the master of them all. The whole story is still one of the marvels and problems in this strange matter of leadership and its causes, and the heights to which, with God's blessing and help, man may rise.

CHAPTER XI

SOME VICTORIANS AND AFTER

Queen Victoria
William Ewart Gladstone
Benjamin Disraeli
David Lloyd George

SOME VICTORIANS AND AFTER

Queen Victoria

In thinking of leadership in the nineteenth century it is not possible to pass over the personality of Queen Victoria. Apart from her general estimable character, what was the occasion that permitted a girl of eighteen to take up the part-guidance of so world-wide a Power? That there was ample occasion is obvious to all. But what *was* the occasion, and what, if any, was the secret? An outline, brief enough, will enable us to see that there was an influence more than ordinary, something that every human soul has not, and an occasion that was in itself compelling, and to the eyes of the world was calling for some strong wise man to see that Britain kept the position that the past generation had won for her.

The long reign of King George, who is now emerging from the depreciatory stage of the Whig historian, had been succeeded by two short and ineffective ones. The twenty years after Waterloo, with the long depression that resulted from the war-depleted treasuries of the world, had left England in a parlous state. There had been years of poverty and misery for many, with few of those social services of to-day to ease the troubles of the poor and needy. The trouble in the countryside as England began to transfer from agriculture to manufactures was increasing, and there were many revolutionary issues, of a kind, however, that needed not repression but diversion into other and more harmless channels. They were times for wise statesmanship, but that statesmanship needed a Crown that could at least sympathise and support the Ministry.

Here then were factors that resembled something of the reign of Elizabeth. Wars being well behind us, the spirit of civilisation was welling up again, not only into the artistic and adventurous side, but in a spirit of human outlook on the rest of mankind and the uncivilised races. Missionary enterprise, not always wise but always fiercely genuine, consciousness of much that was wrong in a world at peace, was welling up. The wilder ways of many of the well-to-do were being frowned down, and the excessive 'respectability' and semi-Puritan spirit that marked early Victorianism was waiting to expand.

But the country was anxious. The great fertility of King George and his good Queen had peopled the Palace with goodly sons, yet by some strange freak of nature when it came to the third generation not one of Farmer George's offspring could give England a surviving male heir. There was not one in the direct succession save the line of Cumberland, which had bartered away its birthright. The little Princess Victoria, little in age and tiny of stature, alone stood before the world as heir to the might of England and that world position which the astounding character of the Duke of Wellington had won for her in the council chambers of Europe as well as in the field. There were even intrigues and talks of a *coup d'état* to secure a male succession. But ministers were clever enough to see that a queen (under their guidance!) was just what the country wanted, and they builded better than they knew. So this rather solemn little maid of eighteen was called from her slumbers in the early morning of a June day to be hailed by her Ministers as Queen of England. And a very good and proper little God-fearing maiden she was, with plenty of ideas behind her demurely brushed hair as to what a good queen should be and do. And the great nation hailed her with affectionate sympathy, the wiser heads, male and female, knowing that the head that wears a crown has many anxious days before it. Thus all the British world made up their minds that she should have as good a ride as they could give her, on the great British horse of power. So there we have the occasion, the unusual occasion, with fate and public opinion out to help.

But this stately, if frail, little person was but eighteen, with the *joie de vivre* deep-seated as it should be, and soon, when not closeted with her first set of Ministers, for whom she showed an affection and courtesy that enchanted all, she was very much the lass, with horses and balls and partners to open her heaven's gate.

It was, as the Victorian ballad has it, with her as with Tseu-Hi:

> What are young girls made of, made of?
> What are young girls made of?
> Ribbons and laces and sweet pretty faces
> That's what young girls are made of.

And such are immense assets to a world that needs uplifting!

And so we galloped to reviews in a general's dress with skirts, and we cantered with merry parties in Windsor Great Park, and we danced the soles off our tiny shoes, and we received ambassadors gravely, and danced quadrilles with them on State occasions, and we ruled over England by the unintelligible mystical feminine charm, added to high spirits and the *joie de vivre* aforesaid, till every old curmudgeon in England felt better and brighter and younger for hearing of it. And that is where this lass came to lead her people, and for it let us praise wise mothers who reared us, and nature which gave her the disposition to be developed.

And when in 1840 she took unto herself a husband, and set the example to all her folk in her expanding Empire, to be fruitful and multiply, then generations of mothers and *patres-familias* stood up and called her blessed, and did likewise. The young matron's physique, endurance and energy were astounding, for within a day or two before and after one of her frequent child-bearings it was horse and hounds again, and State balls and reviews, and all the world applauding. And therein, added to a gravity of demeanour on occasion, lay the secret of the 'it' that lay in Victoria the Good. A very genuine real 'it' it was, and all the while across the China seas little Tseu-Hi, about the same stature, was handling a very different team by means of an 'it' that had no sort of affinity save in the mysticism of femininity, and the flair for the right thing—and both were to set time at naught for several generations.

We need not dwell on the loss of the Prince Consort, and the period, the sadly prolonged period, of retirement, which had the sole advantage of preserving mystery, of which Tseu-Hi understood the value. Time laid his hand heavy on this joyous maiden and ample matron, and the little, stout, pathetic old lady of later days had outwardly little of her who rode and danced rejoicing. Then there came that wondrous reawakening, when, emerging from seclusion for the Jubilee, she became the fetish of the now entirely democratic yet Imperial Britain of the seas. A great story, my masters! worthily told by many great pens, and its coping-stone comes to us in the Jubilee of George and Mary.

William Ewart Gladstone

It has already been suggested herein that Britain from her happy situation in the world rarely lies in want of the dramatic leader of amazing and compelling personality. With her orderly, well-disposed people, a good quick driver at the wheel of a well-running machine is the ordinary need—a fugleman and not a *Führer*. In modern times the only real occasions have been the two great wars—the meteor of Napoleon and the world tragedy of 1914. But at the same time, during that great unfolding of our world destiny that the Pitts, the Nelsons and the Wellingtons had unveiled for us, there are a few magnetic and dynamic persons who can hardly be overlooked in a study of the personality that gives power. From Waterloo to the Marne the crises and difficulties have been those of modernisation, of overcoming the aftermath of wrecking wars and the guiding into new paths.

The outstanding figures are therefore not the leaders in war, but those who for good or for evil must guide a country in peace. The two characters that stand out are William Ewart Gladstone and Benjamin Disraeli, and until we come to the World War we do not see, nor did we need, another dynamic personality. It may amuse those who watch time rough-hew our ends to see the Scot, the Hebrew and the little Welshman lead this stolid, largely Saxon, people. Perhaps the position of Mr Baldwin as a leader at the present time is, behind the scenes, due to his being, from his pipe to his unemotional smile, a typical '*Englander*,' a jolly old Anglo-Saxon, with beer, glorious beer, that has survived hops and heresy and still makes for sturdy worth among us.

The career and cause of Mr Gladstone was, curiously enough, did we realise it, that of the anti-Norman conquest, the removal of, at any rate excessive, privileges from the conquering upper crust and their Church fabric. His following were those of the inferiority complex—Nonconformist, trade and science—and how it came to be so is an extraordinarily interesting study. But it was the Norman upper crust who have held the field in which the complex of uplift grew, and who made this milieu in which commerce and science and energy could build our Commonwealth, or the fruit of the prolific English loins be subsisted. Because the anti-Norman conquest went too far and got too hot about it, and tried to gain its ends by stirring bad blood, the upper crust, that might also be called the armour-plating, rose in their wrath. Because they could throw up no articulate leader who could see farther than a cornfield, they were fain to go, not to the Ghetto as they have perhaps since, but to the ancient courts of the princely Sephardim for a man of imagination and vision, and the guile of a politician, to guide them for a while. In Merrie England you can always watch each poison grow its own antidote, even as does

Nature herself. Cromwell to Charles II., Smithfield to Fifth Monarchy, Gladstone to Disraeli, Pitt to Fox, Corn Laws to Free Trade, and round again to Protection, widdershins, or against the sun, Baldwin to MacDonald, and back again, till the world thinks Albion *perfide*, which is only another word for knowing your own business.

Mr Gladstone came on to the English stage—we were still allowed to speak of England—in 1833, and sat in the House for sixty-three years, was leader of the Liberal Party for twenty-eight years and was four times Prime Minister—the most remarkable Parliamentary career in our history. Descent and origin is such a potent factor in character and career that we should examine it. Though brought up in Lancashire, and cultivating the burr as a matter of policy—a species of that 'flat-catching' herein referred to—he was Scottish on both sides, Lowland on his father's side and Highland on his mother's (Robertson). The auld Gledstanes peel-tower still remains, and it was only in his father's time that the 's' in the name was dropped.

The peel-tower ancestry should have stood for Presbyterianism and sturdiness, and that of his mother for vision and perhaps a trend to Catholicism. Yet this leader of Nonconformity was a staunch follower of the Church of England in its High-Church aspect, had little sympathy with Non-Episcopalian Protestantism, and no leaning at all towards the Church of Rome.

Now as all the world knows, Mr Gladstone was the champion of Liberalism, but though he entered the House in 1833, it was not till twenty-seven years after, that he finally broke with the Tory or

Conservative Party with which he had been identified so long, and to which from his breeding he seemed to belong. The last ten years or so were, it is true, years of weaning, but it was not till 1860 that the break came.

His detractors will tell you that he changed because it was by so doing he saw an opportunity for a greater political career than seemed open in his own party. But the bar of history and perspective will not say so, but rather that he saw with a clearer vision the result of years of education and opportunity, added to the immense numerical increase of the town-bred, yet entirely forceful, commercial and manufacturing classes.

The time had come to cut Nonconformity, that wonderful growing asset of British integrity, from the control of a Church with which it did not conform. No doubt he realised that the Established Church, that had gone through so much and had emerged as part of the original Catholic and Apostolic Church, freed of accretions, was the best rule of life and the best of the 'many mansions,' but he had equally agreed that the free bodies were too important to be in any way subordinated. Hence the anomaly referred to, of the High-Churchman and Anglican enthusiast appearing as the champion of Nonconformist freedom.

The worst that could really be said of Mr Gladstone was that to gain support in the ballot-box he mightily magnified the disabilities and unevenness of life, or at any rate their causes, got far too hot about it, and succeeded in making that bad blood—like his successor in oratory, David Lloyd George—for which there is no real occasion in 'this England.'

Then again the Little England complex referred to, written up against him, the failure to preserve our just dignity and rights, may probably be fairly attributed to him, although the failure to extricate Gordon should not be laid at his door. That eccentric uncontrollable hero was beyond the management of anyone, whenever loosed into 'the blue.' It is the fashion among Liberal writers, when extolling his greatness, to apologise for his share in the Crimean War. That again is part of the constant misrepresentation of historical facts which used to taint lesser Liberalism, as it did the Whig historian. The Russian war was clamoured for by the British public, led by *The Times*. That the war was unnecessary and should have been avoided, like most wars, goes without saying. But the children of Waterloo and the Peninsula had had enough of the Manchester School, and believed, rightly or wrongly, that we, once the arbiters of Europe, were neglecting our rôle. The 'hot air,' the belief in the goodness of the world that did not exist, with which the more vocative Christians were flooding the world after the Great Exhibition of 1851, had revolted John Bull. He meant to have the Tsar climb down, and the diplomatic steps of all concerned were not sufficient. The Tsar's cynical proposal to dismember Turkey had stuck in John's gizzard,[1] so war broke out at a time when, thanks to the influence of the Manchester School, we were quite unorganised and unprepared therefor. It was this that Mr Delane, the powerful editor of *The Times*, should have known.

Assuming that war was unavoidable, the

[1] *Cf.* Abyssinia and Mussolini.

expedition to the Crimea and the naval armada in the Baltic were both good measures. The failures were from causes largely unavoidable, due to the measures of earlier Governments. Further, the British Premier being the kindly soul he was, the Tsar did not believe he could mean business. But whatever we may think, we need not put Mr Gladstone in the pillory for his share therein.

After it, came Mr Gladstone to the Liberal camp, when the Free Trade Era was to make for Britain's greatness. But it was overdone, and now we suffer. It was one thing for the anti-Norman conquest to try to destroy the power of the great landowners. It was quite another to ruin all the Saxon and Danish and Celtic farmers, and destroy the food-growing of this isle.

Nevertheless, Mr Gladstone wielded immense power for many long years, both for good and perhaps for evil. His later weakness in foreign policy may have been due to carrying the burden of a Sovereign both aged and a woman. The important thing to study here is the why and the wherefore of the stupendous influence that Mr Gladstone wielded.

One of his admirers wrote: 'The great poet or the great artist lives as long as his books or his pictures; the statesman, like the singer or the actor, begins to be forgotten as soon as his voice is still, unless he has so dominated the men of his own time, and made himself a part of his country's history, that his personal character is indissolubly linked to the events, the course of which he helped to determine. Tried by this test Mr Gladstone's fame seems destined to endure. His eloquence will soon become merely tradition, for his printed speeches do not preserve his charm. If his books continue to be read, it will be rather because they are his than in respect of any permanent contribution they have made to knowledge. The wisdom of his policy, foreign and domestic, will have to be judged . . . by consequences still hidden in the future. . . . Yet whoever follows the annals of England during the memorable years from 1843–1894 will meet his name on almost every page . . . and will seek to know something of the dauntless figure that rose always conspicuous above the struggling throng.'

Indeed, to those who followed him, 'when he departed, the light seemed to have died out of the sky'—though tens of thousands danced with joy; and such is England—again, what was it that made so many feel as the writer [1] quoted obviously felt?

Let us try to see where lay the power. It has already been said that 'he who drives fat oxen should be fat.' A man such as Augustus described Horace, '*Sessilis Obba*,' 'a squat little pot,' would hardly lead a nation. Mr Gladstone from his youth upward looked the part. Tall, of striking feature, the lines of age developed a striking countenance, and incidentally, of a not negligible importance, the collars, high in front covering the cheeks, that he affected lent themselves to caricature; and the dignified caricatures of Britain make both fame and propaganda. Mr Gladstone was a profound scholar as well as a voracious acquirer of knowledge, and his life before all the world was dignified and upright. His family life was typically English in its harmony, and his means allowed him to live as the English country gentleman, this man

[1] James Bryce.

who was wholly Scot. Dignity, religion, scholarship, family life, these are what the Victorian English and Scots valued.

Courage, both physical and mental, was obviously included in his make-up, and to these were added, without which an English politician cannot become an English statesman, political adroitness and flair, as well as supreme self-confidence. 'I don't mind,' said Mr Labouchere, 'the Grand Old Man having the ace of trumps up his sleeve, but I do protest at his assumption that it was the Almighty who put it there.' Indeed it was only in the matter of getting Queen Victoria into his pocket that his acumen failed him. Such a striking character should have managed to secure her friendship and ensure her sympathy. *Nemo mortalium omnibus horis sapit.*

But all these qualities do not make the man who can lead for many years so large a portion of the British people, essential concomitants though they be. Where else lay the charm? And the answer is *in Oratory*. As already remarked, outside the occasional appearance of a Spurgeon in the pulpit, there have been no orators save Gladstone and Lloyd George. Good speakers? Yes, by the hundred. Orators?—men who could move men not by what they said, but by the way they said it? Only two!

Mr Gladstone, with a magnificent voice of charm over which he had the greatest control, a voice which had developed intense flexibility—joy and anger, scorn, sympathy, derision—up and down the gamut of human emotions could he play. As Mr Bryce has said in the passage just quoted, his written words were dull, and often his facts most unconvincing, yet in his voice lay all that his heart and mind felt and throbbed; in the way that his volume of words indicated form and shape, and depths and feelings—the heaven for height and the earth for depth. That was the secret. Many of his causes were great, but whether they were or whether they were not, he was able to make them appear so, and what he said, that he felt. To the scoffer he was 'intoxicated with his own verbosity,' but that was not what his vast following felt. The basis of it all was sound English quality, the secret was power of oratory, the occasion the uprising of the new world against the tail-end of the Norman Conquest.

Benjamin Disraeli

It is a commonplace to say that Benjamin Disraeli, Earl of Beaconsfield, was one of the greatest men of the Victorian Age, and one of those also who served England better than he knew, but it is not so commonplace to follow the development of his strange and compelling influence and leading. It was not the leading of a new party in the land, not the opening out of Communist or Radical movement. No! It was the rallying together of the children of all those parties and people that had made England what she was, the great landowners, the country gentlemen, the Conservative working man who knew the foundations of wealth and content, and how such as he could share therein. This was the people whom this child of the chosen race, of what Bolitho calls the 'eternal contemporaries,' was to lead back to their own in a Whig world. It was the sons of the men who had won Trafalgar and the Nile, who had stormed Badajos and held back the Guard at Mont St Jean, who feared for that England that they cherished. Since no one else would lead them, miracle of miracles! they turn to a Hebrew, but not, it is true, a Hebrew of the Ghetto. It was to one of the old noble—nay, princely—houses of Israel, as has just been said, one of those who so long found their halting-place in Spain and the *Wadi el Kebir*, which the maps call the Guadalquivir, that they turned, yet it was certainly not to a man after their own heart. Who, then, was this prince and ruler in Sephardim Israel that he should also become a prince of Herodim and ruler in Albion?

The answer is this. Benjamin Disraeli, or d'Israeli, was born in London in 1804. His father, Isaac d'Israeli, was a literary man of cultivated taste and independent means,[1] whose family had come to England from Spain in 1748. He moved in good society, so that the young Benjamin met at his father's house men of importance and attainments. For two or three years after 1821 he was an articled clerk in a solicitor's office, a career that did not appeal to him. Samuel Rogers, the poet, had taken a fancy to him, and had had him baptised at the age of eighteen, to which his family apparently raised no objection. Educated privately, he went to no university, but had the gift of acquiring knowledge and a literary culture of a whimsical kind. He first appeared before the public as an author in 1826, he then being twenty-two, having written *Vivian Grey*, a novel that revealed something of his political aspirations.

[1] He wrote several books, *Curiosities of Literature* being the best known.

During the next ten years several others of no particular note appeared, and it was not till twenty years after his entry into literature that his political novels *Coningsby* and *Sybil* began to attract attention. In 1870, as he was approaching old age, came *Lothair*, to be followed by *Endymion*. Through them all ran a fascinating satire, often mistaken for his Asiatic gift of exuberance and hyperbole. Between 1828 and 1831 he made prolonged travels in the Near East, visiting Syria, Constantinople and Egypt, obtaining some useful information about countries far less known in the West than now.

During the period of his literary career he made his Parliamentary debut, in the Whig interest, as his great opponent did under the Tory ægis. In 1832 he failed to be elected for High Wycombe after the Reform Bill; he also stood unsuccessfully for Taunton and Marylebone. His persistence attracted some attention as he had little backing and influence and his means were but small. It was not that Whiggism appealed in the least, and ere long he came to hate it, but he was apparently, as was Gladstone, searching for some new way of politics more consonant with the changing age and the opportunities of the Reform Bill. By 1835 he was an avowed Tory and under the leading of Sir Robert Peel, but with those leanings to the brave old Toryism when the word meant the Crown and the people against the wealthy and the overbearing. Indeed the trend of his speeches and opinions showed a 'Liberal' tendency. It was not till the year of Queen Victoria's accession that he was successful for Maidstone and appeared in the House.

All the while during this period of evolution we see something of the Eastern side of his descent and of his own unusual outlook. Apart from the extravaganza of his novels and the 'ropes of pearls,' his dress was always fantastic, and his waistcoats of gorgeous hue and design, while his hands were heavy with rings, which was the more marked amongst the sober attire of the age that had outgrown the satins and ruffles of the earlier Georges.

All of which is interesting enough as biography, but as yet leads us nowhere in finding the gift of leadership, of the kind that was to put him at the head of the Tories of England and lead that Conservatism which, while marching sedately with the times, would conserve all that is great and good. The first step in becoming something more than a clever and unusual eccentric—mountebank to his opponents—was his realising that no parties of new thought and progress would be violently evolved, that evolution must be slow and only in the medium of existing schools. We therefore find him subscribing to some extent to party discipline and accepting the party whip. Nevertheless, his clever active mind always compelled him to look at political matters with a new outlook and a whimsical gaze that prevented him settling for a moment into the solemnity of Tory externals. Had it not been for our party system, he and Mr Gladstone might well have rowed in the same boat.

But we are now beginning the period when occasion was to take him also by the hand, as it had taken Oliver Cromwell, and as at the moment it was also piloting the little Victoria and the still smaller Tseu-Hi of China.

The point of cleavage with the usual, and also with his leader, Sir Robert Peel, came with that great divider, the Free Trade question, of which the merits are outside the scope of this thumbnail sketch.

At this time it would seem that Disraeli, if not earlier, had some knowledge of the value of propaganda, for he set the lobbies and the clubs a-talking by challenging Daniel O'Connell to a duel. His rings and his ties and his waistcoat may have had the same object, perhaps subconsciously, in the sublimated Orientalism of this active mind. Perhaps of him more than of any others would his objectors have used, had they known it, the army term of 'flat-catcher,' and England in Victorian days was the happy home of 'flats,' even if, which is possible, it is not so now.

But Peel's conversion to the need for repealing the Corn Laws, however unavoidable in the rapidly changing condition of English population and manufactures, was obviously likely to injure the landed gentry and the great farming peoples who had hitherto been the background of all the might of England and Scotland. Disraeli saw that, if carried to excess, especially the suicidal excess of modern times, all that England depended on at bottom might be jeopardised, as we have at long last been forced to see in a world that has changed once more. With these views he met occasion —he became the only voice available that could say what the Tory Party in the countryside wanted said. When Lord George Bentinck died, in 1848, Disraeli was by far the keenest intellect left in the Tory side of the House of Commons. To him, therefore, came the bulk of the Tories, hiring him at first as men to-day will hire a 'loud speaker,' and then falling under the magic of the man who could speak and interpret. In their turn they made him, through the confidence they gave him, the great exponent of what Britain really cared for. Incidentally, we may perhaps deplore the system which prevented the two great sides joining forces for the greatness of the Empire, without going through that period of empty and false denunciation which so often clouds our British issues, and which sent Mr Gladstone to buy the Irish to get his measures through Parliament.

The premature death of Sir Robert Peel by a fall from his horse prevented a rewelding of the Tory Party, which eventually lost the bulk of the 'Peelites.' This meant that there were few men of note to whom Lord Derby in the Lords could turn to lead his party in the House of Commons, and it was to Disraeli, who alone had the gifts that mattered, that he turned for his leader in that 'other place.' He offered him the Chancellorship of the Exchequer in 1852, Disraeli then being at the effective age of forty-eight. It cannot be said that this elevation of him, whom many among the Tories as well as the Liberals (as they now were) considered a mountebank adventurer, pleased the party. While the Tories fumed, his Budget gave Mr Gladstone, now on the other side of the House, the opportunity for a searching and indeed crushing speech, which produced the resignation of Lord Derby's Government. It was not a good start for the man who provided the occasion, though we can see clearly enough that England then wanted, as it did in Cromwell's time, or as we see the French do to-day, 'duck and green peas for tuppence'—all the luxuries without having to pay the price! It is one of the anomalies of the time that this unusual career should have begun with this lapse.

But then we who have seen the founder of Israel and of the basis of Christianity rising to his position by defrauding his elder brother of his birthright, and deceiving his aged father, can hardly complain. Just as such a bad beginning could be permitted to Israel, so was his first lapse to be forgiven to Disraeli.

For fourteen years, however, was he to taste the bread of discontent and to sojourn in the desert. For fourteen years was he to lead the great Tory Opposition in its striving to prevent the good-hearted, in alliance with the sour-hearted, giving away too much of the inheritance of Britain in their lust for new ways and uplift. For fourteen years did the sons and grandsons of the men of Trafalgar and Waterloo come more and more to look on this scion of the Sephardim as the one who could say their say in not only their language but in a far better one. It is not too much to say that all the legislation in England of this period was the better for the drag that his debating power was able to put on what otherwise might have been a run-away coach.

It is great disciplining to spend a period in the desert, but it is not many who can survive fourteen years thereof and return at the age of sixty-four with all fire and energy and courage intact. It has been said of this long period in Opposition, 'Once or twice in every session he used to rally his forces for a general engagement, and though always defeated, he never suffered himself to be dispirited by defeat,' and here we see the first real indication of an 'it,' a power that was uncanny to the ordinary understanding. The eternal obstinacy and sturdiness under adversity and persecution, that has been the life through the ages of the Chosen, has made both a resilience and a toughness vouchsafed to no other.

The long years were years of great difficulty, for the not unnatural murmurings in Sinai were there, and, even as Moses, he had to face cabals and risings and pestilences. There were times when he dwelt unperturbed on some hilltop almost alone. With Lord Derby's support and that of the new men who had not known of his vagaries and escapades, but saw only his efficient, his uncannily efficient, handling of debate in the Lower House, he came back to power. He had the gift of sympathy, and also of wisdom, in helping and stimulating the young arrival to the House. Then came the opportunity that had taken fourteen years to arrive.

Lord Russell and Mr Gladstone produced a Reform Bill, a Bill which was going farther—when England had three-quarters of a century less popular education and experience than now—than most thinking folk were prepared to accept. Defeated, the Ministry resigned, and Lord Derby came back into power, the Machiavellian (to Liberals) Disraeli behind him, as the hand that rocked the cradle. Next year the fodder was taken from Mr Gladstone's cattle by the Tories bringing in the much-needed Reform Bill in a form that went even farther than that of the previous Government, though perhaps the more controversial points were better wrapped in sugar. The adroit Disraeli piloted it through a semi-hostile House, thereby gaining many adherents in the constituencies, and also the reputation for his party for progressiveness which stood them in good stead on many occasions. Mr Bryce writes of the business thus: 'He had, as he happily and audaciously expressed it, to educate his party into doing the very thing which they had cordially and consistently denounced.' Shortly after, Lord Derby retired from politics, and Mr Disraeli succeeded to the Premiership. He dissolved Parliament, expecting to return in strength after the exhibition of progressiveness that he had just given. Now was to come the great disappointment of his career. To his surprise, and the extreme disgust of his party, a Liberal House was returned, and once again was Disraeli out in the wilderness. Mr Gladstone had 'ate the kid that my father bought for two pieces of money.'

Disraeli was now sixty-four years of age and had suffered a discomfiture which was not unnaturally followed by the grave discontent of many of his supporters.

Then was to be seen the greatness inherent in his character which begins to make clear to us the mystery of his leading. He fought on, undismayed, challenging the Government whenever the battle was worth joining, with all his old tact and with all his own vivacity. Like his race, his courage was only strengthened by adversity. An unexpected diversion came to his aid. The Education Bill of 1874 upset Nonconformity, and for some unknown reason a Conservative tide set in. Perhaps the spirit of his Reform Bill was at last bearing its proper fruit. In 1874, for the first time since 1846, the Conservatives had a strong majority. 'Be the day short or be the day long at length it ringeth to evensong.' Dizzy had come by his own. And now his mental superiority stood out so among his compeers that everything the Government did seemed to emanate from his own commanding brain. A couple of years later, feeling the approach of the years when the strong men shall bow themselves, and the keepers of the house shall tremble, he took himself to the quieter command post of the Lords.

They were troublous times in India and the Near East. Already had he shown his flair for the dignity of Empire when he persuaded the Crown to adopt the title of Emperor (or Empress) of India, a proceeding strongly criticised by those with the horizon of a two-room back. In the Near East there had been the troubles of a Russo-Turkish war, and our constant endeavours to save the 'sick man,' in which Lord Beaconsfield, as he now was, had brought us 'Peace with honour.' He handled wisely, as we now see, the Afghan problem, which his opponents would have shelved. That problem was to make a strong independent Afghanistan. The fact that certain troops and commanders who should not have failed him did so was not the fault of his policy. The result of his campaign on the Afghan frontier was to secure the object of an effective barrier to the march of the 'grey coat horde' and a country quiet for trade. But the venom of the pacifist had then succeeded in upsetting the nerve of this country which had forgotten its destiny. In April 1880 the incantations aforesaid had induced the country to plump for Mr Gladstone once again, and the Government naturally resigned. A year later Disraeli died, prophesying truly enough that Britain never would abandon progressive Conservatism for long.

And that was the end of this astounding story, and again does it leave us wondering where was the secret, or even, as some say, the trick, of his success. Others, as has been said, believed that the secret lay in *Vivian Grey*, and that therein he had but outlined his own career. Granted; but to outline your career at twenty-two and then to follow it are two very different propositions!

Despite his baptism, coming of a Jewish father with no practising habit of Judaism, the religious stimulant could not have been strong within him. Where did he draw his strength? It is true that he wrote, in his *Life of Lord George Bentinck*: 'It is deplorable that several millions of Jews still persist in believing only a part of their religion.' But it has never transpired that Christianity or Judaism held him in a deep grip.

There have been many attempts to solve the mystery, and perhaps we may at this distance be content to say that it was this very mystery, added to self-command in adversity, which made men believe in the depths behind those half-closed eyelids and enjoy the quaint whimsical way in which he disposed of his adversaries' fierce arguments. Most of all, however, does it seem that he rose to power because of the large party in England who found in him their fugleman who could say articulately what within the most of them was but instinctive and inarticulate. A solvent of some of the troubles that hampered his development was the gift of sympathy, that told him that an almost caressing admiration of the Queen, in addition to his respect for her as a sovereign, was the wise card to play. We should not perhaps disregard his private life. His marriage to a wealthy widow many years older than himself, with a suitable town house, removed from him that fear of financial anxiety which may easily assail the politician in Opposition. It also supplied him with the profound adoration which was probably the necessity of his life. To the last days his affection and consideration for his wife was most marked and one of the most admirable of the traits in his character. It was possibly assisted by that innate conception of matriarchy which lies in the Jewish character, and it gave him that peace at home which alone can allow a public man to devote all his anxieties to his career. But such incidents and happenings are but concomitants, the secret lay elsewhere, and it can only be even estimated at this distance by a statement of the facts, from which each must make his own deduction. This is how Bryce states them: 'When all possible explanations of his success have been given, what a wonderful career! An adventurer, foreign in race, in ideas, in temper, without money or family connections, climbs by patient and unaided efforts, to lead a great party, master a powerful aristocracy, sway a vast empire, and make himself one of the four or five greatest personalities in the world.'

Perhaps in some sense Disraeli himself supplied a clue when, in his *Life of Lord George Bentinck*, already quoted, he says: 'An aristocracy is rather apt to exaggerate the qualities and magnify the importance of a plebeian leader'—that certainly is what his political opponents would have said, adding that, in mere justice to their own submission, must they fain do so!

Whatever is said and done, however, still does Benjamin Disraeli, Earl of Beaconsfield, dead more than half-a-century ago, stand as the great eponymic ancestor to the largest of all political parties in England, even if a rising generation must submit to the interpretation of the hero by an Arliss. The fact that he is selected for impersonation may perhaps be the greatest of all tributes, still more so that it is his very greatness of character that supplies the theme. It is a fate that another Prime Minister, even the Duke of Wellington himself, has shared at the same hands.

Had Disraeli lived to see this Jubilee of Grace and of Britain's destiny before the world, he might with justice have claimed, and many would thus render tribute, that he, more than any Victorian, had turned the prow of the great ship of State towards the rising sun of prosperous Commonwealth.

David Lloyd George

Among the few dynamic public men who have arisen in modern times and are worthy to be put in the same case with Gladstone and Disraeli must be included Mr David Lloyd George. It is not a question whether we do or do not admire and approve of his ways and his acts, but of the phenomenon of his rise and of his leading the British Nation and Empire through the critical and final stages of the World War. He had, and has, certain dynamic qualities as a leader. What are they, and what the occasions that called them forth?

We need not dwell particularly on the early career of the little Welsh lawyer, whom some have frequently called the 'Liar from Wales,' save to say that he was conducting for Wales, to some extent, a real or imaginary anti-Norman conquest as had Mr

Gladstone. Like Mr Gladstone, he had and has a remarkably uncanny gift of oratory, but whereas Mr Gladstone, from outside the causes for which he fought and the peoples whom he led, still fought their battle, Mr Lloyd George fought from within his Welsh people. To him their peculiarities, their good and their evil, their clannish ways, their shyness, their power of music, their Nonconformity were known—and perhaps their traditional constitutional weakness—as a man knows himself. Like Mr Gladstone he ever exaggerated his case and grievances, preferred to make bad blood if only he got his way; like Mr Gladstone he has done much good and no little evil in his political career. From Wales he turns to England, and, often losing his head and saying more than he meant, has continued Mr Gladstone's campaign. He has made, as so many of the Liberal and Radical leaders did, the supreme mistake of creating an instrument on which they hoped to play and call the tune, to find that it would fall into quite different hands than he, and they, intended.

Much that he has done remains for ever, much will be forgotten in shame; but the fact remains that he did it, partly because the anti-Norman conquest was not yet finished, and partly because the growing wealth of England made his Socialist schemes feasible.

Those were his occasions, but the gifts were and are, firstly, an amazing power of swaying men's minds with the spoken word, greater indeed than the power of the Grand Old Man himself; secondly, an equally assured power of drive and tenacity. These are the qualities that enable the man to lead for good or for evil. Added to these are an equally remarkable personal charm and magnetic appeal. It is true that many who know and have served him, while admitting the amazing charm of the first personal contact, declare that in every subsequent one they like him less. However that may be, the charm is there, a charm in some ways beyond compare, and by it, by his oratory and by his drive, he stands out among those who lead through uncanny, almost hypnotic, gifts.

In 1908 Mr Lloyd George left the Board of Trade to become Chancellor of the Exchequer, and at first earned the intense distrust of a large part of the more responsible people of England. Before very long indeed this was mitigated as it became known that he was a 'strong Navy' man, however pacific in his desire before the world. In Britain to be a strong-Navy man is to prove your sense of nationality, and much may then be forgiven! In the *Agadir* crisis Lloyd George was on the side of strength. In his informal conversation with the German Ambassador, while peaceful enough, his logical unbending stand on Britain's sea position restored him to the good opinion of those who knew, and with his magnetic address he was able to put the comether on many. We can see therefore how some of the attributes of leadership were taken in with his mother's milk, his power of moving men by speech, his personal charm and address, and then, as he developed himself, his power of 'drive.'

Let us now see him getting away, at any rate for a while, from the atmosphere of mistrust, and coming to the front as the great war-leader, the modern Pitt and Castlereagh. We have seen the attributes with which he was born, and can realise how that quick Cymric mind and lawyer's training had helped him to get to the bottom of things, even if his earlier surroundings militated against his understanding of all the tools that would serve him. We can see too how the inferiority complex that at times exacerbated his actions had impelled his anti-Norman courses.

When the Great War began to rush forward to its unexpected and unwanted outbreak Mr Lloyd George was still at the Treasury. Up to now there had been no greater occasion to call for his qualities than that of engineering a partly bogus demand for emancipation, first of his Wales and then of the classes that the rising wealth of Britain could now do more for.

We need not trace the onrush of the tragedy. Mr Lloyd George himself has told us how the gravity of Britain's war position and contingent liabilities came as a shock to most of the Cabinet. If that was so, it was because of the difficulties of getting Britain, especially Liberal Britain, to face war danger at any time. The pacifist who lives on his own imagination in a world of unreality is as prevalent now as he was before the World War. The inner Cabinet had had to work alone. Mr Lloyd George, shocked and surprised, set himself with his innate drive to see that the armed forces had all the money immediately needed. To an exchequer, even that for our small forces was vast. When the monetary system, not only of the Empire but of the world, seemed to be tumbling about the ears of the frightened City of London, it was the Chancellor who, taking bankers and business men by the hand in deep conclave, did manage to weather, by the now historical measures, the astounding crash that then threatened the money centre of the world. Thus the Chancellor's name, hitherto a bogy and an offence, became installed as a sign of confidence.

Then we come to the munitions drama. We need not accept in its entirety Mr Lloyd George's own account of the situation. The trouble was caused by the Government's own action. It brought Lord Kitchener into the Government as War Secretary without knowing his equation. They, circumstances, and his Lordship, kept on increasing the military forces by waving fairy wands. Army production based on tiny forces never could have coped with such demands. Mass production with a very big 'M' was needed. Lord Kitchener got a striking lesson in the first few weeks that should have shown him. He placed an enormous contract for hutting with a famous contractor. In a few days that confident contractor came to say that he could fulfil it only if Government saw that he got the material; the open market for overseas timber was gone. In fact, the baker would only bake you large supplies of cake if *you* organised his supply and saw that flour, sugar, currants and all constituents were available! Then was the time to face the situation. From day to day would come the message, the army is to be doubled, to be trebled, to be quadrupled—magic words, but without the magic wand of supply being produced. When so late as Whitsun 1915 Mr Lloyd George became Minister of Munitions there was a terrible leeway to make up. Fully in touch with big business, as the years of war finance had made him, his great power of drive was never more apparent, and he did become the great man of the War. As other mentalities wilted and collapsed under the strain, his but grew more forceful, and his imagination ranged more fully. The instinct to go 'large' was his. Mass production was then but partly understood. He made it his own, and he cast his glamour over those he called to serve him. At every stage thus do we see his natural qualities married to this unlimited opportunity, and rising more and more untrammelled to carry the Empire and the *Entente* to victory. Also should we realise that perhaps he alone with his political record could have kept Labour staunch amid all the movements of subversion in progress. We need not even stress his qualities further. We may marvel that all classes should admit this dreaded disruptionist as the one man who could lead them. That is proof enough of the dynamic qualities of this Celtic politician. But lead us he did, by personal qualities and personal efficiency and versatility denied to most men. We know that he made many mistakes. You cannot get on with a job of urgency and emergency without doing so. We may deplore the terms in which it has pleased him to vilify some of those soldiers and sailors who served him so well, and who may go down to history yet as those who saved the Empire from a madman, from the 'madness of his madness when he's mad.' Those behind the scenes know how often a wise hand and head at his side had asked 'How would you feed them?' 'How would you supply them with munitions?' to the wilder flights, when imagination turned from the *impasse* on the Western Front to some attractive chimera engendered by a small-scale atlas and a trust in ravens and cruses of oil. But when all is said and done, and when we have duly deplored the deplorable and the sow's ear in the otherwise marvellous make-up, the hard fact remains.

David Lloyd George, of the Principality, led this great, and at one time stymied, Empire to victory, held up the civilised world, and perhaps even saved it from a worse peace treaty than actually emanated from Versailles. But we must also feel that he was enabled to do this because of the staunch support of the patriotic part of the nation and its leaders, who realised that he, with the democratic support and theirs, would have a free field for his gifts.

It is a quaint reflection for those who watch Nature and Father Time rough-hew our ends, that this leader of worlds should plough his lonely turnip-fields while another with a contemptible war record should be destined to be our bell-wether in our next great crisis. Perhaps it is his own fault; yet ever in the annals of the British Commonwealth must he remain as the man who 'could' and 'did.' Even this very short story brings out, to some extent, for those who follow, the record of a leader's secrets—personality, magnetism, charm, oratory, clarity of vision, drive, abounding untiring over-riding drive. Young man! if you would lead the British in their next great trouble, go thou and be likewise.

CHAPTER XII

BENITO MUSSOLINI

The Italian Risorgimento
Socialism, Nationalism and Benito Mussolini
The World War
The Italy of the Peace
The Fascist Coup d'État

BENITO MUSSOLINI

THE ITALIAN RISORGIMENTO

WHEN the dynamics of leadership and sources and origins thereof are being studied in the post-War age of Europe, the figure of Benito Mussolini, *Il Duce* ('The Duke'), must ever be in the forefront. He and Herr Hitler, in 1935, dominate the Eastern stage of the civilised portion of Europe, and the fact that the chapter of their careers is in the latter's case but beginning, and in the former's still in its course, makes a study thereof fascinating as well as indeterminate. Have the Kings of Orion occupied their minds and bodies for ever, and will they, as did Moses, disappear before God, with their causes still triumphant, or are they destined to come to earth in a devastating spin? The astounding boon that they have been able to confer on their own countries would seem to entitle them to the safest landing, and a jump across the seventh brook to that eighth square where the past-masters enjoy peace and watch their works in harmony, the golden crown of achievement on their heads.

It is obvious that both of them are the products of occasion, which the studies we have made show us to be essential in the bringing of leadership to the place of departure, and to understand Mussolini a brief glance at Italian history is essential for a right perspective. It is to be remembered that Italy as a modern entity but dates from 1870. From the day that Alaric the Goth entered a decadent capital till that year of memory, the Italian peninsula, marked though it be by nature more than any other country for a separate existence, never achieved it.

During the Dark Ages the unfortunate peninsula had seen many unholy masters from the north, Saxons, Franconians, Normans, even for a while the Muslim domination of the Saracens from the East, Byzantines, Carlings, Hungarians, and many another. Since the great cry went round the world, 'Rome falls! Rome falls!' there had been none to pick up the pieces. In the fourteenth century the partition of the old heart of Rome was at its worst. Then appeared a prophet and apostle, in the shape of the immortal Dante. To him the departed glory shone as a light destined to burst forth again, and passages from his cantos are the Fascists' Doxology. On the tenth Fascist anniversary it was at Dante's tomb that passages from the cantos mourning the unnatural divisions of Italy, and reasserting the Imperial destiny of Rome, were declaimed. But many centuries were to pass before Italy was to see the Risorgimento of the nineteenth century. Rent by the Condottièri, parcelled between Spain and Germany and Austria, and later by the French, what hope of a national and reunited Italy did there appear to be? Napoleon, whose Italianity Mussolini emphasises, gave the first sign of hope. Many were the wars, oppressions, revolts and struggles before Rome was entered by real Italian troops, in September 1870. In 1872 King Victor Emmanuel entered, in due and ancient form, 'the very Rome,' king of a united Italy, only wanting the Trentino to complete. But much was wanted in smaller items, such as Trieste. The Papal States, who had no business to have an army, were beaten, but still the Pontifex Maximus refused to be within Italy, and was allowed to be outside: and so he remained, refusing to acknowledge the kingdom and the sovereignty until the Lateran Treaty of 1929.

The new Italian Government had countless difficulties to overcome, and many unsolved problems before it. Curiously enough, it took as its constitution that known as '*Il Statuto*,' promulgated by Charles Albert of Piedmont, in 1848. Round this, Italy's laws and constitutional customs were built up, taking where possible British parliamentary practice as a guide, but, like so many children of the Mother of Parliaments, ignoring or forgetting that Two-Party System which is the mother's strength. Indeed a Parliament is entirely a Nordic institution, which does not run too happily among any Southern people.

From 1872 to 1922, when Mussolini came to save a conflagration and debacle, there had been sixty-seven changes of Government. A thousand different cliques with extra-parliamentary subsidiaries prevented all solid policy from flourishing. It went on during the World War with none to regiment it. Countless good and beneficent measures failed to fructify in this revel of Parliamentarianism gone mad.

But this was not the only trouble. The people of Italy are of very mixed race. The magnificent Sardinian body, born of the old Roman stock who had escaped malarial contamination, was a small one. It sent a splendid small expeditionary force to join the Allies in the Crimea; but it was not Italy. The Greek and Phœnician and all the lesser Iberian, stock of South Italy were different enough from the Sardinian.

When we come to the Great War we find that the natural leaders of the fighting services were not the gentry. The officer cadre did not take pride of social place. This and the weakness of the lesser breeds produced Caporetto, when the Nordic armies of Germania struck at the Allies' weakest spot. It took, if not 'all the king's horses and all the king's men' of England and France, at least a considerable portion of them to pick the Italian army up again.

We need not follow the many vicissitudes of the reunited kingdom or the whirl of international politics which impeded the completion of Italy, nor the events which, depriving Italy of her ancient Tunis, drove her into the Triple Alliance. Throughout the period of her struggles it was always from England that most sympathy came. But it is to be remembered that, while Italy was being brought into the European and world picture by Cavour, Bismarck was doing the same for the North German States.

Socialism, Nationalism and Benito Mussolini

During the years after 1872 that the locusts have eaten, the political virus grew very deep in the parliamentary fibres, although for purposes of convenience the changing of opinions was brought to a fine art. In such soil the Socialist germ multiplied a thousandfold, the old honest Republican party, that disliked the King, but which convenience had maintained, tended to merge into the Left. Those who cherish the chimera that all men should be pulled down, rather than all gradually lifted, grew and scattered throughout the glands of the State. They naturally came into clash with the worthy nationalism, which alone made an Italy possible. Anarchists and Communists swam in the political hotch-potch. So far back as 1892 the Socialist Party formed itself, but wisely threw out its anarchists, and slowly worked for such a kaleidoscopic programme as Socialists charm themselves with. Whatever the good in the programme, it did militate by some mad germ against Italian Nationalism, and it produced that unmitigated evil, class war, unmitigated since it has no attainable goal outside the herring heads of Russian Soviet dietary.

So, in Italy, Socialism ran a vain course, instead of aiming at that gradual redistribution of that wealth which stronger action dissipates like the mountain mist. And then there arose one Benito Mussolini, named after Benito Juarez, the Mexican revolutionary, trained as a village schoolmaster, of stock and strain that had come direct from Roman ancestry, with the countenance of a Roman senator. The dynamic young man set himself to study in Central Europe and Switzerland, disciplined by a poverty that was phenomenal, and a bitter sympathy with all in poverty, passing through the gamut of all such: Anarchism, Communism, the fierce unpractical side of Socialism; but with a gift of sympathy, and the complex of fierce self-pity—a great school if you have the grit and character and good fortune to emerge from it. In comfortable, democratic England the iron does not enter the Socialist's soul enough to emerge as fine-drawn steel. With Mussolini it did—but by the way of eleven imprisonments for offences against an ordered State.

By 1914 Mussolini was the leader-in-chief of all the subversive elements—Socialists, Anarchists, Communists, Moonlighters, Peep-o'-day boys, and every fierce element pupped on misery and despair. In June 1914 a Socialist revolution threatened in Italy. There were strikes, and in June 1914 an armed revolt against the State, in what are known as 'The Red Days,' began. There was a good deal of none too deadly fighting between troops and Socialists. Revolution simmered until the outbreak of the World War, which then saved Italy from her madness, as it saved England from her Irish folly.

For twenty years, remarkable to state, Italy had had one Premier, Giovanni Gioletti, in spite of the inchoate and numerous parties, a prince of the Italian political spirit of *trasformazione*—*i.e.* the merging of principles for convenience. But he had produced a continuation of general policy which had perhaps kept Italy together. During the pre-War parliamentary years, however, a National party was arising, with an astoundingly ambitious programme: the recovery of the Alpine Trentino, Venice, Trieste, Fiume, Dalmatia, little British Malta, North Africa, and no doubt the lost Roman province of Albion! Its precepts naturally were militant, to the accompaniment of sabre-rattling. It has been said that between this group and the Socialists hovered a strange connecting link, the poet Gabriele d'Annunzio, and from this pact we see the birth of Fascism, which is the attempt to weld Nationalism and the better side of Socialism—a process, incidentally be it said, always in process in Britain by the genius of the people. In Italy it was to produce strange but essential storms.

The World War

Then broke out the World War. Reference has been made to the circumstances that sent Italy to the Triple Alliance before the War broke out. Gioletti was still Premier, and saw, or thought he saw, that Italy would profit immensely from Austria and from Germany by neutrality. The Nationalist Party rose in its wrath, and with it, ere long, the Socialists, led by Mussolini of the Roman countenance. Italy must fight or be swamped, thought he: 'To-day war, to-morrow revolution!' War would tear the basis of civilisation into such shreds that revolt and Socialism must follow. But this was not at first. In November 1914 he was expelled from the Socialist Party, and deprived of his post as editor of *Avanti*. Next day he founded *Popolo d'Italia*, to propound his ideas. The resolution expelling him ran: 'Long live Socialism! Down with the War!' Ten days later was founded 'The Fascio of Revolutionary Action.' In January 1915 was started the *Fasci*, and in an incredibly short time over a hundred *Fasci* (group centres), and the movement had become the *Fascista*.

In the meantime, Gioletti, the high priest of neutrality, was bargaining with Germany and Austria, and finally proposed Italy's terms. They certainly ministered to the National idea. But while Italy was outwardly calm, she seethed below the surface. Austria rejected Gioletti's proposals. The *Entente* now offered better ones, knowing that in the seething Nationalism which aimed largely at rescuing Italian minorities from Austrian dominion the *Entente* were on safe ground. On the 26th of April 1915 was signed the secret *Treaty of London*, between France, Italy and *Great Britain*. The spirit that insisted on this had been largely due to Mussolini's dynamic *propaganda*. To the neutralists he had been *anathema*, and early in 1915 had been arrested. In the enthusiasm thus engendered,[1] Nationalists and the Mussolini Socialists marched hand in hand. War was not yet, but in May Gabriele d'Annunzio arrived in Rome. Salandra, the new Prime Minister, sent an ultimatum to Vienna that month, with all the spirit of Italy behind it. But, after the accursed political system of the country, it left Gioletti and the ordinary Socialists free and eager to embarrass their patriotic National Government. They could not bury their own opinions to form a common front. All the while did they toil against victory for their nation, and all the while did the conviction grow in Mussolini's mind that Nationalism and true Socialism were best in wedlock. It took several years for Hitler to propound the same. It was discovered generations ago in Merrie England, when the Tories, the King and the people fought the super-bourgeoisie of the Whigs.

We need not here follow the chequered course of Italy in the World War, save to say that, balked by political intrigue, her army, never at its best development, suffered much by the Russian defalcation and Revolution, and from the hostile group in Italy. The disaster of Caporetto, not far removed from a Sédan, was repaired by the staunch Allies, and the army rebuilt by a new Italian chief, General Diaz. Nevertheless, behind the line, treachery and anarchism were at work in the war factories. Efforts were

[1] The writer was in Italy in the early days of Italian mobilisation, when enthusiasm surged.

made to set up soldiers' and workmen's *soviets*. Austrian planes strewed Socialist propaganda. Yet in the stress and strain of the trench life, that eventually produced real Italian victory over Austria the enemy, there grew up a class goodwill and understanding, with *Italia*—sane Nationalism—as the basis.

The Italy of the Peace

Even the very little that has been said suggests that the phenomenon of Mussolini is somewhat different from that of most of the other leaders whose occasions and gifts have been outlined: Moses overcoming an inferiority complex at the spurring of the Almighty—Alexander of Macedon urged to a career of conquest by belief in his divine origin—Elizabeth leading by some feminine mysticism and a trust in her ministers—Cromwell reluctantly grasping the staff of leader when all others had proved ineffective. Here we have a dynamic personality starting with a bee in his bonnet, calling to his world, and calling from the wilderness before the World War, converted by the *camaraderie* of the battle-line to a national belief in a combination of all classes, with all the story of Italy from Rome and Garibaldi behind him. Occasions enough indeed! But nothing to that to come.

The world had been torn in shreds and the choicest of its young men dead; the accumulated savings of generations scattered to the four winds of heaven; returned soldiers, who had left the ranks thinking of Italy and not of their homes, balked by disorganisation; the old disruptive elements at work intensively.

To the earlier implacable Socialists it seemed that

their opportunity had come. The Reds were hard at it while the Peace delegates were at Versailles.[1] On the 19th of February the 'Italian Unitarian Socialist Party,' the swine who had tried to upset the war factories, concluded an alliance with the Russian Bolshevists and their own Red block. Celebrating the event by a 'Red Day' at Milan, the Italian national flag was torn down, trampled underfoot and insulted, the ex-soldiers abused and spat on, countless revolutionary demands emitted, including the abandonment of the new redeemed frontiers. Similar scenes took place in other important towns and provincial capitals. Four hundred thousand Reds determined to impose their will by surprise bloodshed on forty millions of their countrymen.

Mussolini had no use for Socialism and Communism of the Russian order. He applied his dynamic energy, this Sergeant Mussolini of the brotherhood of brave men, to combat the dire disease forthwith. A month later, with but two hundred supporters, he held his first Fascio de Combattimento, in a small hall in Milan. His original Fascio was but to maintain the principle of unity of the Risorgimento. Now it was to save Italy from a self-incubated pestilence, that same pestilence that, in 1871, France rooted out so promptly in Paris. His original *Fasci* were not dead, and it was urgent to call them into being. Journalist and editor by instinct, *Il Fascio* grew to his hand, the first number bearing the old Æsopian device of a hand grasping the union-is-strength bundle of

[1] This is not the place to talk of Nationalist Italy's disappointment at some of the provisions of the Peace, nor of d'Annunzio's popular filibuster at Fiume.

sticks, far more significant than ever the lictors' rods; the sticks that the Reds would destroy singly. *Il Fascio* contained the Fascist programme, *I Postulati-dei Fasci par la Constituente*, which in brief aimed at a united authoritative Italy, free of all party, all 'dogmas,' all 'mentalities,' and aimed at not only stating the problem, but at dictating the solution.

The lesser breeds of Italy had shown themselves quite unfit to handle the Nordic machine of parliaments; they now needed, under the stress of post-War troubles, a dictator to pull them together. They got one! Mussolini first appealed to his comrades of the battlefields. Demobilisation had thrown them by the tens of thousands on to an unprepared labour market. The trade unions were excluding them by hard and fast union rules.

But Syndicalism and Red labour were organising an orgy of strikes for purely political reasons, nay, purely revolutionary reasons, and also were aiming by various organisations at breaking up the *camaraderie* of the ex-service men. The Government of Italy itself, gassed with the Wilsonian gas, was failing to make a stand. Mussolini addressed all traitors, 'Stand back, you Socialist jackals, it is forbidden to divide the dead!'—and especially did he trounce the already discredited President Wilson.

But cells and spores, even those planted by a Mussolini, take time to grow and spread. The outward story of Italy in 1919 is but the story of strikes, of syndicalism, of the destruction of the capital that is really only credit, of the making the poor man poorer, to make the rich poor. It is easy enough to do the latter, but the corollary is the former, with the Soviet diet of herring heads aforesaid. By way of encouraging everyone, the anarchists took to bomb-throwing, for no apparent reason. The theatres of the innocent were their favourite arena, and Italy was becoming a hell. Now we can see the real occasion that demanded a spirit from the deep. It was at hand in the shape of the dynamic sergeant.

In October 1919, after some months of underground work, Mussolini held his first Fascist Congress. One hundred and forty-eight Fascio centres or cells were represented, with sixty-five more to follow. Each sent five delegates. The Fascists now numbered 45,000. The Congress was timed to precede a coming election, and the policy of an all-Italian universal all-class Nationalism was propounded. The Reds attacked the Conference, and the revolvers popped merrily. Fascism was arresting attention.

As 1919 and 1920 passed, affairs grew worse—the Italian Government was afraid to govern, or timidly accepted Red dictation. Murders and massacres were everyday incidents, the Red Flag flew over factories, battle flags were insulted, ex-officers killed, Red tribunals even executed 'Fascists.' Pitched battles took place in certain towns; Socialists marched out of Parliament when the King entered; horror, bankruptcy, Russian Sovietism, all threatened. Agrarian strikes effected astounding loss to the country. Mussolini's candidates failed to get elected, but without Gioletti's tight-rope manœuvres the various parties of ordinary politics quite failed to grip any sort of affairs. There was no one to bell the cat, and we in England, who have never seen such a state of affairs, cannot realise the hell that was prevailing.

But Benito Mussolini was spreading his Fascist

propaganda, which meant 'All for Italy,' steadily among those who were waiting for a saviour. Gioletti came back, the Gioletti they had driven forth, but the situation was now beyond his adroitness. It was the iron hand behind the heart of faith that was needed. Mussolini was arrested, imprisoned, released; and *Il Popolo*, now eagerly read, had a chequered existence, but it was doing its work. Fascism was growing. The pro-Russian Socialists tried to stage a bloody day for all Italy, and inaugurated it by a ruthless series of bomb explosions in hotels and threatres, in the hope of instituting a Red Terror.

The organising Fascists, however, were growing stronger, and reaction meant more bloodshed. 'Reds who would not shout "Long live Italy" were killed by Fascists, and Fascists who would not shout "Long live Lenin" were killed by Reds; and both Reds and Fascists were alternately coddled and killed by the Government's *Guardie Regie*.'

By November 1920 the first Fascist union, the 'Italian Confederation of Economic Syndicates,' was created at Milan, and the first *Fascio* formed abroad—the former to combat the 'Labour Chambers' in every town, the latter to explain the situation to Italians abroad and to the outer world. The shooting of an ex-service men's leader raised the Fascist anger. Gioletti's sending troops to suppress d'Annunzio at Fiume sent Nationalist feeling surging.

The Fascists tried a revolt, which failed, and many were arrested, but arrests were only the needed fuel. Socialists and Communists now happily quarrelled, but the latter tried to massacre both Fascists and Government troops. At Florence there was a fierce battle, with very many injured. An army lorry was ambushed and fifteen soldiers done to death. Public opinion trended more towards the Fascists, with their cry of 'Italy for all, and all for Italy!' The culminating point really came when, in March 1921, the Anarchists threw a bomb in the Diana Theatre at Milan, which killed twenty and wounded fifty, including many women and children. Milan rose in its wrath to help the Fascist avengers. Then it was that the Fascists began to take on their aspect of the public avengers. But the mischief went on, and the Socialists declared that the territory given Italy by the Peace would not be retained. Nationalist Italian feeling was much exacerbated at German and Austrian propaganda in the acquired territories, everything Italian was ignored therein. Mussolini, now ubiquitous, preached his doctrine: 'We dream of a Roman Italy —that is, an Italy wise, strong, disciplined and Imperial.' Much of that Imperial spirit surges in Fascism—'Roman is our pride and courage.'

The Fascist Coup d'État

In May 1921 came the General Election. Fascists, rejected at the last, now gained thirty-three seats. Benito Mussolini, erstwhile Socialist, ultra-Revolutionary of Republicans, was now heart and soul Fascist—but his Fascism was a union of the nation, all the classes in one. He was now able to carry his programme to the floor of the Italian House—to him the Roman Forum.

The rule of Fascism, however, was not yet. The dynamic figure in the House, despite the occasion calling loud for a leader, was but the leader of a small section. Gioletti still carried out his adroit policy, now outworn, of trying to balance sect against sect, by means of his officials and representatives. But Italy had passed beyond so simple a remedy. By 1922 Fascism was a very definite party, and Mussolini *Il Duce del Fascismo*. Local Fascists in the Alto Adige had to do the duty that the Italian Government shirked, and dismissed Austrian officials and all those who insisted on wearing Austrian uniforms in the ceded districts. In October 1922, 35,000 Fascists assembled in congress at Naples, and Mussolini was everywhere. At a secret conference at Naples the plan for seizing the ineffective Government at Rome, and saving Italy by a *coup d'état*, was adopted, with alternative plans in case of failure. The G.H.Q. of the movement was efficient, and included General R. Bone, a corps commander during the War. 27th October was fixed for mobilisation. Balbo took command of the forces marching on Rome; De Vecchi, chief of the Fascist General Staff, and Grandi were deputed to persuade the King to invite Mussolini to form a Government—no easy task. The Holy See had smelt a rat, and sent to inquire how did Fascism regard the Church. The answer was satisfactory.

On 25th October, De Vecchi and Grandi came to Rome and advised the two Liberal leaders, Salandra and Orlando, to tell the King of the aims of the Fascists, and asked the new Premier, Facta, to resign. Facta temporised, and advised the King to return. On the 27th the G.H.Q., *Il Quadrumvirato*, issued their mobilisation proclamation, asserting the martial law of Fascism, and announcing the aims of Fascismo.

Three columns with reserves, 70,000 strong in all, marched on Rome. The Italian Home Office issued orders, somewhat humorously, for the arrest of *Il Quadrum-virato*, and declared a state of siege. Three hours later this was cancelled. Orlando persuaded Facta to resign, which he and his Cabinet did that night. The King sent for Grandi and De Vecchi, and his first remark was that *he* had not ordered the state of siege! He then asked Salandra to form a Cabinet with Fascist help. Salandra offered Mussolini a Cabinet post. The latter refused, saying that he did not wish to mitigate a Fascist victory. Next morning the King had invited him to form a Ministry.

Travelling through scenes of enthusiasm, he was received by the King, in his black shirt. In answer to the King's greeting Mussolini replied: 'I bring to your Majesty the Italy of Vittorio Veneto, reconstructed by a new victory,' and presented the names of his Cabinet. Blackshirts had by now massed outside the Quirinal, and as the new Prime Minister left there was a demonstration of loyalty to the King, to Italy, and to the new Prime Minister.

50,000 Blackshirts now met at the National Monument to the Risorgimento, where lies also the Unknown Warrior's Tomb, whence the *Duce* made a reassuring proclamation—and moved his Blackshirts out of Rome. They demobilised throughout Italy, and the populace, the forces of order, and the army rallied round the new *régime*.

Outside Italy, Mussolini's apotheosis was a surprise; inside, his influence and name, now famous for several years, brought hope of peace and prosperity. But it was the culmination of three years of the principles of law and order and nationality, instinctively at work against the poison and terrorism of Soviet propaganda, murder and destruction.

The occasion that called for Mussolini was prodigious, and happy a thousand times was the country to find such a character to save it, and rescue a Southern race from a Nordic form of government run mad. But whence the Mussolini? The answer here is clear: the dynamic personality, aflame with the principles of a perfect Italy, turning from the unfledged Socialism of his first ignorant enthusiasms to the great idea of a National Socialism of goodwill and good people. But again let us note the dire occasion of Red ruin that brought him support. Let us note that without his personal energy and force, clear vision, oratory and power of the pen, he could not have filled the bill for a moment. There is no more complete example of the leader born, the prince of dynamics, nor the effect, already noted in the case of Gladstone, of the power of oratory over men's minds. In his case a great cause, and a great tongue and a great pen to explain it. But, as has so often been repeated herein, a terrible occasion as well as a great cause—and hence *Il Duce*.

For the rest, what more? How wise his political and economic measures may be, where his failures, when his successes, do not concern us. It is the magic of *Il Duce* that we are studying. We in homely England do not even now understand what he saved Italy from—we who need not. Were a Stafford Cripps to get sufficient power to be able to pull our house about our ears, we should probably think and act very differently. Were Communists to attempt terrorism, John Bull himself would become *Il Duce*.

But whatever the successes and future of Fascism in Italy, the fact remains that for thirteen forceful years has Mussolini dominated Italy, and does so because the forces of disruption that he has repelled must lie in the grave till a new-born generation can take the helm and, like Moses, he dare hand over his work. *Viva il Duce!*—the man strong to save and lead a derelict people.

If, however, anyone asks: 'How can I be a Mussolini?' the answer is: 'Young man, you must have unfathomable courage and self-confidence, a cause that drives you through fair weather and foul; you must have the gift of oratory and the pen of a master writer. Having these, you must find a country of Southern blood, wracked by its own toxines, and pray for opportunity.'

The Mussolinis and their occasions come not too often, though we must now look to one other somewhat similar personality of our day.

CHAPTER XIII

ADOLPH HITLER AND THE CONCLUSION OF THE MATTER

ADOLPH HITLER AND THE CONCLUSION OF THE MATTER

Adolph Hitler

It is one thing to study the well-documented history of Benito Mussolini and to admit the salvation for the moment of an Italy that was going mad; it is another to feel quite so sure of whether Hitler can follow the same road with a larger problem and a greater people. But the great hypnotic power that has saved that greater people from the abyss has been demonstrated even more wonderfully than in Italy, and it is essential that we should stop to marvel and to inquire. We have perhaps, in our own stress, overlooked the astounding problems which Germany had created for herself, and the social and economical *impasse* for which she was heading. It explains the miraculous coming and acceptance of a man far less equipped by education and experience than Sergeant, Mussolini, B., to lead a people. Corporal, Hitler, A., has little save oratory and a cause of first principles. That oratory could, however, have got him nowhere had not Germany been in abject despair. We shall be forced to admit that it was an occasion strange, unprecedented, and so insistent that almost all could acquiesce in any saviour that made the phenomenon possible.

To see the occasion as it really was, we must disregard the question of the war guilt of Germany, and rather cast our eyes on the hope that failed, that a Germany at peace would become the anti-

Prussian human Germany of the earlier Victorian days. On the principle that the children cannot escape suffering for the sins of their fathers and their leaders, we have looked on the entering of the iron into the German soul as but their punishment before civilisation. But however that may be, there was one fatal error of vision at Versailles, made in spite of warnings from the few that cried in the wilderness. Germany was thrice bankrupt. There were in truth no pips left to squeeze. She had, following her well-known military principle of double or quits, kept on the war in the faint hope of quits at least a year too long. All the internal fat had gone. If you reduce an animal so that its interior as well as its exterior fat be gone it cannot recover. By the end of the War every little corner of hidden reserves had been found and used—recovery was impossible. A firm, a business, and a nation, need working capital. Because of the want of this, and also because France would understand nothing save that, however fiercely Tiger Clemenceau might demand that Germany be treated rough, it would be nothing to what a victorious Prussianism would have demanded of her and England, there was never a chance. The Ruhr, the Sanctions, the coal demand, the collapse of the mark, the ruin of the gentry, the Dawes decisions, they were all but steps on the *descensus averno*. All the influential and military classes were ruined. The industrials quailed before a Socialism which was trending to Communism and even Bolshevism. With Socialists in power, with Jews honeycombing the civil service and educational institutions, the whole of Germany lay quivering for a leader. The nobles and the Junkers, the landowning classes, knew that nothing they could do would stem the slide. The mothers of the intelligentsia and the older gentry saw no hope for their sons. All was a blank wall. Hindenburg and Von Papen could steady the machine perhaps, and keep it on the right road, but they could not drive it on soft soil or find the trail that had been missed. Germany had lost the road in the desert and her soul in the mist. Some day we shall know whether some guiding spirit, some hidden Bismarck, found Hitler and used him, or whether Hitler, prompted by Thor and Woden, found himself. But the phenomenon is intelligible if we realise the social and economic state of Germany, added to the world crash in which the collapse of the Lahausen Wool Combine let the water through the quaking bending levees of world credit. Could rich and poor, labourer and *rentier* be rallied into one gigantic national enthusiasm, to save what could be from the wreck? Now arises Adolph Hitler, ex-corporal, mystic enthusiast, Socialist-cum-Nationalist at heart, uneducated but magnetic, and above all an orator whose voice could reach and sway millions. Even Old Hindenburg, his whole Prussian General's being in revolt against the Corporal, saw it. The bitterest debacle ahead, a nation without hope, rushing for the pit of bankruptcy and Communism, suddenly heard a call and was shown ropes and brakes that could save it. Occasion plus a man of magnetic inherent influence, who could feel an idea and make it live, a rarer and greater than Mussolini—a greater people, a worse occasion, an equally magnetic man—'I will be drowned and nobody shall save me,' and then a flashlight, an arresting flashlight, a boom on the big drum that all could hear, a giant and joint movement of concert.

We may deplore all the concomitants of the resurrection, we may equally deplore the want of vision in all around, yet we should realise that the situation was so bad that there was no room to allow any conscientious objectors, no room to be human to Jews whose ideas fought the Nationalism that alone could save, or to Communists imbued with the mass-murder theories of Russia. If there was any chance that we could ever get where Germany was, Cripps and all his *à bas le Roi* and *conspuez Capital* friends would be beaten out of their souls with rubber truncheons before they led us the same way. We are tolerant because we think we are safe, and 'give the losers leave to prate,' as the old wisecrack has it.

Let us then realise that Germany was rushing from ruin and jettisoning every possible impediment to salvation, without time to reason — we who live in these comfortable victorious common-sense islands.

We need not concern ourselves with wondering how long Hitler can 'get away with it,' whether it is a fact that his sensations are the only thing that can still keep up enough wind to float him. We may deplore that a banging on the military gong was a necessary step in prolonging the winch. Such questions are foreign to the purpose of this brief glance. The fact remains of the direst of occasions, which made his enthusiasm and his gift of oratory essential to salvation. We have seen how the national party of Britain allowed Lloyd George to take the helm in the World War *because* of his magnetic gifts, and because he could bring one part of the nation to heel, while they could guarantee the other. Similar, perhaps, is the story of Hitler. But had not there been this flaming personality available it would have gone more than ill with Germany. A nation bankrupt in spirit and self-respect is a pitiful thing; all hail to the man who can restore it. We may say 'Hail, Hitler! Become human!' and 'God save the King! May we never want such a one!'

THE CONCLUSION OF THE WHOLE MATTER

In this study of some of the world's phenomenal leaders we have struck the same qualities and essentials through the long ages, and we have noticed how most of them have been called from the mass to meet some national urgency—that without the occasion the man of the hour does not often arise. He lies in the chaldron, but is not taken forth for annealing. Of the qualities and forgings there are many varieties, the obvious and recorded mission from unseen power, as of the diffident Moses and his disagreeable clansmen, to that of John Wesley in his prickly chrysalis. There are those born to the glorious purple, such as Alexander of Macedon, with the self-confidence of youth and health and the mysterious mental uplift of possible divine origin — to whom the possible uplift of a Pan-Hellenic enthusiasm, in a cultural even more than an Imperial sense, may have added to the mystical side of his uncanny influence.

In Elizabeth, born to an unstable throne and a fluctuating religious system, seated at times on an anvil hot with pain, the tragedy of her origin, the charm of her youth, the *joie de vivre*, and the sturdy common sense that lay at the back of her mind, the mystery of sex and the essential problem of her marriage, the alternating will and stubbornness of the Tudor, combined to set her, with the backing of Burghley, on the dais among the past-masters.

In Cromwell we see an entirely different set of circumstances. Never perhaps has there been a better case of *nolo episcopari*, never has a man been so called forth by circumstance, and called only because others could not organise and lead. The manner of tried leading is another matter. Never perhaps, behind the snuffle of Calvinism which, while he adopted the humbug as flat-catching, he seriously felt, does the English instinct stand out more clearly—to let things be and go their way, but if interference is necessary, to set one's teeth and make a good job of it. We see it in a small way in the second year of the Crimean campaign, in the downing of Krugerism, in the tardy but quite stubborn realisation of what the World War meant, and in the uprising of 1931 against amateur government.

But behind occasion was the stubborn will once aroused, the personal courage, and the success which marked three of the four occasions of 'Old Oliver's Day.' There must be at the basis certain essential qualities for occasion to call on.

Do we turn to such a strange story as that of Tseu-Hi, Dowager Empress of China, it is occasion thrice accentuated, calling on a character in which national pride and history had formed a subconscious background, drawing too her own inspiration and the trust and fear of her people from the double mystery of sex and the veil.

And so the story goes on, and the causes emerge: Victoria among the people of the newer England, progress and prosperity in her peaceful land, looking forth and giving the go-by to a still unsettled world, with an emblem of simplicity, of righteousness and of domesticity at the fore; Abraham Lincoln, the backwoodsman, born of grit and humour and *Pilgrim's Progress*, called to direct a machine he did not understand in a crisis of immense magnitude, and succeeding by some guiding principle of first causes, to fall to a fanatic's pistol in the hour, hardly of triumph, for a triumph he did not want, but of ending. Among people who settle their troubles by other means than the sword we see the gift of oratory developing occasion and leading the masses, with Gladstone and Disraeli as the exponents.

To crown all in our lifetime, David Lloyd George, the orator and barnstormer, having the gift of drive in a crisis, which made him acceptable even to those who hated his Cymric ways—a man who more than any other had origins comparable to Abraham Lincoln.

If you now ask what is the secret, the answer again must come that the secrets are legion, needing, first of all, occasion; second, something born in the mother's womb, something given of God, and labour and self-discipline unceasing. Even when a man is born with all the gifts and has laboured mighti[illegible] in the equipment, the occasion and the 'it' wi[illegible] almost always be wanting, and we are driven bac[illegible] those of supreme ambition, to remember the co[illegible] clusion of the whole matter. For many of us, t[illegible] of personal ambition in the race of life, must come that consolation already quoted of the drunken Emperor Hien-Fung:

> You played and lost the game,
> Perhaps your share
> Lay in the hour you laughed and kissed,
> Your son may bear the honours that his father missed.

INDEX